Pakistan on the Brink

Pakistan on the Brink

Politics, Economics, and Society

Edited by Craig Baxter

LEXINGTON BOOKS
Lanham • Boulder • New York • Toronto • Oxford

LEXINGTON BOOKS

Published in the United States of America
by Lexington Books
An imprint of The Rowman & Littlefield Publishing Group, Inc.
4501 Forbes Boulevard, Suite 200, Lanham, Maryland 20706

PO Box 317
Oxford
OX2 9RU, UK

British Library Cataloguing in Publication Information Available

Library of Congress Cataloging-in-Publication Data

Pakistan on the brink : politics, economics, and society / edited by Craig Baxter.
p. cm.
Includes bibliographical references and index.
ISBN 0-7391-0498-5 (alk. paper)
1. Pakistan—Politics and government—1988– 2. Pakistan—Economic conditions.

DS389.P3473 2003
954.9105'3—dc22 2003060462

Printed in the United States of America

∞™ The paper used in this publication meets the minimum requirements of American National Standard for Information Sciences—Permanence of Paper for Printed Library Materials, ANSI/NISO Z39.48–1992.

Contents

Preface

Over the course of the last several years, Pakistan has assumed greater interest in world affairs. In October 1999 an elected government, albeit one that was inefficient and corrupt, was displaced by military rule headed by General Pervez Musharraf. Musharraf continued the policy of support to the Taliban government in Afghanistan. With the attacks on New York and Washington on September 11, 2001, by Al Qaeda, with its operational headquarters in Afghanistan, however, the Pakistani government reversed its policy and joined with the United States and others in the movement to remove the Taliban regime and to attack the positions it and Al Qaeda held in Afghanistan. The Taliban government was removed and a new government led by Hamid Karzai was installed in Kabul. Pakistan also permitted the United States the use of its airfields and other facilities. Pakistan has cooperated to a considerable extent in seeking out supporters of Al Qaeda in Pakistan itself.

These events have brought a much closer relationship between the United States and Pakistan. It is the purpose of this collection of essays by scholars of many aspects of Pakistan to study and comment upon these aspects. Relations between Pakistan and the United States, Pakistan and India, and Pakistan and Afghanistan are key to understanding the foreign policy of Pakistan.

President Musharraf was to hold elections in October 2002 and did so. But prior to these elections, he directed numerous changes in the constitutional system that his takeover had suspended. An understanding of these changes and of the elections that took place is necessary for the understanding of the domestic political scene. An important part of this political scene, one that touches the people at large, is the system of local government.

The economy of Pakistan and its prospects for further development must also be discussed. Important to economic development is the educational system. These topics are each discussed by specialists in the field. The historical background—indeed, prehistorical background—is the subject of one chapter, which illustrates the joint working of Pakistani and American archaeologists. The book concludes with a chronology of events in Pakistan from the Musharraf takeover until the elections of 2002.

I wish to acknowledge the assistance and encouragement given by the American Institute of Pakistan Studies. The institute is a consortium of American academic institutions and individual scholars of Pakistan that furthers the study of that country through educational exchange programs. Among these programs is one that enables American graduate students and faculty members to undertake research in Pakistan. Another program sponsors distinguished Pakistanis to visit the United States for lecture tours and interaction with Americans who study Pakistan.

I thank my academic colleagues who have contributed to the book. The assistance of Serena Krombach and her associates at Lexington Books and of Ameena Saiyid of Oxford University Press, Karachi, is gratefully acknowledged. The sometimes onerous task of formatting the book was undertaken by Suzanne Everhart, to whom special thanks is due.

Craig Baxter
Juniata College

1

The United States–Pakistan Entente: Third Time's a Charm?

Devin T. Hagerty

The September 2001 terrorist attacks in New York, Washington, and Pennsylvania transformed United States–Pakistan relations. In the immediate aftermath of the carnage, the Bush administration forcefully enlisted the government of General Pervez Musharraf in the newly declared war on terrorism. Musharraf, who had toppled the civilian government of Prime Minister Nawaz Sharif in October 1999, quickly decided to throw in his lot with the United States. Islamabad withdrew its support for Kabul's dictatorial and repressive Taliban regime and permitted Washington to use Pakistan as a staging area for military operations against the Taliban and Al Qaeda terrorists in Afghanistan. The United States has subsequently resumed large-scale economic and military assistance to Pakistan, in exchange for Islamabad's cooperation in rooting out Taliban fighters and Al Qaeda members operating on Pakistani soil. Officially, Pakistan is now an "indispensable ally" in the war on terrorism.[1]

Does September 11, 2001, (hereafter 9/11) mark the beginning of a sustainable friendship between Islamabad and Washington? Or is it only the latest exchange of vows in yet another brief marriage of convenience between two incompatible states whose strategic interests suddenly converge from time to time? The volatile history of United States–Pakistan relations suggests that this latest peak might eventually give way to a valley of resentment and recrimination. In the 1950s, Pakistan was referred to as "America's most-allied ally" in the Cold War; by the mid-1960s and well into the 1970s, the two countries were allies in name, but friends hardly at all. In the 1980s, Pakistan reprised its role as a "frontline state" in the U.S. grand strategy of containment, acting as a military conduit between the United States and the anti-Soviet *mujahideen* in Afghanistan; throughout the 1990s, Pakistani public opinion seethed at Washington's post–Cold War "abandonment" of Islamabad.

Significant attitude adjustments will be necessary for the United States and Pakistan to liberate themselves from this international political version of bipolar disorder. First, both sides should recognize that there are natural limits to their friendship. Historically, the two countries have been closest when faced with a mutual threat, which is an essentially negative, reactive incentive for cooperation. There is little that links Pakistan and the United States in any positive, proactive way. Put bluntly, postindustrial, liberal Western democracies have little in common with preindustrial Islamic "militocracies."[2] Absent a third-party threat, such as the Soviet Union or Al Qaeda, the best that such disparate countries can expect over the long term is to be friends—that is, to have a number of shared interests and generally warm, but unremarkable, relations. Second, Washington and Islamabad should be realistic about the pragmatic nature of their present entente, and modest about how they portray it to Americans and Pakistanis. If and when the Al Qaeda threat eases—or shifts away from the region—Pakistan and the United States will likely revert to a friendly but limited relationship. The more honestly this is acknowledged now, the less pronounced will be the mutual disappointment later. What this means in practice is that the two governments should resist portraying one another—and their relationship—in the glowing, hyperbolic terms expressed in the 1950s and 1980s.

The remainder of this chapter explores this third and latest round of United States–Pakistan amity. In the following section, I set the stage by briefly examining the state of the relationship prior to Musharraf's 1999 coup. Next, I discuss Washington–Islamabad ties in the Musharraf era, dealing in turn with the last fifteen months of the Clinton administration (October 1999 to January 2001) and the first twenty-two months of the Bush administration (January 2001 to November 2002). In analyzing the contemporary state of United States–Pakistan relations, I focus on four important issues: the war on terrorism in southwestern Asia, Pakistan's nuclear weapons program, the Kashmir dispute, and Pakistan's nascent political reform process. I argue in the chapter's concluding section that Washington and Islamabad *can* forge a sustainable friendship, but only if Pakistan makes much-needed changes in its behavior—even its identity—as a member of twenty-first–century international society.

DECADE OF DISCONTENT

As the previous volume of this series went to press in February 2000, the issues that arose between Islamabad and Washington "were almost entirely negative."[3] Indeed, ties between the erstwhile alliance partners had been severely strained throughout the 1990s. With the 1989 Soviet withdrawal from Afghanistan, Islamabad's rapidly evolving nuclear weapons program replaced the Afghanistan War as the issue of most concern for U.S. leaders interested in southwestern Asia. In October 1990, the George H. W. Bush administration terminated most economic and military assistance to Pakistan, as required by U.S. nonproliferation law unless the president could certify that Pakistan did not "possess a nuclear explosive device."[4] As the 1990s unfolded, Islamabad and Washington grew increasingly distant. While Pakistan perceived itself to have been betrayed by the United States once the Cold War was won, U.S. leaders watched with consternation as Pakistan slipped perilously close to being a "rogue state."[5] Islamabad pushed ahead with its nuclear weapons program, imported ballistic missile technology and materiel from China and North Korea, and actively supported the Islamic insurgents in Indian Kashmir, who often pursued their separatist aims through the use of terrorist tactics like the targeting of innocent civilians.[6] Pakistan also may have assisted North Korea's clandestine efforts to develop nuclear weapons via the uranium enrichment route.[7] All the while, quasi-democratic Pakistani governments came and went, each one seemingly more venal and authoritarian than the last.[8]

In particular, the second half of the 1990s witnessed several developments that had even sympathetic Pakistan-watchers calling the country a failing state.[9] In an attempt to stabilize chronically war-torn Afghanistan, create for itself an additional measure of "strategic depth," and develop valuable trade routes between the Central Asian republics and Pakistan, Islamabad grew increasingly supportive of the fundamentalist Taliban movement in Afghanistan. A group of exceedingly radical Sunni Pashtuns, the Taliban fought their way to power in Kabul by 1996. Once installed in the Afghan capital, the Taliban regime embarked on a program of systematic repression based on an extreme interpretation of the *Sharia*, or Islamic law. In the meantime, Al Qaeda's founding leader, Osama bin Laden, had made his way back to Afghanistan after a five-year stay in Sudan. The Taliban and Al Qaeda soon developed a mutually beneficial relationship: the Taliban provided bin Laden and his associates with a vast sanctuary for their training camps and other terrorist operations, while Al Qaeda became the Taliban's chief source of military and financial assistance. With Afghanistan descending quickly into international pariah status, Pakistan by the late 1990s was one of only three countries that diplomatically recognized the odious Kabul regime.[10]

In May 1998, Islamabad officially lifted the veil on its nuclear weapons program by conducting a series of explosive tests.[11] Of course, Islamabad was responding in a tit-for-tat fashion to Indian nuclear tests earlier that month, but U.S. President Bill Clinton had hoped that Prime Minister Sharif might seize the opportunity to appear courageously restrained in the face of Indian provocation.[12] Because both India and Pakistan had been de facto nuclear weapons states for many years, the 1998 tests only slightly changed the material situation. Symbolically, however, they ushered in a new era of U.S. concern about the possibility of nuclear war in the region. Under U.S. law, the Indian and Pakistani nuclear tests mandated a broad package of economic sanctions against New Delhi and Islamabad, including the termination of all aid other than humanitarian or food assistance.[13] South Asian leaders protested vociferously that U.S. anxiety was the product not of dispassionate analysis, but of unspoken Western ethnocentrism.[14] In 1999, U.S. alarm grew even more when India and Pakistan fought a miniwar in the remote Kargil region of Kashmir.[15] Although a definitive study of the Kargil war has yet to be written, one account by a former Clinton administration official suggests that Pakistan prepared its nuclear weapons for possible use during the conflict.[16]

MUSHARRAF AND CLINTON

On October 12, 1999, Pakistan's Army chief, General Musharraf, took power in a bloodless coup. He suspended the Parliament and pronounced himself Pakistan's new "chief executive." Despite the fact that few Pakistanis mourned the demise of Nawaz Sharif's hapless government, the Clinton administration was compelled by U.S. law to ban foreign assistance "to any country whose duly elected head of government is deposed by a military coup or decree."[17] Pakistan thus became ineligible for most forms of U.S. aid. While some observers have argued that these pro-democracy sanctions had little "immediate impact" because of the preexisting nuclear sanctions,[18] Pakistan felt the sting of Washington's ire when President Clinton waived nuclear-related economic sanctions on India only two weeks after the Musharraf coup.

That the Pakistan Army's latest putsch did not cause a greater rupture in United States–Pakistan relations owes much to the fact that the relationship had already slipped so far during Clinton's second term in office. By October 1999, the Clinton administration was in simple damage-control mode with respect to Islamabad. In contrast, Clinton's foreign policy team was sincerely dedicated to a vigorous strategic engagement with India. Notwithstanding what many Pakistanis assume, this was not a zero-sum matter of Washington "choosing" New Delhi over Islamabad.

Rather, it was that Pakistan was descending into the geopolitical mire and had no compensating strategic value, while India offered much to the United States. Consistent with its overall emphasis on "geoeconomics" and its purported grand strategy of "engagement and enlargement," the Clinton administration engaged deeply with India on economic matters in an effort to leverage India's liberalization program to best American advantage. Although India's rightward political turn concerned some in the administration, the country remained a vibrant democracy, especially by South Asian standards.

On nuclear issues, Clinton had been disappointed when India conducted its 1998 nuclear tests, but his administration quickly adapted itself to the reality that India's great-power aspirations included becoming a full-fledged nuclear weapons state. Deputy Secretary of State Strobe Talbott became a regular visitor to New Delhi, where his talks with Indian leaders focused not on rolling back their nuclear program, but on devising an informal regime to contain it. The Clinton policy urged India (and Pakistan) to do five things in the nuclear weapons realm: sign and ratify the Comprehensive Test Ban Treaty; halt the production of fissile material and engage in the negotiations for a Fissile Material Cutoff Treaty; refrain from actually deploying fully assembled, operational nuclear weapons; stop testing nuclear-capable ballistic missiles; and resist exporting nuclear materials or technologies.[19] Although this represented an ostensibly even-handed approach to South Asian nuclear proliferation, Clinton and his advisers were considerably more concerned with Pakistani than with Indian nuclear developments. After all, Pakistan's economy was in desperate straits, so it might have sought hard currency through nuclear-related transfers.[20] With Islamabad's ever-closer links to international terrorism, Pakistan's nuclear materials could more easily fall into dangerous hands. Furthermore, because Pakistan's military dominated nuclear command-and-control arrangements, civilian authorities could exercise no pacifying effects on a regime that might be tempted to go nuclear in a crisis. In sum, U.S. officials in the late 1990s treated Pakistan as a continuing and serious proliferation challenge, while they tended to view India as if it were a "legitimate" nuclear weapons state like China or, at worst, a country like Israel, which remained outside the nuclear nonproliferation regime but seemed to be a responsible enough nuclear custodian.

While New Delhi and Washington moved inexorably closer during Clinton's final year in office, U.S. and Pakistani interests diverged on nearly all counts. This was vividly illustrated during the president's long anticipated trip to South Asia in March 2000. After five days of substantive bonhomie in India, Clinton spent roughly five hours in Pakistan, where he and Musharraf firmly voiced their starkly contrasting opinions on important issues. On Afghanistan, the Clinton administration pressured Musharraf to distance his government from the Taliban. Fearing a backlash among Islamist elements in Pakistan, the general politely demurred. During his Islamabad meeting with Clinton, Musharraf reportedly "said that he wanted to be helpful but stressed how difficult it was to deal with 'people who believe that God is on their side.'"[21]

With respect to Kashmir, the Clinton administration essentially recognized the bedrock reality of—if not the principle behind—the Indian position: the conflict should be resolved by the two disputants themselves, as per the Simla Agreement of 1972.[22] Significantly, the president made no mention of Kashmir in his well-received March 2000 address to the Indian Parliament, while days later on Pakistani television he exhorted Islamabad to eschew a military solution to the dispute. Clinton could have left no doubt in Pakistani minds about his government's policy: "We cannot and will not mediate or resolve the dispute in Kashmir. Only you and India can do that through dialogue."[23] This meant in practice that the U.S. State Department would offer its "good offices" to help facilitate a settlement, but it would not propose solutions to, or invest political capital in, the dispute. Pushing India any harder than this could derail the promising United States–India engagement process and would likely result in failure anyway. Instead, the Clinton team used quiet moral suasion to help ease the violence in Kashmir. U.S. and other diplomatic pressure may have influenced India's November 2000 cessation of military operations in Kashmir during the Muslim holy month of Ramadan. Pakistan responded in December by announcing that its forces along the Line of Control (LOC) in Kashmir would "observe maximum restraint" and that some troops would be pulled back from the LOC. When armed clashes and militant intrusions slowed, New Delhi extended the ceasefire into 2001. Ultimately, however, Kashmir's main *jihadi* ("holy warrior") groups rejected the ceasefire, and the bloodshed continued.[24]

The Clinton administration's last important official act toward Pakistan occurred in the midst of the late 2000 Bush–Gore Florida election debacle. With most American eyes riveted on the postelection drama, few noticed that Washington had slapped on Islamabad the latest in a long line of missile-related sanctions.[25] On November 21, two-year sanctions were imposed on Pakistan's Ministry of Defense and its Upper Atmosphere Research Organization, "as a result of past Chinese assistance to Pakistani missile programs."[26] The decade between 1990—when the Pressler Amendment was triggered—and 2000 could scarcely have ended on a note more sour. As one contemporary account put it: "the U.S.–Pakistani estrangement has reached its nadir." Pakistan "appears more isolated and forlorn than ever."[27]

MUSHARRAF AND BUSH

By January 2001, when George W. Bush took his oath of office, Pakistan's security predicament—always challenging—was dire. In addition to its poor relations with Washington, Islamabad was also coping with a much more gradual, but still real, erosion of its long-standing strategic entente with Beijing.[28] In the 1990s, the end of the Cold War and China's ambitious economic liberalization program had sparked a vigorous diplomatic push to ease tensions along the country's entire periphery. With Russian influence waning, Chinese leaders placed an especially high priority on normalizing relations with India. Although this Sino-Indian rapprochement has ebbed and flowed, it has been accompanied by a consistently growing divergence of interests between Beijing and Islamabad. Most important, China has appeared increasingly skittish about the prospect of a major war in South Asia. The 1998 nuclear tests and the 1999 Kargil conflict caused demonstrable anxiety in Beijing. Well into the 1990s, Chinese views on South Asian security issues were routinely and adamantly pro-Pakistani; since 1998, Beijing has adopted a markedly cooler tone. Islamabad's adventurousness in Kargil and its failure to crack down on terrorists operating from Pakistani soil have given Chinese leaders a whiff of recklessness that they believe threatens their regional diplomatic posture. As a consequence, Beijing's position on Kashmir has moved toward New Delhi's (and Washington's): India and Pakistan need to resolve their dispute through bilateral discussions, not third-party intervention. And, even though China continues to be a valuable source of conventional military aid, economic assistance, and over-all strategic reassurance for Pakistan, Beijing has been unusually forthright in telling Islamabad that it will not intervene in the event of an Indo-Pakistani war.

Much to Islamabad's dismay, the new Bush administration's South Asia policy hardly deviated from President Clinton's. Indeed, if anything, Bush's new national security team was intent on expanding the regional policy it inherited. India's fast-growing economy, its booming information-technology sector, and its position as a relatively stable, democratic, nuclear power in a volatile region argued for deepening Indo–U.S. ties.[29] Not only that, but some senior Bush administration officials perceived that New Delhi could provide a useful counterweight to Beijing's growing influence in Asia,[30] a perspective that was strengthened by the April 2002 Hainan spy plane incident—the president's first foreign policy test.[31] By way of contrast, Pakistan seemed to offer many problems and few opportunities. Translated into policy, these perspectives dictated maintaining the Clinton line on Kashmir, i.e., urging the disputants to engage in bilateral conflict resolution, while not pushing so hard as to alienate India.[32] Washington did not, however, throw up its collective hands regarding Pakistan. Senior officials were "determined to improve the United States–Pakistan relationship,"[33] without turning a blind eye to areas of disagreement. So, for example, while the United States imposed yet another round of missile sanctions against Pakistan in early September 2001, the administration had also resolved—before 9/11—to lift the remaining 1998 nuclear sanctions.[34]

In the immediate aftermath of 9/11, Washington put enormous pressure on Islamabad to join the war on terrorism. Given that Afghanistan was Al Qaeda's headquarters and that the Pakistan Army—and particularly its Interservices Intelligence (ISI) branch—had a vast store of knowledge about Afghanistan's complex political landscape, the Bush administration viewed Islamabad's support as vital to the antiterrorist campaign. U.S. officials also knew that if they expected General Musharraf to incur the political risks of abandoning a cause many Pakistanis believed in, Washington would have to pay Islamabad handsomely. Initially, in September and October 2001, as the United States prepared to invade Afghanistan, it received from Pakistan airspace rights, access to military bases, and intelligence. In return, Washington waived the remaining nuclear and pro-democracy sanctions; pledged more than a billion dollars in economic assistance, mainly in the areas of health, food, education, democracy promotion, counter-narcotics, and law enforcement;[35] and promised to engineer grant, loan, and debt rescheduling programs through the World Bank, the International Monetary Fund, and the Asian Development Bank. Japan and the European Union soon followed suit.[36] President Musharraf's September 19 speech to his nation left no doubt as to what was at stake for Pakistan. If it did not join the U.S. war effort, the country would be marginalized and isolated. Noting that India had already offered its full cooperation to the United States, Musharraf warned that Islamabad's refusal to toe the line would result in Pakistan's being branded a terrorism-supporting state and in the loss of any lingering international sympathy for the Pakistani position on Kashmir. He also implied, obliquely, that the very survival of Pakistan's hard-won nuclear weapons and ballistic missiles was in jeopardy.[37]

UNITED STATES–PAKISTAN SECURITY COOPERATION

With the victory of anti-Taliban forces in Afghanistan and the installation of a successor regime in Kabul, U.S. attention has shifted to the pursuit of Taliban and Al Qaeda remnants who have fled into Pakistan. Although the nature and composition of the U.S. military presence in Pakistan are closely held secrets, it is clear that the war on terrorism has at least temporarily transformed United States–Pakistan security relations. U.S. forces reportedly operate out of three air bases,[38] the most active of which appears to be at Jacobabad, in Sindh. Some 400 to 500 U.S. military personnel are apparently based at Jacobabad, along with C-130 transport aircraft.[39] U.S. Central Intelligence Agency and law enforcement agents collaborate with the Pakistani authorities in flushing out Al Qaeda and Taliban remnants throughout Pakistan. In the mountainous tribal areas near the Afghan border, U.S. special forces also help the Pakistan Army carry out this mission, an unusual intrusion into a traditionally autonomous region.[40] In October 2002, Islamabad claimed "to have captured and remanded to U.S. custody" some 422 Al Qaeda operatives. Washington and Islamabad have also revived or initiated several organizational mechanisms to plan their security cooperation. Among these are the Joint Working Group on Law Enforcement and the United States–Pakistan Defense Consultative Group (DCG). The DCG, which was suspended after Islamabad's May 1998 nuclear tests, reconvened in September 2002. Its mandate is to coordinate bilateral military activity, security assistance, and anti-terrorist measures.[41] A joint statement after the DCG meeting said that Islamabad's main priorities were "acquisition of U.S. defense stores for improving conventional weapons capabilities" and "measures and conditions for a long-term, sustainable defense relationship between the two countries." U.S. Undersecretary of Defense Douglas Feith noted that Washington has "an interest in enhancing Pakistan's conventional defense capabilities as sought by Islamabad."[42] Initial military sales will reportedly include transport aircraft, balloon-mounted surveillance radars, and, possibly, Unmanned Air Vehicles.[43] In October 2002, the United States and Pakistan conducted joint military exercises consisting of small-arms training and small-unit tactics.[44] Although Islamabad would clearly like to resume a major, long-term military sales relationship with Washington, U.S. officials have been circumspect in this regard, partly out of deference to Indian sensitivities.

PAKISTAN'S NUCLEAR WEAPONS PROGRAM

Revived security cooperation has not erased serious U.S. concerns about Islamabad's nuclear weapons program.[45] Open-source estimates indicate that Pakistan has enough highly enriched uranium for twenty to fifty nuclear warheads.[46] The military tightly controls the weapons, which are believed to be stored in disassembled form, with warheads separated from delivery systems and the warheads' fissile cores separated from the warheads themselves.[47] Islamabad's nuclear weapons are deliverable by both air and ballistic missile. The most capable aircraft in Pakistan's inventory is the F-16. As for missiles, Islamabad deploys three main variants. The Ghauri is a liquid-fueled derivative of the North Korean Nodong missile, with a 700-kilogram warhead capacity and a range of 1,500 kilometers, which would allow it to strike targets in every part of India but the far northeast. The Ghauri went into serial production in 1998. The M-11 is a solid-fueled missile purchased from China, which can carry a 500-kilogram warhead up to 300 kilometers. The Shaheen is a reverse-engineered, solid-fueled Chinese M-9 missile, capable of delivering a 1,000-kilogram warhead up to 750 kilometers.[48]

Between May 1998, when Pakistan tested its nuclear weapons, and 9/11, the United States's main policy objective was to ensure that New Delhi and Islamabad did not let crises escalate to the point where either side would contemplate the use of nuclear weapons. While that possibility remains a major concern, the primary goal of U.S. policy has shifted to ensuring that Pakistan's nuclear weapons or materials do not fall into the hands of terrorists.[49] To that end, Washington and Islamabad have held talks on nuclear security matters, but few details are publicly available. It is possible that the United States can share (or is sharing) with Pakistan information gleaned from its own long nuclear history on measures such as personnel reliability programs, material accounting practices, the storage and transport of nuclear materials, overall site security, and emergency response procedures. While the extent of potential assistance is limited by U.S. obligations under the Nuclear Nonproliferation Treaty, one expert suggests that the "provision of unclassified, publicly available knowledge related to nuclear security and control" is allowable, "particularly if it is not provided on an official basis by the U.S. government."[50] The greatest dilemma for U.S. policy is that measures that are useful from a crisis stability standpoint, such as storing weapons components separately, may actually increase the prospects of nuclear materials falling into terrorist hands.

Another issue of concern for the United States is the possibility that Pakistan, in exchange for ballistic missile technology, may have transferred information, designs, and/or material that would help North Korea develop nuclear weapons using uranium enrichment processes. Accounts of such transfers surfaced in October 2002, and in November it was reported that Islamabad might have continued its nuclear aid to Pyongyang as late as the summer of 2002. As one Bush administration official said in November, "there were still shenanigans going on three months ago."[51] Pakistani officials have repeatedly and vehemently denied these claims, with General Musharraf calling them "absolutely baseless."[52] Pakistan had previously been suspected of attempting to transfer nuclear expertise for financial gain,[53] but the North Korea allegations severely dented Islamabad's protests that it would always be a responsible nuclear power.

THE KASHMIR DISPUTE

The second major challenge for United States–Pakistan relations is the Kashmir dispute.[54] The India–Pakistan conflict over this remote Himalayan region has now festered for fifty-five years, with no end in sight.[55] Indeed, the issue has grown even more vexing over the last decade, with the transnationalization of the Islamic insurgency in Indian Kashmir. The dispute was intractable enough when it was exclusively an Indo-Pakistani-Kashmiri affair.[56] Pakistan could have no hope of wresting Kashmir from India, but it could indefinitely support enough insurgent activity to rob India of substantial blood and treasure. From the mid-1990s onward, the Kashmir war evolved into something entirely different. As one analyst wrote in 1999: "For five years now, the rebels with clout have been cut from the same cloth: based in Pakistan, trained in Afghanistan, and motivated by Pan-Islamic fundamentalism rather than Kashmiri nationalism. Their ranks filled with Punjabis and Pashtuns, Afghans and Arabs, many of the fighters wage war on behalf of a people whose language they do not even speak."[57]

After a period of relative peace, described in a previous section, large-scale carnage returned to Kashmir on October 1, 2001. Terrorists from the Pakistan-based Jaish-i-Muhammad ("Muhammad's Troops") attacked the Jammu and Kashmir legislative assembly building in Srinagar, killing thirty-eight people.[58] Cross-border artillery duels, in abeyance for nearly a year, resumed. Secretary of State Colin Powell and Secretary of Defense Donald Rumsfeld hastened to the region in October and November, respectively, in attempts to calm regional tempers. On December 13, according to the Government of India, Jaish-i-Muhammad (and possibly Lashkar-i-Toiba—"Army of the Pure," another Pakistan-based terrorist group) attacked the Indian Parliament in New Delhi, leaving fourteen dead.[59] The audacious strike at the heart of India's government, far from Kashmir's peaks and valleys, dealt a blow to Indian society not unlike that of 9/11 in the United States. New Delhi responded with outrage, deploying the Indian Army to border positions; putting its combined military forces, including those in Kashmir, on high alert; severing road, rail, and air links with Pakistan; and recalling its high commissioner from Islamabad. In doing so, the Indian government served notice that unless Pakistan reined in its *jihadi* groups, India would do it for them by destroying what it described as terrorist training camps and sanctuaries in Pakistani Kashmir.[60] Ultimately, India moved roughly half a million soldiers—including three armored strike corps—to the parts of Punjab, Rajasthan, and Gujarat bordering Pakistan.[61] Islamabad responded by mobilizing its own armor and three hundred thousand Pakistan Army troops to the adjacent border areas of Punjab and Sindh.[62]

India's compellent strategy was partly aimed at inducing Washington to urge Islamabad to stop supporting *jihad* in Kashmir and India proper. India's arguments were bolstered by President Bush's post–9/11 doctrine of targeting terrorists *and* the states that support them. For its part, Pakistan hoped that the latest crisis would cause the United States to take a more active role in resolving the Kashmir conflict. Islamabad argued that the necessity of mobilizing troops along the border with India would require Pakistan to deploy fewer soldiers in the hunt for Al Qaeda and Taliban forces in western Pakistan. New Delhi's diplomatic strategy was more successful; while Washington urged both sides to back off, it pointedly put Jaish-i-Muhammad and Lashkar-i-Toiba on the Department of State's list of foreign terrorist organizations. In response to Indian and U.S. pressure, General Musharraf made an impassioned speech to the Pakistani people on January 12, 2002, in which he unambiguously condemned the October and December terrorist attacks in India. "The day of reckoning has come," Musharraf said. "Do we want Pakistan to become a theocratic state? Do we believe that religious education alone is enough for governance, or do we want Pakistan to emerge as a progressive and dynamic Islamic welfare state?" Claiming that "the verdict of the masses is in favor" of the latter course, Musharraf pledged that "no organization will be allowed to indulge in terrorism in the name of Kashmir," and that "Pakistan will not allow its territory to be used for any terrorist activity anywhere in the world."[63] It was Musharraf's finest hour, and the national address bought his own domestic antiterrorist war much-needed time and goodwill.

Alas, Musharraf has proved unwilling—or unable—to clamp down completely on Pakistan's *jihadi* groups. In the aftermath of his January 2002 speech, Islamabad arrested some 2,000 militants and closed more than 300 of their offices, but few militants have been prosecuted. Moreover, the leaders of Lashkar-i-Toiba and Jaish-i-Muhammad were released in March and promptly vowed to reinvigorate the Kashmir insurgency.[64] On May 14, terrorists attacked the Indian military base at Kaluchak in Jammu, killing thirty-four people and setting off a full-blown crisis. As one Western reporter described the situation in late May, "preparations for cataclysm advance daily along the Indo-Pakistani frontier. About 1 million soldiers have crowded to the long border, equipped with missiles, tanks, and fighter jets. . . . War-fevered politicians in both capitals organize appeals for national unity. . . . And in the secret military warehouses of both countries, engineers presumably are turning screws on doomsday's reserve force—two crude but functional nuclear arsenals." Indeed, while Vajpayee warned the Indian Army to "prepare for a 'decisive battle,'" Musharraf strongly implied that "if India insists on launching all-out war to attack Pakistan's support for Kashmiri militants, Pakistan is prepared to go nuclear."[65]

Once again, Washington embarked on a frenzy of high-level diplomatic activity to prevent war in South Asia. In early June, Deputy Secretary of State Richard Armitage traveled to Islamabad, where he reportedly elicited a promise from Musharraf to "end cross-border infiltration permanently."[66] Two weeks later, though, Musharraf seemed to backtrack when he told a reporter, "I'm not going to give you an assurance that for years nothing will happen."[67] That having been said, infiltrations across the LOC did decrease during the summer, before rising again in the autumn, "but not to the level that they had been previously, prior to the commitments made by the Pakistani government."[68] All in all, the Indian Army chief estimated that militant crossings declined by about half from 2001 to 2002.[69]

Although the immediate crisis faded in June, the Indo-Pakistani troop buildup lasted until October, when India announced that it would withdraw its forces from the border with Pakistan. The Indian decision came on the heels of state elections in Kashmir, after which "there was no reason to continue a deployment that has placed enormous strains on personnel, equipment, and morale."[70] Pakistan immediately reciprocated the troop withdrawal, but Indian officials were at pains to point out that they would not reduce their military presence in Kashmir. Despite the fact that India and Pakistan nearly fought a major war[71] in the summer of 2002, the conflict grinds on. Islamabad beseeches New Delhi to negotiate over Kashmir and tries to convince an increasingly unsympathetic international community to support its cause. Meanwhile, a senior Indian official says there is "no question of a dialogue with Pakistan as long as Pakistani terrorism continues."[72]

POLITICAL REFORM IN PAKISTAN

A final significant issue in United States–Pakistan relations has been Pakistan's political reform process. When General Musharraf took power in 1999, he pledged to root out corruption and reinvigorate Pakistani democracy. As always, however, it has proved more difficult for a Pakistani military leader to take power than to give it back to the civilians. Prior to 9/11, Washington continued to voice its strong preference for a speedy return to democratic rule in Pakistan; but after the war on terrorism was joined, the issue was not so clear cut. With Islamabad pivotal once again to the success of a war in Afghanistan, the Bush administration was loath to undermine Musharraf's authority. While the general moved to protect his position within the army by shuffling senior officers around, pro-democracy voices in Washington grew muted. Pakistani critics have charged that U.S. dependence on Pakistani cooperation in the terrorism war has only emboldened Musharraf to increase, and perhaps prolong, his power. According to one such analyst, Musharraf "hopes to change the label on his military regime, redefining it as a democracy without altering its substance. Having a military dictator in charge may be good for the current phase of the antiterror war in Afghanistan, though even that is debatable. Regardless, such a situation does not transform Pakistan into the stable ally the United States is seeking."[73] This is a view widely shared by Pakistani elites, many of whom, ironically, have served in the disastrous civilian governments of the recent past.

The official American perspective is different. Although the Clinton administration's position—that "the answer to flawed democracy is not to end democracy but to improve it"[74]—might have been true in normal times, the Bush national security team prefers during wartime to have a friendly dictator in power than to run the risks inherent in the standard messy, Pakistan-style democracy. Thus, while Washington has continued to advocate the restoration of democracy and civilian rule, it has not pushed Musharraf very hard to devolve power. In April 2002, Musharraf's presidency was "legitimized" for another five years in a referendum many Pakistanis denounced as a fraud. In August, Musharraf arbitrarily amended the Constitution in ways that would yield himself increased powers even after new elections for national and provincial assemblies.

The long-promised Pakistani elections were held in October 2002. With many potential and former National Assembly candidates sidelined by a requirement that they be college graduates, Islamist parties ran unexpectedly well. The United Action Forum, a coalition of six Islamist parties known by the Urdu acronym MMA, won 60 of 342 seats in the National Assembly. The MMA tallied 11 percent of the national vote, slightly more than the Islamist parties' previous best of 8 percent.[75] The MMA campaigned partly on a program of opposition to the U.S. military presence in Pakistan. Musharraf's favored party was the Pakistan Muslim League—Quaid-i-Azam (PML-Q), universally dubbed the "King's Party." The PML-Q won 118 seats, a plurality of the vote but well short of the 172 needed for a majority. Former Prime Minister Benazir Bhutto's Pakistan People's Party (PPP) took another 81 seats.[76] At the time of this writing, negotiations over the formation of a new government were ongoing.

Regardless of the government's composition, Musharraf will retain an enormous degree of power. In Pakistan's evolving militocracy, the president can dissolve the National Assembly, and appoint the army chief and provincial governors. Perhaps most important, Musharraf still has firm control over the National Security Council, the army-dominated inner circle of decision makers. Although the Pakistani intelligentsia and many foreign observers complain that the new regime is still essentially a dictatorship, most Pakistanis apparently view a strong executive as a necessary evil, given the corruption and ineffectiveness of previous civilian regimes and their prime ministers. Immediately prior to the October 2002 elections, a BBC-commissioned poll, based on interviews with 2,827 Pakistanis, found that 69 percent of the respondents "thought Musharraf had done a 'good' or 'somewhat good' job" in office. Another preelection survey of more than 6,000 voters, "by the Pattan Development Organization, a Pakistan-based nonprofit group whose research was sponsored by the British government," found that "58.9 percent support Musharraf as president." A summary of the Pattan poll results said that "'an overwhelming majority . . . seem[s] to consider politicians and political parties principally responsible for [the] failure of democracy.'"[77]

The Future of United States–Pakistan Relations

United States–Pakistan relations have been transformed, but not necessarily revolutionized. Changing the fundamental nature of the relationship requires replacing the up-and-down political rollercoaster of the past with a more realistic, modest, sustainable friendship. Over the long term, the United States is committed to building a strategic and economic partnership with India. Although American officials maintain that their South Asia policy is "not a zero-sum game,"[78] U.S. decisions regarding Pakistan certainly will be made with Indian sensitivities in mind. This means that Washington will not soon budge from its position that Islamabad and New Delhi must themselves resolve the Kashmir dispute. It also means that the United States will be unlikely to resume a major military aid relationship with Pakistan. This is not to say that Islamabad and Washington cannot enjoy productive, friendly relations, even after the Al Qaeda threat fades. Whether this happens or not largely depends on fundamental changes in Pakistan's identity and behavior. Several concrete steps would begin to bring about these changes. First, Islamabad should make a permanent, good-faith effort to stem the flow of *jihadi* fighters into Indian Kashmir. Pakistani authorities will be unable to stop all such infiltrations, but India and the United States will be able to distinguish between inability and unwillingness. The real challenge in this regard is that the only source of legitimacy for Pakistani elites today is claiming to "defend the faith" in Kashmir. Implicit in this argument is that Pakistani leaders must instead begin to derive their political legitimacy from domestic sources.

This logic leads directly to the second step: Pakistani decision makers must firmly nudge their political system toward democracy. Pakistani democracy need not be of the freewheeling American variety, but Pakistani citizens must have an institutionalized voice in how their country is run. Pakistan has become the state equivalent of a bionic person: held together by "artificial" parts like external alliances, infusions of bilateral foreign aid, and multilateral financial assistance, instead of developing through the evolution of "natural" processes like economic dynamism and the maturation of political institutions. As was abundantly evident in his remarkable January 2002 speech, President Musharraf recognizes the problem; less apparent is his understanding of the solution. As a third step, Islamabad should forcefully address and begin to reverse the Talibanization of Pakistan. Only through the reformation of the country's educational system will Pakistan be able to develop in such a way as to give its exploding population any real hope for the future. Many of the *madrassas* (religious schools) teach a fanatical form of Islam. Some of the institutions are reported to give a measure of military training.[79] Of course, the pursuit of democracy raises its own dilemmas, both for Pakistan and its friends. As the October 2002 elections demonstrated, democracy can shift power to more Islamist elements who may be cooler to the U.S. presence. But the experiences of Bangladesh, Malaysia, and Turkey show that "Islamic" and "radical" are not synonyms. One reason many Pakistani Muslims have become so radicalized is that they have been excluded from a legitimate role in their country's governance. It is better that Pakistan's Islamist parties pursue their goals via ballots rather than bullets. The war on terrorism should not blind Washington to that fundamental truth.

NOTES

1. "Deepening U.S. Engagement in Asia," remarks by Christina B. Rocca, Assistant Secretary for South Asian Affairs, Department of State, to the American Enterprise Institute, Washington, D.C., October 10, 2002.

2. By this I mean states that occasionally exhibit elements of democracy, such as elections and legislatures, but where the real power lies with the armed forces.

3. Dennis Kux, "U.S.–Pakistan Relations as the Twentieth Century Ends," in Charles H. Kennedy and Craig Baxter, eds., *Pakistan 2000* (Lanham, Md.: Lexington Books, 2000), p 76.

4. Devin T. Hagerty, *The Consequences of Nuclear Proliferation: Lessons from South Asia* (Cambridge, Mass.: MIT Press, 1998), pp 82–83, 172–173. The presidential certification standard was changed in 1995; thereafter, it applied only to military assistance, making Pakistan eligible again for other types of foreign assistance. See Dianne E. Rennack, "India and Pakistan: Current U.S. Economic Sanctions," Congressional Research Service, October 12, 2001, p 2.

5. In the United States foreign policy lexicon of the 1990s, the term "rogue state" referred to countries that: were authoritarian or totalitarian in nature; acted aggressively against their neighbors; sponsored terrorism; sought nuclear, chemical, and biological weapons as well as ballistic missiles; and trafficked in these capabilities.

6. For an overview of Kashmir's Islamic insurgency at the end of the 1990s, see Jonah Blank, "Kashmir: Fundamentalism Takes Root," *Foreign Affairs,* 78:6 (November–December 1999), pp 36–53.

7. Stephen Fidler, "Suspicions Deepen over Islamabad Connection," *Financial Times,* November 1, 2002. The possibility of Pakistani nuclear assistance to North Korea emerged publicly in October 2002 and will be discussed below.

8. For details, see Dennis Kux, *The United States and Pakistan, 1947–2000: Disenchanted Allies* (Washington, D.C.: Woodrow Wilson Center Press, 2001).

9. Manzoor Ijaz, "Stop Pakistan's Fall into Nuclear-Armed Failure," *International Herald Tribune,* May 4, 2000.

10. Ahmed Rashid, *Taliban* (New Haven, Conn.: Yale University Press, 2000). See also Kux, "U.S.–Pakistan Relations," pp 72–73.

11. For details, see Devin T. Hagerty, "Kashmir and the Nuclear Question Revisited," in Kennedy and Baxter, *Pakistan 2000,* pp 86–88.

12. On Sharif's difficult decision, see Devin T. Hagerty, "South Asia's Big Bangs: Causes, Consequences, and Prospects," *Australian Journal of International Affairs,* 53:1 (April 1999), pp 22–23.

13. For a complete list of the penalties, see Rennack, "India and Pakistan: Current U.S. Economic Sanctions," p 2. Between July 1998 and October 1999, a number of laws were passed that gave the president authority to waive these sanctions.

14. For example, see Jaswant Singh, "Against Nuclear Apartheid," *Foreign Affairs,* 77:5 (September–October 1998), pp 41–52.

15. See Hagerty, "Kashmir and the Nuclear Question Revisited," pp 90–95.

16. Bruce Reidel, "American Diplomacy and the 1999 Kargil Summit at Blair House," Center for the Advanced Study of India, Philadelphia, Pa., 2002.

17. Rennack, "India and Pakistan: Current U.S. Economic Sanctions," p 4.

18. Kux, *United States and Pakistan,* pp 354–355.

19. K. Alan Kronstadt, "Pakistan–U.S. Relations," Congressional Research Service, October 28, 2002.

20. We now know that Clinton administration officials had strong suspicions in the late 1990s that Pakistan and North Korea were engaged in some sort of nuclear–barter arrangement. See Fidler, "Suspicions Deepen over Islamabad Connection."

21. Kux, *United States and Pakistan,* p 357.

22. Of course, the Simla Agreement itself is now subject to sharp disagreements between New Delhi and Islamabad. See Devin T. Hagerty, "Kashmir and the Nuclear Question," in Charles H. Kennedy and Rasul Bakhsh Rais, eds., *Pakistan 1995* (Boulder, Colo.: Westview Press, 1995), pp 174, 180. For an insightful discussion of why the Kashmir dispute remains intractable, see Mohammed Ayoob, "South Asia's Dangers and U.S. Foreign Policy," *Orbis,* 45:1 (Winter 2001), pp 123–134.

23. Robert Wirsing, "Kashmir in the Terrorist Shadow," *Asian Affairs* (London), 33:1 (February 2002), p 2 of Internet version.

24. Kronstadt, "Pakistan–U.S. Relations," p 3.

25. For a brief history, see Devin T. Hagerty, "China and Pakistan: Strains in the Relationship," *Current History,* 101:656 (September 2002), pp 287–288.

26. Kronstadt, "Pakistan–U.S. Relations," p 3.

27. Ashley J. Tellis, "South Asia," in Richard J. Ellings and Aaron F. Friedberg, eds., *Strategic Asia: Power and Purpose, 2001–2002* (Seattle, Wash.: National Bureau of Asian Research, 2001), p 238.

28. This paragraph draws liberally on Hagerty, "China and Pakistan: Strains in the Relationship," pp 287–289.

29. See Edward Luce and Stephen Fidler, "A Fine Line," *Financial Times,* June 1, 2001, and James C. Cadd, "An Unexpected Chance to Get Down to Fundamentals," in *A New Equation: U.S. Policy Toward India and Pakistan after September 11,* Working Paper No. 27, Carnegie Endowment for International Peace Global Policy Program, Washington, D.C., May 2002.

30. For an analysis of the new administration's perspective on India, see Dennis Kux, "India's Fine Balance," *Foreign Affairs,* 81:3 (May–June 2002), pp 94–95.

31. On April 1, 2002, a Chinese F–8 fighter jet collided with a U.S. EP–3 reconnaissance plane over the South China Sea. The U.S. aircraft made an emergency landing on China's Hainan Island, igniting an intense, eleven–day diplomatic row between Washington and Beijing.

32. General Musharraf, who had declared himself president of Pakistan in June 2001 met with the Indian prime minister, Atal Behari Vajpayee, at Agra in July. The talks ended in deadlock, as symbolized by the adversaries' failure even to issue a perfunctory joint communique. For details, see Radha Kumar, "Untying the Kashmir Knot," *World Policy Journal,* 19:1 (Spring 2002), pp 11–24.

33. Pakistan Television interview with Richard Haass, Director of Policy Planning, U.S. Department of State, Islamabad, October 31, 2002.

34. Lewis A. Dunn, "Balancing Nuclear Security and Nonproliferation in South Asia," in *A New Equation: U.S. Policy toward India and Pakistan after September 11*, p 23; Zamir Akram, "Pakistan–U.S. Relations after 9/11: A Pakistani Perspective," *Georgetown Journal of International Affairs* 3:2 (Summer/Fall 2002), p 117.

35. The promised U.S. assistance will make Islamabad Washington's fourth largest air recipient. Hussain Haqqani, "America's New Alliance with Pakistan: Avoiding the Traps of the Past," Policy Brief No. 19, Carnegie Endowment for International Peace, October 2002, p 7.

36. Kronstadt, "Pakistan–U.S. Relations," pp 6–7, 10.

37. "Text: Pakistan President Musharraf," *Washington Post,* Online, September 19, 2001.

38. Akram, "Pakistani–U.S. Relations after 9/11," p 118.

39. Khalid Hasan, "Pakistan Agreed to Long–Term Use," *Daily Times,* October 29, 2002.

40. Thomas E. Ricks, "Pakistani Casualties Raise War's Stakes," *Washington Post,* June 27, 2002.

41. Kronstadt, "Pakistan–U.S. Relations," p 1.

42. Ihtashamul Haque, "U.S. to Help Raise Conventional Arms Capability," *Dawn,* Internet Edition, September 28, 2002.

43. "Pakistan to Buy UAVs from U.S.," *Daily News,* October 3, 2002; Kronstadt, "Pakistan–U.S. Relations," p 11.

44. "Gen. Franks Holds Talks with Musharraf," *The News,* Internet Edition, October 19, 2002.

45. For a more extensive historical background, see Hagerty, "Kashmir and the Nuclear Question," and Hagerty, "Kashmir and the Nuclear Question Revisited."

46. Robert S. Norris and William M. Arkin, "Pakistan's Nuclear Forces," *Bulletin of the Atomic Scientists* (January–February 2002), pp 70–71; M. V. Ramana and A. H. Nayyar, "India, Pakistan, and the Bomb," *Scientific American,* December 2001, pp 72–83.

47. Lee Feinstein, "When Policy Priorities Converge: U.S. Relations with India," and David Albright, "Securing Pakistan's Nuclear Infrastructure," in *A New Equation: U.S. Policy toward India and Pakistan after September 11,* pp 10, 33.

48. Ramana and Nayyar, "India, Pakistan, and the Bomb."

49. Dunn, "Balancing Nuclear Security and Nonproliferation in South Asia," p 24.

50. Ibid., p 25. For a comprehensive of the technical and political/legal aspects of U.S.–Pakistan nuclear security cooperation, see Albright, "Securing Pakistan's Nuclear Infrastructure," pp 37–41.

51. Glenn Kessler, "Pakistan's N. Korea Deals Stir Controversy," *Washington Post,* November 13, 2002.

52. "No N–Ties with DPRK: Musharraf," *The News,* Internet Edition, October 19, 2002.

53. United Nations arms inspectors discovered an Iraqi intelligence document that contained a 1990 offer of Pakistani nuclear weapons assistance, including bomb design information, to Iraq. Ramana and Nayyar, "India, Pakistan, and the Bomb," p 83.

54. For background, see Hagerty, "Kashmir and the Nuclear Question," and Hagerty, "Kashmir and the Nuclear Question Revisited."

55. Western media estimates put the number killed in Kashmir since 1989 at 33,000. Rama Lakshmi, "Kashmir Politics at 'Crucial Stage,'" *Washington Post,* November 17, 2002.

56. As I wrote in 1998: "Neither country has been willing to compromise on Kashmir, partly for strategic reasons, but also because to do so would be to deny the legitimating ideology on which each state was founded. Pakistan's two-nation theory held that the subcontinent's Muslims could safeguard their political rights only through the formation of a separate country. For Pakistanis, the idea of a Muslim-majority state falling within Indian borders is anathema, as it repudiates the two-nation theory and thus the entire basis for the creation of Pakistan. Indian leaders' secular ideology rests on the successful incorporation of all minorities, including Muslims, into the Indian political order. A Pakistani Kashmir would be an insult to Indian secularism. If Muslims's rights cannot be protected in Kashmir, they are subject to doubt throughout India. Kashmir is a zero-sum test for each state's legitimating ideology: one's validity invalidates the other." Hagerty, *Consequences of Nuclear Proliferation,* p 67.

57. Blank, "Kashmir: Fundamentalism Takes Root," p 42.

58. Kronstadt, "Pakistan–U.S. Relations," p 9.

59. For background on these groups, see Kumar, "Untying the Kashmir Knot," and Jessica Stern, "Pakistan's Jihad Culture," *Foreign Affairs,* 79:6 (November–December 2000), pp 115–126.

60. Kux, "India's Fine Balance," pp 98–100.

61. John Lancaster, "Pakistan to Follow India in Removing Troops from the Border," *Washington Post,* October 18, 2000.

62. John Lancaster, "India to Remove Some Forces from Border with Pakistan," *Washington Post,* October 17, 2002. The oft-quoted figure of 1 million Indian and Pakistani troops facing off against one another included troops in Kashmir.

63. President Pervez Musharraf's address to the nation, January 12, 2002. (Available at http://www.pak.gov.pk/President_Adresses/President_address.htm.)

64. Kumar, "Untying the Kashmir Knot."

65. Steve Coll, "Between India and Pakistan: A Changing Role for the U.S.," *Washington Post,* May 26, 2002.

66. Rahul Bedi and Anton LaGuardia, "Pakistan Steps Back from the Brink," *Daily Telegraph,* June 8, 2002.

67. "Musharraf: Here's What I'll Do," *Washington Post,* June 23, 2002.

68. Spokesman Richard Boucher, State Department Daily Briefing, October 31, 2002.

69. "Infiltration of Terrorists into J&K Down by Half: Army Chief," *Hindustan Times,* November 8, 2002.

70. Lancaster, "Pakistan to Follow India in Removing Troops from Border."

71. Musharraf said was "very close." "Musharraf: Here's What I'll Do." Vajpayee called it "a touch-and-go affair." "Vajpayee: Keep Your Promise," *Washington Post,* June 23, 2002. U.S. Assistant Secretary for South Asian Affairs Christina Rocca stated that the two sides had "barely averted war." "Deepening U.S. Engagement in South Asia."

72. Lancaster, "India to Remove Some Forces from Border with Pakistan."

73. Haqqani, "America's New Alliance with Pakistan," p 2–3.

74. Ibid., p 3.

75. Mandavi Mehta and Teresita C. Schaffer, "Two Elections: New Hopes and Old Frustrations," *South Asia Monitor*, No. 52, Center for Strategic and International Studies, November 1, 2002; Akram, "Pakistan–U.S. Relations after 9/11," p 116.

76. "National Assembly Party Position," *Dawn*, Internet Edition, November 4, 2002. Bhutto could not contest the election as she faces corruption charges and lives in exile.

77. John Lancaster, "Pakistanis Return to Polls with Cynicism," *Washington Post*, October 6, 2002.

78. Boucher, State Department Daily Briefing.

79. See Stern, "Pakistan's Jihad Culture." Samina Ahmed writes that "in the absence of public schooling, nearly a million Pakistanis are being educated in *madrassas*, where they are indoctrinated and trained by religious extremists." "The United States and Terrorism in Southwest Asia: September 11 and Beyond," *International Security*, 26:3 (Winter 2001–2002), p 91.

2

The Ongoing Conflict: Pakistan and India

Thomas P. Thornton

Among the world's trouble spots, only the dispute between Arabs and Israelis rivals that between India and Pakistan. Both have caused multiple wars, both date from the early post–World War II years, and both continue with unabated virulence. Hopes that the passage of time would reduce conflict and bitterness have proven vain; indeed, the intensity of conflict is in both cases at least as intense as it was in previous decades and solutions have turned out to be elusive. Josef Korbel, writing about the Kashmir dispute in 1954 observed "the two governments would agree on one matter only, namely, that neither wanted to stop the fighting without certain conditions which were respectively unacceptable to the other. On both sides there was an absence of that which is the paramount prerequisite for negotiation among any group of countries: a semblance of [goodwill]."[1] The remark has lost little of its validity in either case.

There are of course marked differences between the two. While Israel and (in varying combinations) the Arabs actively sought the involvement of the United States and Soviet Union in their conflict, India, with few exceptions, adamantly rejected the idea of any sort of outside involvement in its differences with Pakistan generally, and in the Kashmir dispute specifically. Pakistan, the weaker party, knew that only the involvement of outside forces, whether the United Nations, fellow Muslims, Americans, or Chinese, might give it the added strength necessary to confront India. As years passed, however, India was increasingly able to assert its position bilaterally and in international forums.

Both disputes were caught up in the politics of the Cold War, but there were notable differences. The former Soviet Union was always odd man out in the Middle East and hence played a dog-in-the-manger role there. After the Tashkent mediation of 1965, Moscow was increasingly a status quo power with regard to South Asia. Since the United States was also not interested in promoting conflict, Cold War dynamics generally tended to moderate conflict between India and Pakistan. There were exceptions, of course (the 1971 war being the most extreme), and there was always some Cold War overlay on South Asian regional matters, but the emptiness of allegations that Indo-Pakistani conflict was a product of global politics is demonstrated by the fact that the regional conflict has long outlasted the United States–Soviet Union Cold War.

Also, while both disputes have seen marked variations in intensity, there was a relatively "long peace" in South Asia that the Middle East never enjoyed. For over a decade—from the Shimla meeting in 1972 until the late 1980s, the Kashmir dispute was quiescent and thus much of the intensity and danger was taken out of the larger conflict between Pakistan and India. Whether or not Indira Gandhi and Z. A. Bhutto had agreed at Shimla to a long-term Kashmir settlement is unclear; what mattered more was that the dispute seemed to have been relegated to a very back burner.

KASHMIR REEMERGES

By the mid-1980s it appeared that the Kashmir dispute had been "settled" as much as it ever would be. India was in firm control of the Vale, the Kashmiris had apparently accepted their lot, and Pakistan was at worst sullen. India and Pakistan were preoccupied with domestic affairs and regional matters including Afghanistan and Sri Lanka. Outside actors such as the United States, the USSR, China, and some of the Muslim states, had no interest in stimulating Indo-Pakistani tensions and either avoided talking about Kashmir or urged the parties to work things out peacefully on their own. India's goal of excluding outside involvement in the region looked as if it might be attainable.

This stasis broke down badly at the end of the 1980s. Even as the Cold War was drawing to a close, the subcontinental conflict took on a new life. The trigger was a series of heavy-handed political moves by the Indian government that so outraged the Kashmiris that they launched a campaign of open resistance against Indian domination. This time it was not Pakistan that put the issue on the international agenda but the Kashmiris themselves—a situation that presented the Indians with a much more difficult challenge. Indian repression was extensive and severe, raising international criticism of Indian human rights practices. Soon enough, of course, Pakistan began to lend political, manpower, and material support to the insurgents and the atmosphere rapidly deteriorated.

The fact that the Cold War was coming to an end changed considerably the international setting of the renewed Indo-Pakistan dispute. No longer could India automatically expect full support from Moscow, nor could Pakistan have confidence in Washington or Beijing. More generally, the restraining framework that the United States–Soviet Union rivalry had provided for the previous decades could no longer be assumed. If neither of the Cold War enemies had much remaining political interest in the region, they might well stand by if India and Pakistan once again had at each other.

The Indian and Pakistani nuclear tests of 1998, coupled with their growing hostility, raised alarm signals throughout the world and revived external interest in the region. The United States especially sought to cap the nuclear genie and defuse regional tensions. The fact that nuclear weapons were now an open factor in the India–Pakistan equation opened new vistas for some Pakistani strategists. Drawing on the belief that mutual deterrence had kept the United States and Soviet Union from going to war, they reasoned that a general war between Pakistan and India was equally unlikely, and that Pakistani provocation of India would be low risk. Certainly Pakistan was much inferior to India even in nuclear capability, but parity is not essential for deterrence.

Another change that was taking place was the growing importance of India on the international scene. This was partly because of improved Indian economic growth and the spread of globalization, but also the fact that new equations were emerging as the Cold War paradigm disappeared. In the course of President Clinton's second term, Washington began to show an increasing interest and, at the same time, nations of East Asia that had largely ignored India over the previous years began to extend a tentative hand of cooperation. Pakistan was enjoying no such upswing in its international position; on the contrary, its role had slipped perceptibly as it lost its status as a frontline state in the Cold War, lagged economically, and was increasingly subject to internal disorder.[2]

To Lahore and Back

Even aside from the nuclear tests, the last year of the old century was a dramatic one. The visit of Prime Minister Atal Behari Vajpayee to Lahore, where he met with Prime Minister Mian Nawaz Sharif, was the most promising moment in ties between the two countries for decades. The two sides seemed genuinely committed to finding a peaceful settlement to the Kashmir problem that, in turn, could perhaps open the way to genuine peace and cooperation on the subcontinent. Observers were encouraged by the fact that each nation enjoyed credible, democratic leadership. Even while the two prime ministers were meeting, however, Pakistan's military leaders were laying plans for action that would catastrophically set back the relationship.[3]

In spring, forces based in Pakistan moved to cut a crucial Indian supply line in the Kargil area of Kashmir and enjoyed initial success. As so often happens in Pakistani policy, however, a seemingly brilliant tactical move was but a first step into strategic disaster. The Indians responded with full military force, making it clear that the nuclear stalemate would not deter them from defending their strategic interests. Equally unfortunate from the Pakistani point of view was international reaction. Islamabad had probably expected that the international community, fearful of a nuclear outbreak on the subcontinent, would intervene and force a compromise solution that would almost inevitably further Pakistan's interests. This did not happen, however, and outside, primarily American, pressure compelled Pakistan to withdraw ignominiously. While the Indians had suffered heavy casualties, their military and political victory at Kargil was a galvanizing factor for Indian pride and determination not to yield to Pakistani pressure. Given the fact that the Kargil adventure was undertaken at the very time the "Lahore spirit" was being cultivated, New Delhi understandably saw the affair as a clear example of Pakistani treachery.[4]

The Kargil events had political repercussions in both countries. In India, it ensured the return of a strengthened Bharatiya Janata Party (BJP) in the Indian general elections. In Pakistan, it was one of several factors contributing the October 12 coup in which army chief General Pervez Musharraf deposed Nawaz Sharif. Indians profess to be loath to deal with military governments (in Pakistan at least) and in addition, Musharraf was the man who was presumably planning the Kargil assault even as Vajpayee and Nawaz Sharif were exchanging toasts in Lahore. Musharraf's initial gestures of goodwill—pullback of some of the Pakistani troops along the border and a call for an equitable, unconditional, and result-oriented dialogue that emphasized Kashmir as the core issue—found no resonance in New Delhi. India sharply denounced undemocratic Pakistan in the Commonwealth and forced the cancellation of the annual meeting of the South Asian Association for Regional Cooperation (SAARC) as a way of keeping Pakistan isolated. The message was driven home by India's refusal (except for the 1999 World Cup) to play cricket against any Pakistani team. An agreement reached by military commanders in November to avoid cross-border shelling that endangered civilians was only a modest ray of light.[5]

Relations took a further downward turn on December 24 when an Indian civilian airliner was hijacked by an Islamic militant group based in Pakistan. There ensued a long odyssey that ultimately ended on December 31 in Kandahar, Afghanistan, where the hijackers released the passengers in return for three prisoners whom the Indians held for terrorist activities. The entire affair was a humiliation for India, which of course reflexively accused Pakistan of being behind the hijacking. Pakistan hinted darkly that the entire affair had been a provocation staged by Indian intelligence. Soon afterwards the Indians arrested four individuals in Mumbai who, they claimed, had connections to Pakistan's Interservices Intelligence directorate (ISI) and to the Harakat-ul-Ansar organization that carried out the hijacking. International observers were less than convinced by the Indians' evidence, and Indian demands for the extradition of the hijackers themselves, two of whom were by this time appearing publicly in Pakistan, went unheeded. Whether the Pakistan government was itself directly involved remains open to question, but the broad mass of Indians are convinced that it was.[6] As Devesh Kapur points out, the combination of Kargil (where Pakistani misbehavior was manifest to the Indians), and Kandahar (where they suspected it) had a striking effect not only on Hindu nationalists, but across the whole Indian political spectrum. It confirmed the belief that Pakistan, and in particular the Pakistani military that was once again in power, could not be trusted.[7]

The dialogue between the two countries stagnated during the ensuing months and the Indians, following the Kandahar hijacking, asserted that further negotiation was conditioned on Pakistan's stopping cross-border incursions of militants into Kashmir. Since the government in Islamabad cannot even with the best of intentions completely control cross-border movement, New Delhi had a ready-made tool for controlling the pace of any renewed dialogue. And, of course, whether Islamabad had the "best of intentions" in this regard is certainly open to dispute. The Pakistanis for their part seemingly pushed for negotiations but only if the centrality of the Kashmir dispute is accepted by India. As if to punctuate their hostility, each party resorted to arresting (and occasionally roughing up) diplomats of the other side, declaring them spies, and expelling them—which of course led to reprisals in kind. Killings within Kashmir and fighting along the LOC, including the Siachen glacier, continued at a deadly rate.

The broader change in the relative positions of India and Pakistan was highlighted by the visit of President Clinton to the region in March. The tense atmosphere was sharpened by the slaughter of thirty-six Sikhs in Kashmir which India blamed on the Pakistan-based Lashkar-i-Toiba.[8] Clinton spent five days in India in an atmosphere of warmth and cooperation; he stopped in Pakistan only long enough to deliver a television address that resembled a lecture to recalcitrant schoolboys. If Pakistan had ever basked in American approval, this was clearly no longer the case. American policy had made clear a preference for India that was not unconditional, but undoubtedly strong.

Hopeful Initiatives from Kashmir

A break in the logjam came during the summer of 2000—not initially from Islamabad or New Delhi, but from within Kashmir. First, the Legislative Assembly in Kashmir called for a restoration of the state's autonomy, but this fell on deaf ears in Delhi. Then, on June 24, the Hizb-ul-Mujahidin, a Kashmiri resistance group, called for a three-month cease fire within Kashmir and talks with the Indian government. India was loath to enter into any negotiations to which Pakistan would be a party and insisted that talks be held within the Indian constitution (i.e., excluding any fundamental change in status for Kashmir). The various parties maneuvered gingerly through these political minefields but ultimately no agreement was possible on either point and the Hizb abandoned its offer on August 8. While the offer came to nothing, it did set the wheels of negotiation back in motion and caused both India and Pakistan to explore greater flexibility, at least in their approach to the question of Pakistani involvement in talks between India and the Kashmiris.[9]

The last months of 2000 showed surprising signs of promise, as the government of India implemented on November 27 a unilateral ceasefire for the month of Ramadan. Pakistan responded in a positive manner, stating on December 2 that it would act with maximum restraint. Islamabad went on to urge the Indians to negotiate with the All Parties Hurriyat Conference (APHC), an umbrella organization of Kashmiri political parties, and Foreign Minister Abdul Sattar did not insist on Pakistani participation in the talks. Tensions along the line of control lessened considerably although violence within Kashmir—presumably caused by groups that were unwilling to accept the idea of a ceasefire—continued and caused considerable casualties among Indian security forces. Particularly troublesome was an attack on the Red Fort in Delhi, mounted by the Lashkar-i-Toiba on December 22, 2000. A further discordant note was arguing back and forth of whether or not APHC members could go to Pakistan for discussions that might lead to fruitful trilateral dialogue. The Indians refused permission to four of the APHC members; under the circumstances, the other four delegation members refused to go, putting the prospect of talks again on hold. India did, however, extend the cease-fire until January 26, 2001, and then once more until February 19. Looking back over the past several months, Zaffar Abbas wrote in the *Herald* that the two countries were witnessing "unprecedented gestures for peace." He was exaggerating and little had been accomplished beyond posturing, but the two sides seemed to have come a remarkable distance since Kargil.[10]

The year 2001 thus started off with some promise. On January 15, India conveyed its desire for a summit meeting with Pakistan under the helpfully vague rubric of a "composite dialogue" and the proposal was repeated a month later in a speech by President Narayanan. Meanwhile, on the occasion of a devastating earthquake in the Indian state of Gujarat, Pakistan sent some relief goods and on February 8, President Musharraf called Prime Minister Vajpayee to express his condolences. This was the first contact between Indian and Pakistani leaders in twenty months. A week later, the two countries agreed to stop targeting civilian areas in the cross-border shooting that remained an everyday occurrence along the LOC.[11]

UN Secretary General Kofi Annan's call for Pakistan and India once again to take up direct talks was widely echoed by other world leaders. Then on May 23 Vajpayee invited Musharraf to come to India for discussions, even though Indians were not convinced that Pakistan had made sufficient effort to halt infiltration of terrorists into Kashmir. Musharraf accepted the invitation on May 29, indicating that the talks did not have to be concerned exclusively with the Kashmir issue. Each side thus seemed willing to finesse the matters that had proven so troublesome before and soon thereafter the groundwork began to be laid for the Agra Summit.

THE AGRA SUMMIT

The meeting between the two leaders generated a vast amount of publicity, wild speculation, and excessive expectations. Much was made of the fact that the two leaders were well positioned to come to an agreement. Their respective bona fides on the Indo-Pakistan issue was unquestioned in the eyes of most of their countrymen and each seemed to be genuinely interested in making progress. There were, however, profound disagreements, especially over how Kashmir was to be handled, and both sides engaged in extensive "public diplomacy" to position themselves for the meeting.[12]

Musharraf, accompanied by his wife and a substantial delegation, arrived in New Delhi on July 14 and spent the day on a mixture of protocol calls and, to the delight of the media, a visit to the home where he had lived in Delhi when a boy. Over Indian objections, Musharraf also met with a delegation from the APHC. The following day he proceeded to Agra, where he and Vajpayee got together privately, followed by a meeting of their respective delegations.

Prospects for a successful outcome fell victim to the assiduous spin-doctoring engaged in by each side. The first discordant note was sounded by the Indian information minister who, in her briefing on the private bilateral talks, did not include Kashmir among the topics covered; the Pakistanis were irritated and refuted her statement. Negotiations on a joint declaration that would bridge some of the gaps between Pakistan and India nonetheless continued on into the early hours of the following morning.

It was now the Pakistanis turn to use the media in a disruptive manner. Musharraf held a meeting with a group of Indians on the morning of the 16th in which he stressed the centrality of the Kashmir issue and dealt with other issues, ranging from the Indo-Pakistan War of 1971 to the prospects for joint confidence-building measures, in ways that were offensive to India. Although it had been a closed meeting, the Pakistanis passed a tape of the meeting on to Star TV and within a short time it was relayed into every South Asian television set. As the *Herald* pointed out, the interview was a media coup, but a diplomatic faux pas that raised the ire of the Indians, who in turn released Vajpayee's opening statement to the summit that had stressed the terrorism issue but did not mention Kashmir. (They also made sure that Musharraf did not have a press conference upon his departure.) Two further meetings were held between the two leaders and the delegations continued work on a statement during the day. They seemed tantalizingly close to success, but were unable to find mutually acceptable wording on Kashmir and terrorism. Late in the evening Musharraf flew back to Pakistan empty handed.[13]

In the immediate aftermath of the summit, diplomats on both sides sought to put the best face on the outcome, noting that Vajpayee had accepted an invitation for a return visit to Pakistan and the dialogue would continue. The summit was a failure, however, and strengthened the hands of hard-liners on either side who always expect the worst from such a meeting and do everything they can to bring such an outcome about. Even Vajpayee would soon be claiming that Musharraf had no intention to pursue a path of friendship[14] and others would trumpet the outcome as a success, in that the Indians had not capitulated to Pakistan as (they argued) had been the case in previous summits. Beyond leaving a bad taste in everybody's mouth, Agra soon slipped out of memory as, essentially, a nonevent.

THE WORLD REORDERED

The post–Cold War order involved the emergence of new issues, such as nuclear weaponry, that only partially provided the kind of global paradigm that the

United States–Soviet Union rivalry had offered. For the greater part, conflicts such as that between India and Pakistan could be sorted out on their own merits. The September 11th attacks on the World Trade Center in New York and the Pentagon marked a major shift back to globalism. It brought home that there are destructive forces transcending national and regional boundaries and the United States, in the person of President George W. Bush, manipulated it much the same way earlier American presidents had manipulated the Cold War. Terrorism was declared to be the defining global issue and the slogan "If you aren't with us you're against us" was resurrected as a guide for American policy.

This new globalism was nowhere as evident as in Washington's approach to South Asia. As the emotion-laden but vague word "terrorism" shot to the forefront of international attention it played into the zero-sum politics of the region. The hijackers who piloted their flying bombs were evidently members of Osama bin Laden's Al Qaeda, which was based in Afghanistan under the protective wing of the Taliban regime. The Taliban, for its part, had essentially been created and brought to power by Pakistan and other *jihadi* remnants, if not Al Qaeda itself, were supplying many of the shock troops of the Islamist rebellion within Indian-held Kashmir.

India was quickly among the most enthusiastic supporters of the United States, demanding that Pakistan be branded a terrorist state since it was the transit route and perhaps also the sponsor of "terrorists" who went to Kashmir. While India could be wholeheartedly "with us" in the cause of terrorism, it could portray Pakistan as "against us." (The Israelis and Russians saw similar prospects in enlisting more U.S. support against Palestinian and Chechen "terrorism.") Given the already evident predilection for India that had carried over from Clinton to Bush, New Delhi had the highest hopes for the American role in South Asia. Rather than adhere to the Nehruvian premise that the United States was best excluded from South Asia, Vajpayee and his foreign minister, Jaswant Singh, embraced an American regional role. India had seemingly found a new international mooring to replace at least part of the gap left when non-alignment became an anachronism.

It would not, however, be that simple. General Musharraf was faced with a dreadful choice. He could maintain Pakistan's lines to the Taliban and keep the pressure on in Kashmir, but the cost would be throwing the United States into the arms of India. Or, he could throw his lot in with the Americans, allowing Pakistan to be used as a springboard for the attack on Afghanistan, and withstand Islamist outrage within his own country as best he could. Musharraf chose the latter course and in return was showered with considerable American generosity. Pakistan moved from being a frontline state against Communism to a frontline state against terrorism. For the Indians, this meant that they would be at best one of two American allies in South Asia, not in the privileged position they had hoped to attain. As Arun Swamy commented India confronted "a simple fact of geography. Pakistan bordered on Afghanistan, India did not."[15]

On October 1, at the time of a visit by Secretary of State Colin Powell to India, terrorists attacked the Legislative Assembly in Srinagar, leaving twelve dead. India blamed Pakistan, making more than the usual threatening noises. Particularly disturbing were suggestions that the American attack on the Taliban regime in Afghanistan provided a good model for how India should deal with terrorist groups based in Pakistan.[16] The United States wanted to avoid an open conflict in South Asia that would not only have nuclear overtones but would also distract from the war on terrorism, and Powell apparently convinced the Indians that they should refrain from military action against Pakistan as long as there were no more major terrorist attacks. Under reported pressure from the United States and the United Kingdom, Musharraf called Vajpayee to express his condolences and promised to investigate whether there was any Pakistani involvement.[17]

The two sides exchanged ambivalent statements about renewed dialogue: On October 17 Vajpayee stated that Kashmir is indeed the key to Indo-Pakistan relations and needed to be discussed, but added that overall negotiations could not be conditioned on Kashmir. Later in the month, he renewed India's position that talks were pointless as long as Pakistan supported terrorism. The Pakistanis sent a demarche to India on October 23 protesting "provocative statements" but followed this up a week later with reassurances that they wanted to resume the Agra dialogue.[18]

Despite international and regional concern, it does not appear that either side was seriously thinking of war. Even though the events of September 11th provided a new context, signals were generally ones of exasperated patience on the Indian side and something more than minimum concern for restraint by the Pakistanis. Inside Kashmir itself, violence continued at a high level during 2001; reportedly over 100 Indian security personnel and 2,000 "militants" were killed in fighting within the disputed state.[19]

THE ATTACK ON PARLIAMENT

On December 13, tensions took a quantum leap toward the abyss. Militants from the Lashkar-i-Toiba and Jaish-i-Muhammad launched an attack on the Parliament building in New Delhi. Although casualties were low, the symbolism of an assault on the heart of the Indian government went far beyond anything that had happened previously and roused the anger of all Indians; it was for India a mini–September 11th. Vajpayee described it as "transgressing the limits of patience" and, taking his cue from President Bush, declared that India would "liquidate terrorists wherever they are." Other countries echoed his demand that Pakistan end all activities of the Lashkar and Jaish inside Pakistan. Rhetoric notwithstanding, the Indian government apparently decided that, rather than resort immediately to high-risk means such as cross-border strikes and hot pursuit, it would orchestrate a program of political and military pressures. New Delhi recalled its envoy to Islamabad and cut transport lines to Pakistan, including the withdrawal of permission for Pakistani aircraft to fly over India. Most important, by Christmas, Indian troops had begun to move towards the Pakistan border—even some pulled away from the Sino-Indian front—in a show of strength and intimidation.[20]

The Indians were seeking to make clear that Musharraf could no longer bask in international approbation as a stalwart in the war against terrorism in Afghanistan while still supporting the *jihad* in Kashmir. His initial reaction cautioned against adventurism and offered a joint probe of the attack—and, of course, added the usual dark hint that the entire thing might have been an Indian conspiracy. By year's end, however, he froze the assets of the Jaish and Lashkar and banned the two organizations. Pakistan did not recall its envoy to New Delhi and continued to take the position that talks were desirable, perhaps at the upcoming meeting of the SAARC heads of government in Kathmandu. Vajpayee dismissed the idea of a joint probe and declined a meeting in Kathmandu (although a brief encounter did take place). On January 11, Indian Chief of Army Staff Padmanabhan announced that his forces were ready for war.

Musharraf delivered a speech on January 12 that appeared to mark a watershed in Pakistani policy. Although it addressed primarily internal Pakistani matters, it promised to root out the *jihadi* culture that was proving so costly to Pakistan and Musharraf promised specifically that no organization would be allowed to engage in terrorism in the name of Kashmir. It went far toward addressing the criticisms that Indians and others had leveled against Pakistan and Vajpayee welcomed it, saying that if the Pakistanis were to "shed their anti-Indian mentality," India would be willing to go more than halfway in negotiations. First of all, however, Pakistan must back up with action its intention to stop cross-border terrorism.[21] In the meantime, military pressure continued unabated and soon as many as a million troops would be facing each other across the border. Pakistan called for talks about a phased withdrawal of troops, but Indian Defense Minister Fernandes ruled that out. Secretary Powell's January 16th offer of U.S. assistance in facilitating talks bore no fruit although American concern probably helped to keep the temperature down.[22]

The course of the next several months is enigmatic. Both sides built up their forces, uttered threats, said that nuclear war was unthinkable but then equivocated, and pleaded their case before the court of international opinion. Whether war was ever imminent is something that probably only a few Indians know, for the Indians held the initiative in what they came to call their strategy of "coercive diplomacy."[23] The danger of an Indian attack had to be fully credible if the Pakistanis were to be intimidated in this war of nerves and—at least as important—international opinion was to be mobilized to put pressure on Pakistan to do better in fulfilling his commitments. Assuming that Pakistan did all that it could to seal off the border (an assumption the Indians were never willing to make in public at least), India was very successful. While a continuing parade of American emissaries to South Asia did caution India and urge it to the negotiating table, that was a minor irritant compared to the pressure they put on Pakistan to rein in the militants and the ensuing decline in infiltration. Indeed, by using the emissaries as conduits for Pakistani promises of good behavior, New Delhi enlisted the United States in overseeing that behavior. India had—especially after September 11th—learned to manipulate external involvement to its own advantage. There was a potential political cost to be paid in that once Americans and others were involved, they would start involving themselves in the politics of the Kashmir problem, but New Delhi evidently felt that it would be able to handle these pressures.

Musharraf during those months continued to protest that Pakistan was doing everything possible to restrain the militants and pointed out that he was incurring high political costs not only for his Kashmir policy but also for stalwart support of American policy in Afghanistan. The initiative was however with India, and Pakistani policies during the period were essentially reactive.

The situation took a dangerous turn when, on May 24, terrorists from a previously unknown group perpetrated a deadly attack at Kalchuk in which twenty-four Indians, mostly civilians, were killed and forty-three injured. General Padmanabhan demanded action and the United States was called upon to put still more pressure on Pakistan. Vajpayee lashed out angrily and Pakistan was told to withdraw its high commissioner and was reportedly given two weeks to end cross-border terrorism and disband training camps. Attempting to defuse the situation, Musharraf in a May 27 television speech reiterating his promises to rein in the militants and used the visiting British foreign minister to transmit his renewed pledge to New Delhi. Indian foreign minister Jaswant Singh dismissed the promises as unconvincing. The whole affair had something of a set piece, with all actors behaving predictably.

Yet June was a crucial month. On the one hand, there were actually positive signs. Pakistan arrested twenty-four militants late in the month and promulgated an ordinance that would control the *madrassas* (although Musharraf had to backtrack soon). Pakistani aircraft were again permitted to fly over India, Jaswant said that maybe Musharraf's promises were a step forward, the Indian high commissioner returned to Islamabad, and Defense Minister Fernandes recorded a "perceptible decline" in militant activity. He ruled out any deescalation of the confrontation, however, and there is general agreement that during June the danger of a war was at its highest and international concern was most intense. The Indians soon claimed that Musharraf was backing away from his promises and American officials hastened to get still more Pakistani reassurances.[24] But the war that seemed imminent to many did not come about and was probably never meant to. An intriguing story in the *New York Times* suggested that the Indian business community played a significant role in restraining the government from setting out on a course that could have been ruinous for the economy.[25] New Delhi denied this, but in the increasingly interdependent world of economics (not to mention nuclear weaponry) no Indian government could consider war except under the most dire circumstances.

For the remainder of the summer the Indo-Pakistani relationship remained on hold. In late July, Secretary Powell visited South Asia and continued the American balancing act by urging India to take further deescalatory steps and reminding New Delhi that Kashmir was again on the international agenda; in Pakistan he observed that cross-border infiltration had not completely stopped, but that tensions had lessened. Although acts of violence (including the slaughter of twenty-eight civilians in Jammu on July 17) took place and dire accusations were hurled, the focus was the next stage of India's strategy, state-level elections to be held in Kashmir in the autumn. Both the United States and the United Kingdom indicated that they would avoid new initiatives until the elections were over.

Part of Powell's message (and that of others who followed him) was that Pakistan should not attempt to disrupt the elections that, India hoped, would produce a new government in Kashmir that the people respected and with whom New Delhi could deal. Pakistan, for its part, was also busy planning for nationwide elections. Incidents continued for the next several months and India maintained its coercive diplomacy posture at full strength, declaring that a violence-free election was a precondition for demobilization along the frontier and political dialogue. Although Musharraf expressed contempt for the Indian electoral process he did agree in August to rein in violence and the run-up to the elections was, by the standards of Kashmir, not especially violent.[26] There was, according to Indian sources, a significant military action in the Malchi sector of the LOC in August, which Pakistan denied, and late in the month U.S. Deputy Secretary of State Armitage cautioned the Pakistanis concerning some increase in cross-border activity. Armitage added, however, that he felt that the Pakistani government was not behind the infiltration and the United States declined to brand Pakistan a terrorist state, as the Indians repeatedly demanded.[27]

Meetings between Indian and Pakistani officials at SAARC meetings produced at least a minimum degree of civility, even while the governments continued to level charges at each other. Exchanges were particularly vitriolic following the massacre of worshippers at a Hindu temple in Gujarat in September that India blamed on Pakistan-based terrorists, and an unseemly exchange of accusations between Musharraf and Vajpayee at the United Nations General Assembly session. A moment of no little embarrassment came in September, when militants[28] within Pakistan told a *New York Times* reporter that the Pakistani government continued to permit them to cross into Kashmir, a charge which Islamabad promptly denied. There was little doubt that infiltration continued and that probably at least some elements of the Pakistani government condoned it. The level was enough for the Indians to continue their coercive posture but not so outrageous that it provoked a war.

India increasingly realized that it had achieved about as much as it could hope for from its coercive diplomacy. The huge forward deployment was costly in terms of manpower and financial resources and its utility increasingly questionable since the likelihood of India actually starting a conflict by this point was barely credible. India had shown its determination and, in a sense, won the "Fourth Indo-Pakistan War"[29] by forcing Pakistan to foreswear direct support to Kashmiri insurgency (even granting some slips in practice). Now, however, Washington and others were beginning to focus increasingly on Indian intransigence rather than the diminished *jihadi* activity. As the Kashmir elections approached, policy remained in a state of suspended animation awaiting the answer to two questions: first, would Pakistan-based militants make a major effort to disrupt the polls, and second, would a sufficiently free and fair election take place so that the resulting government could become a negotiating partner.

ELECTIONS AND BEYOND

The election process in Kashmir did in fact provide sufficiently positive answers to both of these questions so that India could announce, on October 16, that it would pull back troops from the forward positions they had occupied since early spring along the international border. Pakistan called the move a "step in the right direction" and followed suit the next day. India would not, however, reduce its presence along the LOC in Kashmir nor would it engage in a dialogue with Pakistan until support for terrorism had stopped.[30] The redeployments were an important step in that they marked the end of India's coercive diplomacy, implying that negotiation with the new Kashmiri government and later with Pakistan could now take precedence. They did nothing, however, to change the basic shape of the dispute nor, despite a mood of euphoria following the elections, was there any indication that New Delhi had a clear idea of how to extricate itself from its negative posture on negotiations.[31]

At the Lahore meeting, the two countries seemed to be taking charge of their own fates. Although mutual suspicions still ran high and each carefully kept an eye on international opinion, they had positioned themselves to come to an agreement that would be virtually independent of external considerations. The South Asian international system was poised to assert a degree of autonomy and attain a degree of stability that had eluded it for decades.[32] Even if the expectations of Lahore were inflated, Pakistan and India were going in the right direction, toward settlement and away from military conflict.

In the past four years, however, the situation has changed radically. First, the credible threat of violence became the dominant means of communication between the two states. Negotiations are rejected by India and advocated by Pakistan mainly for tactical advantage. Important bilateral matters ranging from trade and water sharing to the status of the Siachen dispute have fallen by the wayside and apparently there is not even any significant back-channel contact. Relations between these two giant neighbors are totally sterile. When announcing the decision to reduce forces on the border, Defense Minister Fernandes described the action as unilateral since "we don't interact with Pakistan."

Second, both India and Pakistan have mortgaged their policy to the opinion and actions of outsiders, notably the United States which has again become globalist and interventionist in its global "war" on terrorism. The push factor is no longer the bugbear "communism" but the new concern "terrorism;" the pull factor remains the same—Indo–Pakistan hostility. Whenever the political temperature rose in 2002, American representatives scurried off to South Asia to tend the fragile regional balance in ways reminiscent of a generation earlier. India was praised for its forbearance but urged to reduce military pressure on Pakistan while Pakistan got its good chit for retraining militants but was urged to do better. These comings and goings became the benchmarks of South Asian policy that were highlighted in the regional press, more than any constructive initiatives of India and Pakistan themselves.

To the extent that South Asians have the initiative, it has been individuals and organizations more than governments. Inside Kashmir, the government of India has been unable to pacify the Kashmiris, thus perpetuating a running sore that drains India's resources and is an irresistible target for involvement by Pakistanis. The Pakistan government is unable to control what goes on in terms of Muslim extremism within its borders; it has little hope of keeping members of these groups from crossing into India even if it wanted to. Thus, persons committed in one way or another to the Kashmiri cause have been able to seize much of the initiative. Perhaps a new state government emerging from the fall 2002 elections will show a way forward. Meanwhile the two nations that came so close to gaining mastery over their own affairs at Lahore have let slip the keys to their own future.

NOTES

1. *Danger in Kashmir,* revised edition (Princeton, N.J.: Princeton University Press, 1954), p 132.

2. See Christian Wagner, "Indiens Weltpolitische Rolle," in *Internationale Politik*, 3/1997, pp 1–8. On Pakistan's foreign policy: Thomas P. Thornton, "Pakistan: Fifty Years of Insecurity," in Selig S. Harrison, et al., eds., *India and Pakistan: The First Fifty Years* (Cambridge: Cambridge University Press, 1999). Pakistan's sensitivity to the shift can be seen in its sharp reaction when Southeast Asian nations put more pressure on it than on India to solve the mid-2002 crisis (*Dawn,* August 2, 2002). Note: All references to South Asian daily newspapers are to Internet editions.

3. The events of this period are described in some detail in my "A Long Way to Lahore: India and Pakistan Negotiate," in Charles H. Kennedy and Craig Baxter, eds., *Pakistan 2000* (Lanham, Md.: Lexington Books, 2000).

4. See Amelendu Misra, "The Centrality of Kashmir in Indo-Pakistan Security Dynamics," *International Politics,* 38:2 (March 2001), p 110. On Kargil more generally, General Ashok Krishna and P. R. Chari, eds., *Kargil: The Tables Turned* (New Delhi: Manohar Publishers and Distributors, 2001), and Bruce Reidel, "American Diplomacy and the 1999 Kargil Summit at Blair House," *Center for the Advanced Study of India*

Policy Paper Series 2002 (Philadelphia: University of Pennsylvania, 2002). (Accessible online at http://sas.upenn.edu/casi/reports/ReidelPaper051302.htm.)

5. Rajesh M. Basrur, "Nuclear Confidence Building in the Post-Kargil Scenario," in Moonis Ahmad, ed., *The Challenge of Confidence-Building in South Asia* (New Delhi: Har-Anand Publications, 2001), pp 424, 426.

6. *Asian News Digest* (continuation of *Asian Reporter,* hereafter *AMD*), pp 84, 86. Also *South Asia Monitor,* No. 18, February 1, 2001, and *India Today,* January 19 and March 1, 2000.

7. Devesh Kapur, "India in 1999," *Asian Survey,* 46:1 (January–February 2000), p 206.

8. *India Today,* March 20, 2000.

9. *South Asia Monitor,* No. 25, September 1, 2000, and *Herald* (Karachi), August 2000, pp 261ff.

10. *India Today,* December 18, 2000; January 15, 2001; January 29, 2001. Also, *AND*, pp 851, 858, and Zaffar Abbas, "Inching Toward Peace," *Herald,* January 2001, pp 84ff.

11. *AND*, 906, 918, 1181,

12. See *India Today,* July 9 and July 16, 2002.

13. For analysis of the Agra Summit see Zaffar Abbas, "Reality Checkpoint on the Road to Peace," *Herald,* August 2001, pp 64–69; *India Today,* July 30, 2001; and Teresita Schaffer and Mandavi Mehta, "The Agra Summit," *South Asia Monitor,* No. 36, August 1, 2001. The extent of Indian irritation is reflected in J. N. Dixit, "India–Pakistan Relations," in a special issue of *India Quarterly,* 57:2 (April–June 2001). Virtually all of the contributions to the issue give a disturbing gauge of Indian bitterness over the meeting.

14. *India Today,* July 28, 2001.

15. Arun Swamy, "India in 2002: A Year of Living Dangerously," *Asian Survey,* 47:1 (January–February 2001), p 174.

16. *India Today,* October 20, 2001. Later, Indians would cite President Bush on Iraq as justifying a preemptive Indian strike on Pakistan.

17. *AND,* 1509.

18. *AND,* 1542. According to the *Telegraph* (Calcutta), October 18, 2001, Vajpayee's October 17 statement went further than any previous Indian statement in acknowledging the gravity of the Kashmir dispute.

19. *India Today,* December 13, 2001.

20. Ibid.; also, *AND,* 1668. For a highly dramatic interpretation of the events of late December, see *Herald*, January, 2002, pp 32ff.

21. Indian officials reportedly specified that not only was border-crossing to be ended and camps be dismantled in Pakistan, but Islamabad had to order an end to all activities inside Kashmir and also to stop all wireless communications associated with the militants' activities, *News* (Karachi), August 7, 2002.

22. In this point and others in this paragraph, the analysis follows Mandavi Mehta and Teresita C. Schaffer, "India and Pakistan: Can Crisis Become Opportunity," *South Asia Monitor*, No. 42, February 1, 2002.

23. The concept and its execution are discussed by Jasjit Singh in *Indian Express,* July 31, 2002. Also K. Subramanyam in *Times of India*, June 24, and P. R. Chari in *The Hindu,* July 11. For Pakistani interpretations, see M. A. Bhatty in *Dawn,* August 8, 2002, and S. J. Burki, *Dawn,* July 2, 2002.

24. In a June 17, 2002, *Newsweek* interview, Musharraf denied that he had given any pledges about cross-border activity; the U.S. Embassy in New Delhi stated, however, that Musharraf had given American officials such a promise, *AND,* 2100.

25. Thomas Friedman, *New York Times,* July 11, 2001.

26. According to Shekar Gupta, *Indian Express,* October 19, 2002, during the first nine months of 2002, incidents and casualties among Indian forces were at half the level of the previous year. See also opinion pieces by Ragavan, K. K. Katyal, and Raja Mohan in *The Hindu,* of July 14, July 22, and October 10, 2002, respectively.

27. *AND,* 2245, 2246, 2252.

28. *New York Times,* September 20, 2002; Pakistan News Service, September 22, 2002.

29. The phrase is from the Pakistani journalist M. B. Naqvi, writing in the *News,* cited by K. K. Katyal, *The Hindu,* June 24, 2002.

30. *The Hindu,* October 16, 2002; *Daily Times,* October 17, 2002.

31. American Ambassador Blackwill in New Delhi lost no time in telling the Indians that the ball was now in their court and that they should move forward to negotiations with Pakistan. Interview with *Indian Express,* October 19, 2002.

32. On this concept and its application in South Asia, see Thomas Perry Thornton, *The Challenge to U.S. Policy in the Third World: Global Responsibilities and Regional Devolution* (Boulder, Colo. Westview Press, 1986), especially pp 23–26 and chapter 6.

3

In the Shadow of the Past: Pakistan's Afghan Policy

Rasul Bakhsh Rais

There are complex factors rooted in history, religion, and overlapping ethnicity that bind Afghanistan and Pakistan together. Despite political disputes, porous and largely undefined borders, and tribal affiliations have kept the flow of goods and people through the mountain passes uninterrupted. Neither the authorities in Kabul or in Islamabad have ever tried, or whenever they tried to so do under the pressure of events, succeeded in stemming their movement. The reason is very simple, the historical patterns of migrations, market integration, and interdependence of local communities and their transborder networks have significance beyond the narrow calculus of national interest. Even when rulers in both countries were displeased and angry with and hostile to each other, goods and people kept moving in both directions. This makes them sort of natural allies both in hard and good times. But it would be wrong to conclude that Afghanistan and Pakistan are indispensable to each other.[1] Iran and the Central Asian states have important stakes in the adjacent regions of Afghanistan, and for that reason have evolved significant links essentially with the non-Pashtun ethnic communities of the country.

For the past quarter century, successive bouts of war in Afghanistan that have devastated its economy, society, and state institutions have further deepened linkages, contacts, and a sense of common stakes of Afghanistan and Pakistan in stability and peace in that country. But parallel to a feeling of common stakes is the issue of conflicting definition of what is common between the two countries. This has been the most fundamental and critical problem in Pakistan's relations with Afghanistan primarily for two reasons. First and foremost, Afghanistan as a nation and country has remained fragmented along regional, sectarian, and ethnic lines, and no group there could authoritatively claim to represent national interests. Politically polarized and divided as the Afghan groups have been in at least two but generally in more than two camps, their material and political need to seek foreign support, and the involvement of great powers and regional states with them have always made it difficult to reach an understanding with Pakistan on what was common between the two countries and what was not. As a result of internal confrontation among them, the issue of commonality of interest became the function of the nature of ties of Pakistan with a particular Afghan group or set of groups. It is therefore not only the ethnic definition of what is good for Afghanistan, which in any case cannot be separated from groups' interests in political power, but also choices Pakistan made in the Afghan game. Pakistan's images as a friend or enemy of Afghanistan have therefore been largely determined by the degree of closeness to any specific group and degree of material assistance it provided to fight its rivals.

Pakistan was more open in providing assistance to all Afghan groups that joined the resistance movement against the Soviet forces than it was after Moscow withdrew its forces in 1989. Even during that period, some of the Afghan groups, particularly non-Pashtun groups from the north of the country complained that Pakistan was playing favorites and it leaned heavily toward the Hizb-i-Islami (Party of Islam). Such complaints were not without substance. Those handling Pakistan's Afghan policy in the Interservices Intelligence (ISI) and some in the Foreign Office found the Hizb and its leader Gulbaddin Hekmatyar closer to their political and military objectives. More significantly, there was deeper trust and understanding with this party than with anyone in the Afghan resistance. The strategic swing was more visible when the *mujahideen* took over control of power and the balance in Kabul shifted in favor of Jamiat-i-Islami and its leaders, late commander Ahmad Shah Masud and Burhanuddin Rabbani and their allies. No country in a situation of conflict with a political and security agenda of its own while competing with other regional rivals can pursue an even-handed policy. Pakistan's Afghanistan policy was no exception to the general dilemma that states bordering on a troubled country with a legacy of interventions by outside actors face.

Analysts and diplomatic historians will continue to probe the question as to why Pakistan become a major player in the second "great game" in Afghanistan. There are many answers to this question, and all of them are loaded with the political, ideological, and security preferences of the person who tries to answer it. Generally speaking, Pakistan's response to the Soviet invasion was shaped by a combination of political interests of the regime at that time and its vision of both Pakistan's and the region's security. As all such strategic decisions are based on careful assessment of the national, regional, and international environment, late general Zia-ul-Haq and his associates were quite clear about the costs and benefits of the choice that was made. The voices at the time that argued neutrality and nonintervention were subdued by the pervasive desire in the country to free Afghanistan. Pakistan earned international acclaim and the gratitude of millions of Afghans who sought refuge in the country and of their leaders for the courage and steadfastness that Pakistan showed in assisting them in liberating their country.

That was the best period in the entire history of relations between the two countries. As the common enemy withdrew from Afghanistan, the Afghan groups began to fight one another to control fragments of territory and stake claims in Kabul for greater share in power. Could Pakistan leave Afghanistan to the Afghans and only extend them help indirectly to resolve their problems peacefully and to itself face the legacy of that war? In hindsight, that seems to be the most rational, pragmatic, and least costly option. But those who were handling Afghanistan at that time thought that Pakistan had earned the right to stay as a dominant player to contest the growing influence of rival powers, including creeping influence of its eastern neighbor, India. Pakistan presented its objectives in Afghanistan as a friendly, stable, and integrated Afghanistan. The latter two best could be left to the Afghans and Pakistan could effectively pursue the first by appearing to all contestants in the Afghan power game as neutral. That was not the case. Pakistan dug itself too deeply into Afghan politics that grew quite deadly and ferocious. While denying it publicly, Pakistan was on the side of the Taliban, and those who suffered gravely in the northern and western parts of the country were justified in accusing Pakistan of intervention and supporting their enemies. The world community was equally concerned about Pakistan's connection with the Taliban that provided a physical base to transnational Islamic militant networks. For the Taliban, Pakistan was a friend, a critical ally, and a strategic partner; but for the non-Pashtun groups in the Northern Front, it was a hostile power intervening to advance its own interests. This chapter will trace the evolution and development of Pakistan's Afghan policy with a focus on the changes that the tragic events of September 11th and international war against terrorism led by the United States have forced upon it. Our basic premise is that Pakistan's multiple links, proximity, strategic interests, and long history of involvement make it a central player in Afghanistan both in a condition of war and peace.

PAKISTAN'S KEY ROLE

Pakistan has played a key role in the Afghan conflict both during the Soviet war and after the collapse of the Marxist regime in Kabul. On a broader level, therefore, Pakistan's Afghan policy may be analyzed in three distinctive phases: the war of resistance against the Soviet occupation, intergroup Afghan civil war, and the post-Taliban politics and security. In the first phase that started with the Soviet invasion in December 1979 to the Geneva accords, which were signed in April 1988, Pakistan's goals centered on vacating the Soviet occupation and helping the *mujahideen* replace the Marxist government in Kabul. The sudden collapse of the Najibullah regime in April 1992 was a turning point both in the political history of Afghanistan as well as in Pakistan's policy toward that country. A unified and friendly Afghanistan under a broad-based government has been the main concern of Pakistan since 1992. In understanding Pakistan's role one has to look at a wide array of domestic, regional, and international factors that shaped its responses to the political and military situation in Afghanistan.

Pakistan staged counter-intervention in Afghanistan under two considerations. First was domestic and the other related to the security situation created by the Soviet intervention. Domestically, the military regime of General Zia ul-Haq was isolated and under tremendous stress from the political forces in Pakistan that wanted him to hold elections and transfer power to the elected government. Internationally, his regime was seen as brutal and illegitimate. But the Soviet intervention next door in Afghanistan changed all that. The military regime exploited the Afghan situation very effectively to gain domestic and foreign support. The foreign support came mainly from the United States and her regional and European allies. Internally, Zia was able to structure an alliance of right-wing religious political parties that shared his view of the Afghan situation and supported his drive for Islamization of the Pakistani society.

On the other hand, Pakistan's security concerns about the Soviet military engagement in Afghanistan were genuine. What would be Moscow's next move if it succeeded in stabilizing the political situation in Afghanistan? How far would the Soviet Union go in encouraging and supporting an allied Afghanistan to raise historical claim over the Pakistani territories in the Northwest Frontier Province (NWFP)? Would the Soviet Union use Afghanistan as a base to incite and aid ethno-national movements in Pakistan? These were some of the troubling questions that Pakistan faced. Pakistan had sufficient reason to fear the Soviet motives. Moscow had been quite hostile to Islamabad for joining the American security alliances during the Cold War. It supported Pakistan's rival, India, in the war of 1971 and emerged as India's major source of modern weapons and defense technology. Two assumptions defined the Pakistani decision to stand up to the Soviet superpower. One, the scale of the national uprising in Afghanistan was such that no amount of Soviet atrocities—fashioned on the pattern of Eastern Europe—could succeed in suppressing the resistance. Second, the Soviet Union could be forced out of Afghanistan by raising the economic and military costs of its occupation and counterinsurgency campaigns. At the same time, Pakistan responded favorably to any suggestion of a negotiated settlement on two conditions. First, it would not recognize the Soviet-backed regime, nor would it hold any peace talks directly with its representatives. Second, the Soviet Union would unconditionally withdraw its forces from Afghanistan. After tremendous costs to itself and destroying much of Afghanistan, the Soviet Union made virtue out of necessity in agreeing to quit Afghanistan by February 1989 under the Geneva Accords. Pakistan greatly succeeded in achieving its objectives in the first phase of the Afghan conflict.

Pakistan's interest in Afghanistan and its involvement with the *mujahideen* groups did not end with the departure of the Soviet forces because its objectives were not confined to getting the Soviets out of Afghanistan alone. The Soviet-backed government headed by Najibullah was still in power to which Pakistan was not willing to either concede legitimacy or enter into any deal for settling the political future of that country. The Soviet factor even without its strong military presence continued to trouble Pakistan and its Afghan *mujahideen* allies. Not only had the Soviets dumped a large quantity of arms while leaving the country but also they continued assisting their Afghan clients. Pakistan's next move was to install a *mujahideen* government in Kabul. It combined military attacks against the border towns like Jalalabad and secretively supported coup plans to get Najibullah out. Under the negative symmetry, meaning that the United States and the Soviet Union would cease giving any assistance to their respective Afghan clients, the Najibullah regime began to crumble from within.

The political changes within the Soviet Union sealed the fate of Afghan communists. Pakistan assembled all the Afghan groups to agree on power-sharing arrangements and form an interim government in April 1992.[2] The meeting produced the Peshawar Accords under which first Sibghatullah Mojeddadi and then Rabbani were installed as interim presidents.

A new phase of civil war began in Afghanistan when Rabbani refused to step down when he ran out of tenure toward the end of 1993. In fact, his faction and that of Hekmatyar had been at war from the very beginning when Rabbani refused to share power with Hekmatyar. Rabbani also used force to eject other groups from Kabul, which included Hizb-i-Wahdat and the Jumbesh-i-Milli led by Uzbek warlord Abdul Rashid Dostum. Pakistan kept shifting its support from one Pashtun group to another in order to put pressure on Rabbani to honor the Peshawar Accord and stop the tilt of his transitional government toward India and other regional powers. The Ahmad Shah Masud and Rabbani were unhappy with Pakistan for supporting their rival the Hizb and its leader during and after the war of resistance and wanted to use Iran, Russia, and India as new levers to contest Pakistan's influence in the Afghan politics. Pakistan repeatedly reminded the duo of the sacrifices it made for liberating their country and supporting them by giving shelter to refugees and arms and money to their forces. It seems these leaders were not punctilious about expressing gratitude to a former benefactor while locked in a bitter struggle for power. In a fit of anger over the killing of four Afghan hijackers of a school bus in Islamabad, they organized an attack on the Pakistan Embassy in Kabul, put it on blaze, killed one employee and injured many others including the ambassador in the summer of 1994. The relations with Pakistan became frosty thereafter and Pakistan began to explore other possibilities along with supporting Hekmatyar. Pakistan was more concerned about Rabbani and Masud inviting Indian technicians and intelligence operatives in air force and other military installations. The creeping back of Russian and Indian influence in an Afghanistan that had been liberated partly by its money and blood in its own streets at the hand of the Afghan communist and Soviet intelligence agencies was the last thing Pakistan could expect to happen.

THE TALIBAN

Pakistan was too eager to open up an Afghan route to Central Asian states, see the return of 3 million refugees on its land, but without peace among the warring Afghan factions and stability it could gain neither of the two. Pressures that it exerted on the Rabbani government through Hekmatyar further pushed the transitional government toward Iran, Russia, and India that were eager to support Rabbani against his Pashtun rivals with whom Pakistan had greater influence than with any other ethnic group. With new bouts of civil war, fragmentation of the country, and different regions being controlled by rival warlords, the internal conditions in Afghanistan further worsened. The *mujahideen* commanders who were loosely affiliated with the major resistance parties without the lever of arms and money funneled through Pakistan became autonomous actors. They turned to arms and drug trafficking and taxing transport and extorting businessmen as new sources of revenue. The central authority of the Rabbani government became confined to a few sections of the Kabul city, which itself remained under constant rocket attack. This city suffered devastation only after the fall of the Najibullah government in April 1992.[3] Ordinary Afghans who saw some sign of hope with the departure of the Soviet forces and then after the fall of communist regime were utterly frustrated to see their country go through another phase of destructive war. Frustration with the former resistance parties and their leaders, former commanders by then turned into warlords, was widespread and genuine among the Afghan population inside the country and living in exile. It was perhaps more so in the vast and greatly fragmented and divided Pashtun areas than in other regions because they had suffered greater destruction and physical dislocation than any other group in the country. While the former *mujahideen* parties kept fighting turf wars in and around Kabul, the ethnic and local warlords divided the country into fiefdoms and kept the restive population under control at gunpoint.

The excesses of the local warlords in the south of the country in the Kandahar region attracted the attention of the local clergy members that had gone back to teaching Islam to their old and new Taliban (students) after waging war against the Afghan and foreign communists. The leading clergy or *ulema* of Afghanistan were part of the resistance movement and were at the forefront of mobilizing support for the war and recruiting young fighters from their *madrassa* (Islamic school) networks. During the Soviet–Afghan War they closed down their religious institutions in the country arguing that fighting in the holy war against the Soviets that had invaded the country was more urgent both in religious as well practical terms than mere imparting education. The *ulema* in Afghanistan have had a strong social base, more perhaps in Pashtun areas than other regions, but there, too, *sufi* (mystic) and *madrassa* associations existed and local population showed tremendous reverence to them. It is a contentious issue whether the local chieftain or the religious scholar enjoyed more respect, loyalty, and following in the Pashtun territory.[4] But the fact is *ulema* in the Pashtun society have emerged an integral part of the power arrangements and their sphere of influence has expanded with the spread of Deobandi or Wahabbi religious beliefs and practices.

The war against the Soviet Union forced leading Afghan *ulema* and their students to fight part time and to replicate their *madrassa* institutions in and around the refugee population in Pakistan. They concentrated mainly in the Pashtun areas of Balochistan and the NWFP where they not only had coethnic groups but also former teachers, colleagues, and peers as the main support base. The local communities, the refugees despite difficult economic conditions, the Islamic Nongovernmental Organizations (NGOs) and charities from the Middle Eastern countries financed the maintenance and expansion of the *madrassa* networks. They were the only large-scale educational institutions that gave shelter, food, and education to hundreds of thousands of orphans who had nobody to take care of them. Most of the later-day Taliban were graduates of these *madrassas*, who grew up and socialized in a purely religious and conservative environment. Their world outlook, ideology, attitude toward other religions and sects of Islam, views about the West, and political culture were shaped at a very impressionable age. Never had they been exposed to any alternative view of religious or world affairs. The mental and intellectual conditioning was quite firm before they took up arms against their political foes in Afghanistan.

The tradition of settling the question of power through armed struggle is as old as the formation of the Afghan state itself; but such armed incursions were always led by the tribal chiefs, members of the oligarchy, or the Afghan kings themselves. In some cases, they enlisted the support of the clergy for giving religious sanction to their quest for power, but kept them in secondary position. Seldom were they involved directly or in a leading position in waging a war to capture political power in the country. Why did the Taliban that included the top clergy and their students take up arms and succeed in capturing Kabul, defeating the *mujahideen* rivals and bottling up the forces of the Northern Front in a narrow corner of the country? This question is at the center of all studies done on the rise of the Taliban movement in Afghanistan. But it is always the answer that separates them all. The most convenient explanation of their emergence and quick victories is that it is Pakistan that equipped, financed, and guided their struggle for advancing its own interests. We cannot dismiss the Pakistani factor in the growth and military success of the Taliban movement. Pakistan's political and strategic interests and the situation in and around Afghanistan pushed it toward the Taliban and it emerged as the most vital source of support for them. The support included diplomatic recognition and allowing the Taliban to use Pakistani *madrassa* and mosque networks to raise funds and recruit fighters. Did the Arab and Pakistani contingents in the Taliban militia make any difference is a controversial matter? Their presence alone suggests that foreign actors in Afghanistan were deliberately allowed to join the struggle for political considerations. There was hardly any check from the Pakistani side on the cross-border movement of war fighting materials, equipment, vital life supporting resources, or movement of men in either direction. What type of financial or military assistance and at what scale the government of Pakistan extended to the Taliban is not publicly known, but no serious student of Pakistan's Afghan policy would rule it out. In the absence of public scrutiny and lack of transparency in the dealing of the governments in such matters, the information remains prerogative of the few. While it helps the policy of concealing facts, it also hurts in creating an exaggerated and inflated assessment of a country's involvement. Pakistan is no exception to this. Pakistan's contribution to the Taliban both official as well private, political, or economic, in the way of hard materiel assistance or in the shape of soft social support, evidenced by the constant flow of Pakistani and Arab fighters was perhaps substantial. But our contention is that foreign support such as Pakistan extended to the Taliban movement should not obscure us from the internal and regional environments that shaped the Taliban movement. Almost every analyst of the Taliban phenomenon has focused on the religious and ideological aspects ignoring ethnic considerations behind the popularity of the movement. Why was it that the Taliban militia expanded in the Pashtun parts of Afghanistan like a whirlwind, captured it without a single fight, and rolled on to occupy Kabul? Where did the Pashtun warlords, the former *mujahideen* fighters, and the local chieftains go? There was a strong resentment among the Pashtun that the power in their country had passed on to Tajiks and that there was no leader or party that could deliver it back to them. The decade-long war against the Soviet Union had transformed ethnic relations, and this change could be viewed as more significant than either the defeat of Communism or ofcommunists in Afghanistan.[5] The Taliban was the only organized force with religious zeal to do exactly what the Pashtuns wanted, and for that reason they threw their strength behind them. Some would also argue that the Afghans were exhausted by the war and that they had hardly any will to fight the new force or had hardly any love left for the Masud–Rabbani combine in Kabul to do anything. The political and military vacuum in the country, the loss of hope in the *mujahideen* parties, political fragmentation, and chaotic economic and security conditions played a significant part in the popularity of the Taliban.

Pakistan was an important regional player in the Afghan power game, and, as indicated previously, it supported the Taliban movement to checkmate its regional rivals and keep itself in a position of greater influence than others. Pakistan's public posturing regarding Afghanistan asserted that Pakistan sought a unified, peaceful, and friendly Afghanistan. This three-in-one strategy has continuously defined Pakistan's Afghan policy for more than two decades. It has argued that a politically fragmented, anarchical, and unfriendly Afghanistan would menace Pakistan's security environment. Even during the reign of the Taliban Pakistan tried to promote the idea of negotiated settlement that would bring about a broad-based government and sharing of power among all Afghan groups. It sought involvement of the United Nations in brokering peace among the Afghan groups.[6] Its diplomats kept shuttling between Mazar-i-Sharif, the power center of the northern coalition, and Kandahar, the political base of the Taliban movement to bring the two sides to a negotiating table.[7] Also, Pakistan made several efforts to convene a conference of regional countries to promote a consensus on the political future of Afghanistan. In all these efforts, Pakistan faced tremendous difficulties from its Islamic neighbors and the Afghan opposition to Taliban rule. Iran, Tajikistan, Uzbekistan, and Turkmenistan all accused Pakistan of supporting the Taliban movement. Iran, another player with a long history of involvement and regional ambition, was quite vehement in peddling the theory that Saudi Arabia and the United States financed the Taliban movement and that Pakistan played the role of an intermediary between the Taliban and these countries.[8]

Pakistan's interest in the Taliban government was pragmatic. They were strong enough to provide stability in the Pashtun areas of Afghanistan, which was a matter for Pakistan's security. They ended the Indian influence from Afghanistan and raised its hope for a gas pipeline from Turkmenistan and trade with Central Asian states. But supporting the Taliban was not without domestic and foreign policy costs. At the domestic front, Islamic extremism and its links with the Taliban grew menacingly and it raised the fear of Pakistan going under the influence of religious political parties. This has somewhat materialized with the electoral success of the Mutahidda Majlis-i-Amal (United Action Council) or MMA, a coalition of religious parties. Even in the defeat of the Taliban they have increased their political space and have emerged as a dominant force in Balochistan and the NWFP. Their success is partly based on sympathy for the Taliban and on anti-American sentiment, but largely it is due to popular disenchantment with the nationalist and mainstream political parties. Pro-Taliban feeling still runs deep in Pakistan and well beyond the Pashtun territories. It will remain an important force in the political process of Pakistan whatever shape it takes in the coming years. In the area of foreign policy, although strategic partnership with the Taliban placed Pakistan in a somewhat better position, the alliance gave rise to other complex problems. Rivalry with Iran and Central Asian states grew in intensity and at unmanageable levels. The world community saw Taliban rule as extremely harsh, medieval, and discriminatory toward women and minorities. Pakistan's association with them caused major image and policy problems. The Taliban rule that was essentially security oriented did not earn any international support for reconstruction of the country, a result of which millions of refugees could not be repatriated. In the end, involvement with the Taliban proved to be a messy affair for Pakistan. At the end of the day, Pakistan gained very little from its policy of Taliban support. Pakistan's dream of opening up to Central Asia remained unrealized. Rather, there was a sentiment of passive hostility against Pakistan in that region for the support Pakistan gave the Taliban. The United States, European countries, and even China, its closest ally, were offended by Pakistan's failure to influence policies or politics of the Taliban on any issue. Even in the face of international isolation and harsh criticism Pakistan found it extremely difficult to extricate itself from pro-Taliban policy, changing tack only after the Al Qaeda terrorists with links in Afghanistan struck the Pentagon near Washington, D.C., and the World Trade Center towers in New York on September 11, 2001. The tragic events changed some of the fundamentals of world politics and Pakistan, since a backer of the Taliban could not escape tremendous impact on its domestic and foreign policy orientations.

PAKISTAN'S DEFINING MOMENT

The fast movement of events in the wake of terrorist attacks in New York and Washington presented Pakistan a difficult diplomatic terrain to negotiate. Essentially, it had only two options: to stay an ally and supporter of the Taliban or to join the American-led international coalition against terrorism. Realistically, there was no medium to these two alternatives, since even genuine attempts to find a neutral course would have earned hardly any credibility with the world community and would have damaged Pakistan's national security interests. Triggered by public anger, humiliation, and the scale of human tragedy, the immediate reaction of the United States left Islamabad no room to maneuver.

It would be overemphasizing the point that statecraft, strategic decisions, and pursuit of national interests require prudence, cool reflection, and careful weight of the cost and benefit of various alternatives. This amounts to what, in policy-making jargon, is known as rational choice theory. By calculating the risk and payoff of the two options and after consulting with every section of the power structure of the government, General Pervez Musharraf made the right decision in supporting the United States' new war against terrorism—directed against Pakistan's former ally, the Taliban. It was a timely decision dictated by Pakistan's prudence and difficult circumstances. Any delay or margin of error would have taken the initiative away from Pakistan and perhaps might have pushed Pakistan to the brink of diplomatic and even strategic disaster. The government, understanding the gravity of the situation, the intensity of the international revulsion against terrorism, and the global sympathy and support for the United States, could easily read the grave dangers that wavering, hedging out, and riding on the public's emotions could pose to national interests.

A misstep would have provided India the opportunity to lead a formidable international coalition of forces against Afghanistan, placing Pakistan on the hit list. Had such a situation unfolded, Pakistan might have suffered incalculable losses that could have included destruction of its nuclear assets. In Pakistan's immediate interest turning its back on the Taliban and going along with the United States meant the collapse of India's attempt to categorize Pakistan with the Taliban as a source of international terrorism and declare Pakistan a rogue state. Pakistan's decision to fight a common war against terrorism brought it back to the center stage, and, for the second time in twenty years, it is a frontline state, this time against international terrorism. The nature of war against the faceless enemy, who may be living next door and may have the ability to cause colossal damage, required strategic partnership with countries like Pakistan that are close to the sources of trouble

Therefore, Pakistan was a natural choice as a strategic partner in the war against terrorism. Pakistan has assisted the United States and other allies in a variety of ways, offering its bases for reconnaissance and rescue operations, logistic support to the American troops operating in Afghanistan, intelligence resources, and airspace for strikes against the Taliban and Al Qaeda targets. There are two other important areas of cooperation that also need to be mentioned. First, the denial of Pakistani territory to the retreating Taliban and Al Qaeda fighters was a crucial step in preventing them from claiming sanctuary from their comrades in Pakistan. For this purpose, the United States and Pakistan set up joint patrolling of the borders, and Islamabad deployed troops in some areas of the tribal belt bordering Afghanistan for the first time in history. Pakistani concentration on the Afghan border swelled to 100,000 troops along its border around Tora Bora in March 2002, when the United States was conducting its largest military operation against the Taliban and Al Qaeda forces in eastern Afghanistan.[9] The substantial number of Pakistani troops that remain there are assisted by the technical means provided by the United States in checking infiltration. In such a difficult, long, mountainous terrain, it was a difficult operation that succeeded in netting hundreds of Al Qaeda members. All the same quite a few members of Al Qaeda did succeed in crossing over the border to take shelter in Karachi and other densely populated towns. The second important and perhaps long-term impact of Pakistani cooperation with the United States relates to the hunt for terrorists hiding in Pakistan. Through joint operations the Pakistani authorities and the FBI have arrested several leading Al Qaeda members. Since so many of them are on the run and now there is evidence that Pakistani religious extremists have terrorist networks of their own to organize attacks against foreigners and Western interests in the country, the joint Pakistan–United States operations against them may continue for some time.[10] The fight against terrorism in Central Asia is going to be of long duration, and Pakistan will remain a critical participant until the situation in Afghanistan stabilizes and the region around it, including Pakistan itself, makes a peaceful transition to stable political order.

SEEKING NEW PARTNERSHIP WITH AFGHANISTAN

It has been a difficult task for Pakistan to forge new ties with the new rulers of Afghanistan for a number of reasons. Pakistan's image as a strong supporter of the Taliban and considerable evidence that it allowed supplies of materiel and Pakistani men to assist the religious militia to defeat their ethnic and sectarian rivals in Afghanistan have proved a psychological barrier in the way of accepting Islamabad as a partner. The leaders of the Northern Front in particular have been overtly hostile, for they attributed their human and territorial loss, human suffering, and misery indirectly to Pakistan.[11] The late Ahmad Shah Masud and his followers from the Panjsher valley now holding major positions in the Hamid Karzai administration considered Pakistan responsible for unending civil war and their war against the Taliban as a war of national liberation. The animosity among them against Pakistan runs very deep. In June to July 2002, there were a number of stories, confirmed by Central Asian diplomats, circulating in the national and international press that Northern Front warlords sold out thirty or more Pakistani prisoners to India who were flown out from Dushanbe, capital of Tajikistan.[12] This caused outrage in Pakistan and has further strengthened the view that the Northern Front leaders carry a chip on their shoulder in dealing with Pakistan and its citizens. They kept thousands of Pakistani Taliban in their private prisons, tortured them severely, and later released them on receipt of payment of huge ransoms by their family members.[13] The released prisoners have told unthinkable stories of torture and reported how thousands of them died in containers without a single hole to breathe. Every Pakistani Taliban, whatever his motivation to go and fight against the Northern Front, violated Afghan sovereignty; but the view in Pakistan and among the government circles is that they should have been treated as prisoners of war with all the rights and punishments under the international law. There are still Pakistani prisoners in the captivity of the warlords and even the intervention of the Karzai government has not succeeded in getting them released. Karzai and many of his advisors and cabinet ministers from the Pashtun areas have been eager to mend fences with Pakistan and start a new chapter. Karzai chose Pakistan as his first foreign destination after assuming the chairmanship of the Afghan interim administration. While visiting he asserted that "we, Afghan, have nothing but goodwill for Pakistan, and it is from the heart. We don't have to put it into writing or express it in any other form."[14]

Pakistan on its part has tried to reassure all factions in Afghanistan that it has a new outlook and that it would neither side with any faction nor would it allow its territory for any hostile action against the new government in Kabul. During the period from launching of the military strikes to the Bonn Accord among the Afghan groups in December 2001, Pakistan tried to seek assurances from the United States and other partners in the war against terrorism that its interests in Afghanistan would not be neglected. While political stability, political and economic reconstruction, and peace are not new but old concerns of Pakistan, it wanted better understanding and accommodation of the interests of the Pashtun majority in the post-Taliban political arrangements. Islamabad used its influence indirectly and by pushing the idea that the neglect or alienation of the Pashtun majority would not bring about stability and peace. The feeling of alienation among the Pashtuns does exist but with Hamid Karzai as head of the transitional government and co-optation of other Pashtuns into decision-making, power-sharing arrangements are better than at any other time during the past twenty years.

The Northern Front leaders who hold key positions in the new government have slowly reassessed the need to forge relations with Pakistan on pragmatic grounds. It was in part the influence of Karzai and in part a gesture of goodwill to Pakistan on the part of Abdul Rashid Dostum, Uzbek warlord, that he released 400 Pakistani prisoners in May 2002 in addition to the 500 that he released earlier.[15] They understand better than they did before in the early 1990s that the economy of eastern and southern parts of Afghanistan is integrated with that of Pakistan. Pakistan offers the most economical, short, and safest transit route and is a major source of supplies for reconstruction of physical infrastructure. And there are still 1.8 million refugees on Pakistani soil waiting to be repatriated. The existing problems, including the fight against terrorism and the prospects of Afghanistan's economic revival and stability are tied with Pakistan more than any other neighbor. Pakistan has made conscious efforts on a sustained basis to cultivate relations with the new leaders of Afghanistan. It has been a strong advocate of assisting Afghanistan's recovery in the world forums and has itself pledged $100 million in assistance over a period of five years.[16] It has already disbursed $18 million. It has allowed liberal donation and sale of wheat from its surplus stocks and other supplies on a regular basis and has allowed its ports, roads, and railways to be used for all reconstruction activities.[17]

Relations between the two countries have improved substantially. The government leaders of the two countries have been regularly visiting each other and they are engaged in high-level consultation. Some of the dust of mistrust and bitterness is gone, but they have to work more to get the shine in their bilateral relations. For this they have taken the route of economic cooperation in furthering mutual interest. There are good signs that they are succeeding in this respect. The bilateral trade is up. In July to November 2002, Pakistan exported goods worth $165 million to Afghanistan compared to $185 million in the entire 2001 to 2002 financial year.[18] Imports from Afghanistan also registered increases during this period from $55 million for the previous year to $27 million for the first four months.[19] The two countries have revived the Turkmenistan, Afghanistan, and Pakistan gas pipeline project which was thrown into cold storage after UNOCAL, a United States–based consortium of companies withdrew from the project. They signed a landmark tripartite agreement on December 27, 2002, to construct a 1,400 kilometer pipeline from Daulatabad gas fields in Turkmenistan to Multan in Pakistan. The $2.7 billion project would immensely contribute to the economy of Afghanistan and integrate the economies of South and Central Asian regions. The pipeline is planned to be extended in the future to the central areas of India.

There are a number of problems that the two countries have yet to resolve. Repatriation of refugees, release of Pakistani prisoners from Afghan jails and transit trade facility will be at the top of the coming years' agenda. Pakistani prisoners are being released, though at a slow pace, and Pakistan is not averse to punishing those involved in crimes against Afghan citizens. They have reached an understanding to expedite a process that will include release of Afghans from Pakistani prisons. The issue of refugees is troublesome. Pakistan has hosted more than 3 million of them in the past, and there are still an estimated 1.8 million in the country. Most of the refugees wish to return home with or without assistance from the United Nations High Commission for Refugees that has been funding their return. Over 1.2 million have gone back voluntarily during the past year. But the flood of returning refugees has already caused economic and social problems, since the interim government lacks the resources to rehabilitate most of them. Recently, Afghanistan and Pakistan reached an agreement to facilitate refugee repatriation in phases over the next three years. Conditions of war, peace, and economic opportunity will determine whether refugees return home to Afghanistan or stay in Pakistan or whether more reenter Pakistan or not. Therefore, Pakistan's vital interest lies in the stability and peace of Afghanistan, removing the burden of the refugees on Pakistan's labor market, utilities, and services.

The transit trade issue is as old as the independence of Pakistan. Landlocked Afghanistan has right of transit through Pakistan, which Pakistan has recognized through a bilateral agreement of 1965. On occasions, Pakistan has terminated this facility or tried to control the list of items that Afghanistan can import through Pakistan for political and economic reasons. In recent decades and years, it is the issue of the reexportation of third-party back to Pakistan that has been causing massive damage to its local industry and revenue—revenue that could otherwise be collected in customs duties. The volume of this informal trade, also involving Pakistani traders and connivance of custom officials, is estimated to be worth about $3 billon. Afghanistan wants unfettered transit trade, while Pakistan wants to ensure that whatever is imported through Pakistan stays in Afghanistan and is consumed there. There is a running dispute on the list of items that Afghanistan can import. This will continue to be a problem until Pakistan orders itself, because most of the Afghan transit goods are sold openly in its markets.[20]

CONCLUSION

All the neighbors of Afghanistan have direct interest in the reconstruction of Afghanistan as a normal state, country, society, and nation. War in Afghanistan has adversely affected the economies, societies, and security environment of the region. Building a safe society and functional state institutions and reviving the economy of Afghanistan would benefit all of its neighbors; but perhaps Pakistan is likely to gain the most because of greater integration of economies among the bordering provinces and an extensive transit trade network. While thinking about reconstruction, one must remember that Afghanistan is a multilateral project that needs the positive involvement of all state actors who have the capacity to influence its internal politics and security.

Afghanistan's neighbors, including Pakistan, have long exploited the internal fragmentation and intergroup rivalry in order to advance their own strategic interests. The situation of Afghanistan after the departure of the Taliban with the international community's focus on economic and political reconstruction is radically different. At the moment, Afghanistan's neighbors are somewhat neutralized by the presence of American forces and those of other partners of the coalition against terrorism. But they retain an intrusive capacity because of their proximity; entangled geopolitical and economic considerations both benefit and harm Afghanistan's rebuilding process. The policy choices of Afghanistan's neighbors determine their future stability, peace, and reconciliation as much as do the choices of the Afghan factions and that nation's ability to resolve divisive issues within its own borders. Judging from the past history of Pakistan's involvement, war and peace would greatly impact Pakistan's own future stability and economic growth as it would that of Afghanistan itself.

Pakistan's involvement in Afghanistan for more than two decades leading to the establishment of the Taliban regime, and now its frontline position in the war against terrorism that has targeted the Taliban, its former allies and partners in Afghanistan, raises serious questions about the efficacy of its foreign policy today which stands in stark contrast to what it was before September 11th. That tragic event gave Pakistan a good excuse to change the direction of its Afghan policy. But its involvement with the Afghan groups locked in internal struggle for power has left Pakistan with fewer friends and more enemies in Afghanistan, particularly among the literate urban middle class and non-Pashtuns. As Afghanistan is itself on the course to national recovery, so are its relations with Pakistan. There is a growing realization that the two countries are inextricably linked to each other in a number of important ways. It is to be hoped that the forces of history, ethnicity, markets, and logic of profit would bring the two peoples closer and that the flow in both directions would remain constant. Among the many lessons that Pakistan can draw from its Afghan experience, one stands out very clearly: The free-spirited Afghans want friends, not masters.

NOTES

1. Marvin G. Weinbaum, "War and Peace in Afghanistan: The Pakistan Role," *Middle East Journal*, 45:1 (Winter 1991), pp 71–85.

2. *Dawn*, April 25, 1992.

3. The Najibullah regime collapsed on April 16, 1992, when he agreed to step down under a UN peace plan brokered by Benon Sevan.

4. Akbar S. Ahmed, *Pakistan Society: Islam, Ethnicity and Leadership in South Asia* (Karachi: Oxford University Press, 1993), pp 71–99.

5. Anwar-ul-Haq Ahady, "The Decline of the Pushtuns in Afghanistan," *Asian Survey,* 35:7 (July 1995), p 621.

6. Rashid Ahmad Khan, "Prospects for Peace in Afghanistan," *The Nation,* July 15, 1997.

7. *The News,* July 14, 1997.

8. See John-Thor Dahlburg, "Washington Supporting Taliban?" *Dawn,* October 6, 1996.

9. "Pakistan Deployed 10,000 Troops," *Dawn,* August 2, 2002.

10. "Plot to Kill U.S. Diplomats Foiled," *The News,* December 16, 2002.

11. A. Siddique, "Anti-Pakistan Gambit in Afghanistan," *The Nation,* October 12, 2001.

12. "A Heinous Deal," editorial, *The Nation,* July 3, 2002.

13. Rahimullah Yusufzai, "The Stir of Echoes," *The News,* August 8, 2002.

14. *The Nation,* February 9, 2002.

15. *The News,* May 6, 2002.

16. *Dawn,* December 9, 2001.

17. In August 2002, Pakistan announced donating 50,000 metric tons of wheat in installments and immediately sent 900 metric tons. *The News,* August 6, 2002.

18. Pakistan's financial year runs from July 1 to June 30.

19. *The News,* December 17, 2002.

20. Khaleeq Kiani, "Islamabad, Kabul Fail to Remove Trade Differences," *Dawn,* May 17, 2002.

4

Reconstructing the Constitution for a COAS President: Pakistan, 1999 to 2002

Zulfikar Khalid Maluka

There is an oft-quoted gibe in the parlance of Pakistan's political and constitutional system. A father and son brought a plant from the nursery and planted it in the lawn of their house. After some time the son began questioning his father about the liklihood of the plant growing fully and yielding fruit. The father replied, it shall definitely grow and yield fruit, but when it strikes roots in the soil. The son's usual query and the father's reply continued for some time. One day the son bluntly told his father that the plant was not striking roots in the soil! How do you know that, my son? Because I check it off and on by uprooting it, was the plain reply of the son! This perfectly fits in the saga of the politico-constitutional malaise and military interventions in Pakistan.

The 1990s saw political instability, social divisions, continuous fragmentation of society on sectarian lines, constant strife from within, and security threats from without Pakistan. The democratic interlude, 1988 to 1999, witnessed scuttling of the political process by the partial, exploitative, and partisan role of the army and the presidents. The elected governments remained hostage to the army's excessive interference and its tight grip on the country's three pillars of national security—that is, Kashmir, Afghanistan, and the nuclear weapons. Politically, a game of musical chairs had endured for a whole decade. Prime Minister Benazir Bhutto went out, Mian Nawaz Sharif came in. Premier Nawaz Sharif went out and Ms. Bhutto came in, and then for the second time Sharif was in. Between 1988 and 1999, various governments were dismissed in rapid succession, and not a single government was allowed to complete its stipulated constitutional term. The serial dismissals of governments in 1988, 1990, 1993, and 1996 demonstrated the capricious manner in which Article 58(2)(b) of the Constitution was applied by the presidents. This was despite the claim of striking a balance between the powers of the prime minister and the president. Each dismissal of the government at the behest of or nod of the military establishment, carried with it wild corruption charges leveled by every successive caretaker setup against the outgoing politicians. The unrelenting personal accusations and corruption charges against the politicians in general, and leaders of the out-going regime in particular, left deep imprints on the national psyche.

During the span of two and half years, after assumption of the office of the prime minister, Mian Muhammad Nawaz Sharif remained vindictive toward his political opponents, Ms. Bhutto's Pakistan People's Party (PPP), and, indeed, pushed them against the wall. Sharif's self-serving actions seemingly weakened the roots of democracy, and the political process failed to mature. For keeping himself in power and breaking or bending state institutions to his liking, Nawaz Sharif got passed rigid amendments in the 1973 Constitution, making it almost impossible to remove the government through the usual constitutional process. He sent packing a chief justice of the Supreme Court, two naval chiefs, and two army chiefs (the second being General Pervez Musharraf, who, however, refused to go).

In February 1999, Nawaz Sharif's initiatives for the normalization of relations with India bore fruit. Prime Minister Atal Behari Vajpayee visited Lahore and a joint communiqué known as the Lahore Declaration was signed between the two neighbors. The initiative for good relations did not last long and both India and Pakistan found themselves locked in a military confrontation on the Kargil heights in the disputed region of Jammu and Kashmir. The unfolding confrontational scenario vividly indicated that the Kargil hills were captured in a surprise move by the Pakistan Army in the name of Kashmiri *mujahideen*. Consequent of this adventurism, the aggressive Indian propaganda was so lethal and poignant that even old and close friends like China did not support Pakistan on its military initiatives in the Kargil heights.

Finding his country in a physically adverse and psychologically tense international–regional milieu, Prime Minister Nawaz Sharif paid a visit to Washington and pledged to the American administration to withdraw the army from Kargil hills, unilaterally. In the wake of these developments, those, too, of its own making, Pakistan suffered humiliation, diplomatic and political isolation, and a military setback for its misadventure on the Kargil issue. The Kargil crisis had led to simmering differences between Prime Minister Nawaz Sharif and the GHQ (General Headquarters) over fixing responsibility for the enigmatic initiative, the former claiming total ignorance for such a confrontational course with the neighboring country.

The brewing tension was exacerbated when the Interservices Intelligence (ISI) chief, Lt. General Khawaja Ziauddin visited the United States along with the Punjab chief minister Shahbaz Sharif. On their return to Pakistan, the U.S. State Department had warned both the political and military actors in Pakistan to refrain from making any extraconstitutional moves to overthrow the democratically elected government. Such developments notwithstanding, differences had cropped up between the army and the Sharif government over the issue of posting defense personnel to intelligence services. A one-on-one meeting of Lt. General Tariq Pervez, a Quetta-based corps commander and cousin of federal minister Raja Nadir Pervez, with the prime minister without prior permission or even knowledge of the Chief of the Army Staff (COAS), added fuel to the fire. Lt. General Tariq Pervez was immediately removed from military service by the COAS, General Pervez Musharraf. There were widespread rumors and apprehensions within the army circles that Nawaz Sharif was maneuvering to cause a division within its ranks.[1]

ENTER MUSHARRAF

On October 12, 1999, Sharif appointed his relative, the ISI chief, Lieutenant General Khawaja Ziauddin to the post of the COAS, and dismissed General Pervez Musharraf in a surreptitious move. The army refused to accept the command of the Sharif-appointed new COAS, and moved out of the barracks to take direct charge of the country for the fourth time in its history. The Sharif initiative was sudden and unexpected, as he, on September 28, 1999, had extended General Pervez Musharraf's tenure of office up to October 6, 2001, and apparently conciliation had been effected between the two. The dismissal of the COAS, General Pervez Musharraf, was made public when he was airborne and returning from an official trip to Sri Lanka. The formalities of making Lt. General Khawaja Ziauddin the COAS and dismissal of General Pervez Musharraf were carried out, yet the army corps commanders did not acquiesce to the new situation. Commenting on Nawaz Sharif's interference in military affairs, a former law minister in the late Bhutto cabinet opined that Sharif "had the habit of shooting himself in the foot. This time he shot himself in the mouth."[2]

Unlike the past military interventions, martial law was not imposed in the country. On October 14, 1999, General Pervez Musharraf proclaimed emergency and declared himself chief executive of Pakistan. The term "emergency" is present in the 1973 Constitution, and proclamation of emergency was used to make the military intervention acceptable in the changing circumstances and to give it a benign political appearance to the outside world. Like General Zia's military takeover, General Musharraf declared that the 1973 Constitution was held in abeyance, that the National Assembly, the Senate and the four provincial assemblies stood suspended, and that the government was dismissed. The presidency was not touched initially. Deviating from his past practice of calling himself the chief martial law administrator (CMLA), General Pervez Musharraf preferred the corporate world title of chief executive of the country, equating himself to the prime minister. Contrary to General Zia's military setup, the military junta did not paint a rosy picture of holding elections within ninety days, thereby implying, that the regime intended to stay longer.

In his television address on October 17, 1999, General Pervez Musharraf announced the following seven-point agenda to be achieved by his regime: (1) rebuilding national confidence and morale, (2) strengthening the federation with the removal of inter-provincial disharmony and restoration of national cohesion, (3) revival of the economy and restoration of the investors' confidence, (4) ensuring law and order and dispensing speedy justice, (5) depoliticization of state institutions, (6) devolution of power to the grassroots level, and (7) ensuring swift and across-the-board accountability.

SHARIF IN THE DOCK

During the detention of Mian Nawaz Sharif and his close associates, a criminal case—based on FIR No. 201/1999, under Sections 120-B, 402-B, 324/365 of the Pakistan Penal Code, read with Section 7 of the Anti-Terrorist Act (ATA)—was registered with the Karachi Airport Police Station, for the hijacking of the airplane in which General Musharraf, his family, and other passengers were traveling from Colombo to Karachi. They were indicted for their conspiracy "to physically eliminate and murder the COAS, General Pervez Musharraf, and 198 passengers onboard flight PK 805, with deliberate criminal intent [that] is apparent from the act, conduct, and orders/conversations of persons, including the then prime minister, Mian Nawaz Sharif." All the accused persons were further charged for their attempt to "engineer, conspire, and cause the crash of flight PK 805" and "strike terror in the passengers," and, as such, Nawaz Sharif and his accomplices "committed heinous criminal offences, including high treason."[3]

Accused of criminal conspiracy, hijacking, and waging or abetting war against Pakistan, Nawaz Sharif, like his predecessor Prime Minister Zulfikar Ali Bhutto, was brought to dock before the Anti-Terrorist Court in Karachi. Along with Nawaz Sharif, six others, Shahbaz Sharif (his brother), Ghous Ali Shah (heading the Sindh province), Saifur Rahim (accountability chief), Shahid Khaqan Abbasi (MNA and chairman of the national air carrier, PIA), Saeed Mehdi (senior bureaucrat) and Rana Maqbool (inspector general, police) stood to face trial on the same charges. Before the commencement of the trial in the plane hijacking case, the military regime had amended the Anti-Terrorist Act, 1997, through an Ordinance, on December 2, 1999. The amendments pertained to expanding the scope of offences under the jurisdiction of the Anti-Terrorist Court, which were previously not triable by it. The amendments were openly criticized by the PML(N) leadership on the touchstone of being Nawaz-specific, and Musharraf was accused of his determination to procure the conviction of the deposed prime minister.[4]

Scathing criticism of amendments in the antiterrorist law not-withstanding, Nawaz Sharif and his party leaders objected to their trial by the Anti-Terrorist Court as being incongruous with civil liberties. Such objection was a classical example of history's irony because his government was the architect of these courts and the Anti-Terrorism Act, 1997, itself.[5] On its proclamation, the political parties and human rights activists vehemently opposed the law as infringing on civil liberties, with its overwhelming provisions against the due process of law. For instituting such courts, Nawaz Sharif was accused of advancing his personal agenda and giving vent to his vendetta against his political opponents.[6] The law was impugned before the Supreme Court in the case of *Mehram Ali vs. Federation of Pakistan*,[7] and the Court declared the various provisions of the Anti-Terrorism Act invalid. The main thrust of the Supreme Court judgment was that these courts were not working under the direct supervision of the High Courts. After a few months of the announcement of judgment in the *Mehram Ali* case, terrorist acts in Karachi obliged the Nawaz government to promulgate a new Ordinance XII on November 20, 1998, wherein calling the armed forces in aid of the civil administration, and the trial of civilians by military courts, was provided. Despite claim of the federal government that constitution of military courts was a provisional and temporary measure for controlling terrorist activities, the matter was brought before the Supreme Court in the case of *Liaqat Hussain vs. Federation of Pakistan*.[8] On the touchstone of constitutional provisions, Ordinance XII of 1998, providing for the establishment of military courts, was struck down by the Supreme Court.[9] However, the Supreme Court laid down guidelines for dealing with terrorist cases, expeditiously.

On such pursuance of the antiterrorist law and special courts constituted thereof, the military regime retorted to the Nawaz objections that he and his government had enunciated the law and the courts, and that he and his close colleagues had defended them before the Supreme Court, thus he had no right to object to his prosecution under the same law and by the same courts. Given the mind-set of the military regime, prima facie there was no chance of Nawaz Sharif being acquitted in the hijacking case, but there was also the remote possibility of awarding him capital punishment, as provided under the offences for which he was charged. The Special Judge, Rehmat Hussain Jaffri tried the former prime minister, and on April 6, 2000, while acquitting all the coaccused, awarded the sentence of life imprisonment to Nawaz Sharif. Appeals both against the acquittal of others, and the sentence, were filed before the Sindh High Court. Having been convicted in the plane hijacking case, Nawaz Sharif and his brother Shahbaz Sharif were shifted to the Attock military fort situated on the northern fringes of the Punjab province, where he faced trial under the National Accountability Ordinance, 1999, on charges of corruption and corrupt practices.

NOVEL EXILE

On December 10, 2000, the nation witnessed another drama in the form of Nawaz Sharif and his whole family's exile to Saudi Arabia. The government asserted, "the decision" of exiling the former prime minister and his family members "has been taken in the best interests of the country and the people of Pakistan."[10] Interestingly, neither the people of Pakistan knew anything about the decision, nor the "interests of the country" for which the secret deal was devised, were ever disclosed. Nawaz Sharif along with his family's eighteen members, including his wife, parents, and brother Shahbaz Sharif boarded the Saudi Royal jet specifically brought for this purpose, for onward journey and landing at Jeddah, Saudi Arabia, to a red carpet welcome. Whereas the Sharif family members "were in a daze at the unexpected twist of fate that had brought them together on the tarmac to freedom," his negotiated "departure into exile sent shock waves across the country and heaped humiliation on his supporters who believed he would return to power soon."[11]

The deal with the military government had resulted in the commutation of Sharif's life sentence, forfeiture of $8.3 million assets, his staying out of politics for the next twenty-one years and exile from Pakistan for ten years. The Saudi Crown Prince Abdullah, joined by the rulers of Qatar and the UAE, had brokered the deal with the military government, and the move reportedly had the American blessings as well.[12] Neither in the national or international law, was there any legal precedent of such an exile. The move was seemingly motivated politically, rather than being a legal one. The Musharraf government, in view of the mounting criticism from the media, lawyers, and political groups, tried to justify the Sharif clemency and exile as having been effected on "humanitarian grounds."[13]

Pardoning and exiling of Nawaz Sharif had called into question the credibility of the accountability drive of the military government. Another important legal question involved in the whimsical move regarded the validity of the verdict of the Special Court and the trend of appeals before the Sindh High Court. The matter was sub judice before the Court, and the compromise could only be affected through the Court, which was a necessary party. The province of Sindh in general and the PPP's leadership in particular criticized the exile issue on the touchstone of "double standards"—that is, convicted Punjabi Prime Minister Mian Muhammad Nawaz Sharif was pardoned and sent intto exile while Sindhi Prime Minister Zulfikar Ali Bhutto was made to languish in jail and was eventually hanged.[14]

MILITARY PICKS ON THE JUDICIARY

Initially, the military regime did not touch the judiciary and it was allowed to exercise its constitutional jurisdiction, except being barred from challenging the Proclamation of Emergency or issuing any writ against the chief executive. The judges of the higher courts were not required to take oath of allegiance to the Provisional Constitution Order (PCO). The question of the administration of oath to the judges came up in January 2000, when the new chief justice, Justice Mian Ajmal of the Peshawar High Court, had been appointed, and it was agreed between the chief justice of Pakistan and the military regime that he would take oath as provided under the 1973 Constitution. Earlier on December 31, 1999, the military government had reaffirmed through the Oath of Office (Judges) Order

1999, that the judges of higher courts would take their oath under the 1973 Constitution.

Ousted Prime Minister Nawaz Sharif and his party leaders opposing military takeover filed various petitions in the Supreme Court on October 12, 1999, under Article 184(3) of the Constitution. The petitioners prayed for the restoration of assemblies and civilian government. The military regime seemingly panicked when these petitions were entertained by the Supreme Court and fixed a hearing for January 31, 2000.[15] Notwithstanding the apprehensions of the military regime regarding the remote possibility of adverse findings by the Supreme Court on the October 12, 1999 takeover, some key figures in the Musharraf government wanted to settle personal scores with a few judges.[16]

In the fourth week of January 2000, the military government decided to administer a fresh oath of office to the judges of the superior courts, and to that end, the chief justice of the Supreme Court, Saiduzzaman Siddiqui was summoned by General Musharraf and was asked to consider and discuss the matter with his fellow judges. Despite persuasions to the contrary, the chief justice and his close associates in the judiciary remained reluctant to accept the regime's decision. On January 26, 2000, the military regime invited the judges to take oath anew under the PCO. The junta did not allow the chief justice to go to the Supreme Court building in Islamabad, and the judge's colony was virtually cordoned off by security personnel on that day. Evidently, the chief justice was stopped from going to the Supreme Court lest he might persuade his colleagues to reject the PCO and the new oath. On that day, as many as 89 out of 103 judges of the Supreme Court, High Courts of the four provinces, and the Federal Shariat Court took oath under the PCO. Six Supreme Court judges and the rest belonging to High Courts either refused to take oath or were not invited to do so by the military regime. Only seven judges of the Supreme Court took oath under the PCO, and the senior-most among them, Justice Irshad Hassan Khan, was appointed as the chief justice of Pakistan. The rationale behind the whole move was to ensure the feeling of security in the corridors of powers, without any legal hitch or affront by the legal community, though forcing the PCO oath on the judges was an act of misuse of authority by the regime. Regardless of the benefits accruing to the regime, the institution of the judiciary stood damaged beyond repair.

Whether the constitutions were abrogated or held in abeyance, certainly they gave birth to a new legal order based on the PCO or presidential orders (POs). In the case of Zia's martial law, the judges of superior courts were administered oath of office twice, which was entirely and radically different from the one contained in the 1973 Constitution. The rationale behind administering the oath was to circumscribe the jurisdiction of the higher courts to refrain from adjudicating the new legal order. The oath taken by the judges under Order No. 1 of 2000 promulgated by the military government definitely created a new situation for the judges. Contrary to their original oath under the 1973 constitution, the judges swore that they would discharge their duties and perform their functions honestly and to the best of their abilities and faithfully in accordance with the Proclamation of Emergency of October 12, 1999, the Provisional Constitutional Order No.1 of 1999 as amended. They further swore that they would abide by the provisions of the PCO and the Code of Conduct issued by the Supreme Judicial Council. Thus the judges of the superior courts swore to protect and abide by the "new legal order."

RETURN OF STATE NECESSITY

On May 12, 2000, the Supreme Court, headed by Justice Irshad Hassan Khan, delivered judgment on the petitions filed by the leaders of the ousted civil government against the military intervention, etc. Given that the Supreme Court judges had been administered oath under the PCO and that the Musharraf regime sat firmly in the saddle, nothing else was expected except the judgment style as *Zafar Ali Shah vs. Pervez Musharraf, Chief Executive of Pakistan,*[17] was delivered. The Supreme Court in its judgment declared General Musharraf's dismissal by the ousted prime minister as void and of no legal effect and gave the chief executive three years' time to fulfill his seven-point agenda. Besides giving the military leader the power to amend the Constitution, "the Supreme Court, in its eagerness to validate the military regime, ventured into matters [that] were not even an issue before the Court."[18] Such matters pertained to the declaration of the dismissal of the COAS, the status of judges who refused to take oath as "closed and past transaction," fixing of the tenure of the regime, and authority to amend the Constitution, etc.

The judgment in the *Zafar Ali Shah* case and the declarations made therein by the apex Court are devoid of any legal and constitutional sanctity and floated in a presumptive atmosphere of unrealities. The judgment agitated against the Court's earlier verdict in a case reported as *Asma Jilani vs. Government of Punjab,* wherein it was held:

> The courts do not decide abstract, hypothetical, or contingent questions or give mere declarations in the air. The determination of an abstract question of constitutional law, divorced from the concrete facts of a case, floats in an atmosphere of unreality; it is a determination in a vacuum, and, unless it amounts to a decision settling rights and obligations of the parties before the court, it is not an instance of the exercise of judicial power.[19]

The judgment is seemingly devoid of any judicial propriety, for the following reasons: (1) When the military leadership held the 1973 Constitution in abeyance, the Supreme Court and the High Courts stamped the situation or new legal order with judicial sanctity by swearing their oath of allegiance to the PCO. The military leadership asked the higher judiciary to take the new oath for the protection of the PCO, and it readily conceded. (2) The cases of judges, who either refused to take oath or were not invited to take oath, were declared to be "passed and closed transaction[s]," which meant that they were the product of the old legal order based on the 1973 Constitution, which was not only held in abeyance but was at the mercy of the new legal order. The assertion of the judgment—that taking the new oath to protect and abide by the PCO of the military government made no difference at all—is unfortunately not true. For removing the judges, there is a procedure provided in Article 209 of the Constitution, and that procedure was not adopted, because the Constitution was held in abeyance, and it was dependent on the wishes of the military general to take recourse to certain provisions and ignore others. (3) The judges stood removed or retired, because they did not accept the new legal order or, for that matter, the new legal order did not deem it proper to retain them in its capricious fold. (4) The judges of the apex court who could not protect the 1973 Constitution (as per their oath of office) and who readily took the oath for protecting and abiding by the new legal order could not put a legal and constitutional clog on the wielders of the new legal order for effecting changes in the 1973 Constitution. (5) The judges virtually abandoned the 1973 Constitution when they took oath of fealty to the PCO or, more bluntly, to the general and his flourishing military rule.

Finally, there is a marked difference between the *Begum Nusrat Bhutto* case[20] and the *Zafar Ali Shah* case. In the *former*, the Supreme Court dismissed the petition as being not maintainable. Far from making any loud declarations, the Supreme Court "expected the CMLA to redeem his pledge" of holding elections at the earliest. In the latter, the Supreme Court not only declared that the petitions were maintainable, but also made lengthy declarations far from reality. The judges, who could not protect the 1973 Constitution as per their oath, empowered the general to effect amendments therein. It can be looked at from another angle: How could the apex Court, which was the product of the 1973 Constitution, empower someone other than the properly constituted legislature under the same Constitution to effect changes in it?

REMOVAL OF THE PRESIDENT

In the wake of the military coup, holding of the 1973 Constitution in abeyance, and administration of the new oath of office to the judges, President Muhammad Rafiq Tarar was the only constitutional officer untouched by the PCO. However, the coup-maker decided to remove the president in June 2001 and assumed that office.[21] The Supreme Court in the *Zafar Ali Shah* case held in part:

> That the 1973 Constitution still remains the supreme law of the land subject to the condition that certain parts thereof have been held in abeyance on account of State necessity; . . . [and t]hat the Superior Courts continue to function under the Constitution. The mere fact that the Judges of the Superior Courts have

> taken a new oath under the Oath of Office (Judges) Order No. 1 of 2000, does not in any manner derogate from this position, as the Courts had been originally established under the 1973 Constitution, and have continued in their functions in spite of the Proclamation of Emergency and PCO No. 1 of 1999 and other legislative instruments issued by the Chief Executive from time to time.[22]

A plain reading of the aforementioned conclusion of the Supreme Court indicates that the supreme law in the country was the 1973 Constitution. However, such a conclusion of the Supreme Court was negated by the removal of President Muhammad Rafiq Tarar and assumption of the office by the chief executive under the PCO. The former chief justice Saeeduzzaman Siddiqui opined: "There cannot be two supreme laws operating in the same field. If one law is supreme, the other has to be subordinate to it. Therefore, the PCO has to be read as suconstitutional legislation. If it is subconstitutional legislation, then it cannot amend or curtail the Constitution, itself."[23] Despite holding the Constitution as supreme law, the very chief justice who was the author of the judgment, administered the oath to the military ruler, as president. If, as per judgment of the Supreme Court, the Constitution was the supreme law of the land, then it provided for the removal of the president in a particular manner. This act of the military ruler and the chief justice was in direct conflict with the judgment.

NATIONAL ACCOUNTABILITY BUREAU ORDINANCE, 1999

Ensuring swift and across-the-board accountability was part of the seven-point agenda of the military government, and it was in pursuance of this objective that on November 16, 1999, the National Accountability Bureau Ordinance, 1999 (Ordinance No. XVIII of 1999), was promulgated, which has been amended five times. This ordinance repealed the Ehtesab Act, 1997, and the post of the chief Ehtesab commissioner. In pursuance of the provisions of the ordinance, the National Accountability Bureau (NAB) was established with a serving lieutenant general as its chairman. The NAB Ordinance commenced the process of accountability from January 1, 1985. The ordinance provides that the NAB will deal with all cases of corruption, corrupt practices, and willful default in payment of loans and government taxes. All the offences falling within the purview of the NAB law have been made nonbailable, and punishments prescribed include imprisonment, fines, and disqualification from holding public offices and seeking loans from government-sponsored financial institutions. Serving armed forces personnel were excluded from the application of the NAB Ordinance. The military-enacted law allowed the NAB officials to detain the accused up to ninety days.

Over a dozen constitutional petitions were filed in the Supreme Court, challenging the vires of the NAB Ordinance, on the grounds that it was ultra vires of the Constitution, principles of separation of power, violated fundamental rights, provided the authorities with draconian means of dealing with an accused and his property, and created a parallel judicial system in the country, thereby empowering the executive to perform judicial functions. The Court, after hearing arguments for and against the NAB Ordinance, struck some of its harsh provisions and directed the military regime to suitably amend it, vide its judgment: *Khan Asfandyar Wali vs. Federation of Pakistan.*[24] These directions mainly related to the appointment of the NAB chairman by the president in consultation with the chief justice, his removal under Article 209 of the Constitution, tenure of office for three years, allowing the accused the right of transfer of any pending reference, special treatment to women accused, provision relating to the withdrawal of a case from the Accountability Court, auditing of the accounts of the NAB by the auditor general of Pakistan, etc. The court further held that the constitutional jurisdiction vesting in the High Courts under Article 199 of the 1973 Constitution could not be taken away or abridged or curtailed by the subordinate legislation of the NAB Ordinance. The provision of the Ordinance, so far as it ousted the power of the higher courts from exercising jurisdiction, whether under Article 184(3) or 199 of the Constitution, was declared ultra vires. The chairman of the NAB was restrained from meddling in the financial settlement arrived at between a creditor and debtor through the State Bank of Pakistan. In the *Khan Asfandyar Wali* case, the Supreme Court upheld its earlier direction contained in the *Zafar Ali Shah* case to accelerate the process of accountability in a coherent and transparent manner, justly, fairly, equitably, and in accordance with law.

Far from taking concrete and impartial steps aimed at the eradication of corruption, the NAB has shown "open bias in picking up cases of politically undesirable persons, on the one hand, and turning a blind eye to charges against pliable politicians, on the other."[25] Ostensibly created for stemming the rising tide of corruption and wanton acts of corrupt practice in the government, in reality the institution, while treading the footprints of the demised Ehtesab Bureau, has been employed overwhelmingly for politically motivated prosecution. Notwithstanding the insinuation against the NAB for being monetarily corrupt, it has a questionable record to its discredit. Judging its performance, many opine that "instead of impartially investigating cases of corruption in order to facilitate the return of social and psychological equilibrium to society, and allowing the country to leave behind the sour memoirs of a murky past and move ahead, NAB's actions have often been accused of being against the business and investment interests of the country."[26]

The shady deal with Nawaz Sharif, his surreptitious exile and amnesty to his whole family punctured the NAB's credibility. Several politicians such as Aftab Ahmed Khan Sherpao and others contested the NAB cases in the Accountability Courts, yet secretly struck political compromises with the military government. Deliberate delay in and lack of any legal action against politicians (enjoying notoriety for corruption, tax evasion, and loan defaulting), who were supporting the

Musharraf regime, took the steam out of the NAB law, as well. An Awami National Party leader and former federal minister in the Sharif government, Azam Khan Hoti, was sentenced to fourteen years imprisonment on the allegation of having received kickbacks in the installation of telephone booths on the Islamabad–Lahore Motorway. Under pressure from the U.S.-led coalition in Afghanistan, the Musharraf regime pursued an anti-fundamentalist agenda, though willy-nilly, and it needed political allies in the adjoining Northwest Frontier Province (NWFP). The convict, Azam Khan Hoti (from the NWFP) moved a bail petition before the Lahore High Court, where his appeal against the sentence was pending. The counsel of the NAB supported Hoti's contention on the plea that "bad health justified his release on bail."[27] Subsequent to his release on bail, Hoti with his "bad health" was seen moving around in motorcades and attending political meetings of his party. On the other hand, Senator Gulsher from the NWFP, despite severe paralysis, was denied the concession of bail on the same plea, which was vehemently opposed by the NAB.[28] The NAB's false claims of adhering to high standards of neutrality and transparency were contradicted by its discriminatory treatment meted out to various categories of persons with varying political affiliations. A pointer to such an assertion could be Admiral Mansurul Haq, who was let off in a grotesque manner in a plea bargain.[29]

Though first NAB chairman Lietuenant General Syed Muhammad Amjad Ali had a clean image, excessive interference from above for political expediency and other parochial considerations impeded the accountability process. His removal as chairman is said to be the result of his obtaining documentary evidence for launching a full-scale enquiry into six major defense deals involving about twenty retired top military brass including former chiefs of army staff, two naval chiefs, and air force chiefs in the purchase of tanks, submarines, Mirage fighters, and army jeeps.[30] Such a course left the military regime unhappy with him. The NAB made no secret of its intense distaste for politicians opposed to the Musharraf rule. Nothing discredited the anticorruption pursuits more than the NAB's venom against opposition politicians, political partisanship, and victimizing selected targets, while leaving out the most blue-eyed boys in the ranks of the promilitary government (PML[Q]), the Pakistan Muslim League (Quaid-i-Azam).

ARMY MONITORS

Besides promulgation of the NAB ordinance to net and deter political opponents and the civil bureaucracy from challenging and questioning the writ of military rule, the regime introduced on November 15, 1999, a novel system of army monitoring teams to draw performance and evaluation reports on civil officers and their workings. The rationale for the induction of army monitors was to improve the efficiency of civil officers. The monitors were required to receive input from the field and pass it on to their top military brass for policy formulation. Notwithstanding the ostensible purpose for which the monitors were installed, the scope of their activities was practically widened and no departmental civilian posting or transfer could be made without prior clearance from the military officers. The monitors began to be equated with panacea for all the ills and curses prevailing in the civil bureaucracy. In the first year of military rule, 2,500 officials of various ranks were facing enquiries on the report of monitors, and 1,000 officers of the Central Board of Revenue were suspended. Characterizing them as corrupt officials, the military regime promulgated two ordinances, that is, Removal from Service (Special Powers) Ordinance 2000, and the Civil Servants (Amendment) Ordinance 2000, providing for the expeditious dismissal of corrupt and inefficient officials, and for the premature retirement of inefficient civil servants. When their hectic efforts and snooping could not gather tangible evidence of corruption against the suspended employees of the Central Board of Revenue, they were sheepishly reinstated in service. The military government's irresponsible conduct in the form of malicious campaign, loud drum-beating of corruption charges, and poisonous propaganda against the suspended officials in the media, left them socially at a disadvantageous position.

Bias Floating on the Face of Record

In March 1998, the chief Ehtesab commissioner under the Sharif government had registered Reference No. 30/1998 before the Lahore High Court against the former prime minister, Benazir Bhutto, and her spouse, Senator Asif Ali Zardari. The then chief justice, Rashid Aziz Khan, constituted a bench comprising Malik Muhammad Qayyum and Syed Najmul Hassan Kazmi for its adjudication. The allegation against the couple was that by abusing their authority as holders of public offices in collusion with each other and with Societe General De Surveillance SA (SGS), they had sanctioned the SGS contract for preshipment inspection, and thereby received kickbacks and commissions resulting in loss to the public exchequer.[31] While excessively and visibly manipulating the Court proceedings, the Divisional Bench of the High Court held both Ms. Bhutto and her husband guilty of offences of corruption and corrupt practices, and awarded them jail terms of five years each and a fine of US$8.6 million. Both were disqualified as legislators.

Benazir Bhutto and her husband assailed the judgment before the Supreme Court. Besides raising serious legal lacunae, the impugned judgment was assailed on the basis of bias of the judges who succumbed to inducements and pressure of the government. It was argued that Chief Justice Rashid Aziz Khan; Senator Saifur Rehman, who was in charge of the Ehtesab Bureau; Khalid Anwar, law minister; and Judge Malik Muhammad Qayyum were clandestinely in league with each other to secure the conviction of the appellants at the behest of the then prime minister of Pakistan, Nawaz Sharif.[32] The impugned reference was pending at the principal seat of the Lahore High Court, which was subsequently transferred to its Rawalpindi Bench, because Benazir Bhutto and her husband had residence at Islamabad. During the trial, Malik Muhammad Qayyum managed to have the reference heard by the bench he headed even at Rawalpindi. The transfer order of the reference against Ms. Bhutto was deliberately misinterpreted inasmuch as if the Ehtesab Bench was ordered to be transferred to Rawalpindi rather than the reference itself. On such contentions, the Supreme Court held that:

> It appears from the record that notifications were issued by the then learned Chief Justice, Lahore High Court, from time to time to enable Malik Muhammad Qayyum, J. to visit Rawalpindi to hear Ehtesab Reference No. 30 of 1998 and to be present on each and every date of hearing of the aforementioned Reference. It supports the contention of the learned counsel for the appellants that Reference No. 30 of 1998 was virtually "chased" by Malik Muhammad Qayyum, Judge, and the exercise had caused substantial financial loss to the State exchequer. The "chase" thus given amply demonstrates the keen interest of Malik Muhammad Qayyum, Judge, to impose himself on the matter and take it to its end according to his preconceived notions.[33]

Besides Malik Muhammed Qayyum's self-imposition on the reference, the Supreme Court also noted other glaring examples of his prejudice against the former prime minister and her spouse while adjudicating the case. A few weeks before the Supreme Court was scheduled to hear Ms. Bhutto's appeal against her conviction, *The Sunday Times* (London) sensationally disclosured the existence of more than one dozen tapes of telephone calls between Malik Muhammad Qayyum, Khalid Anwar, and Saifur Rehman that were wiretapped by the Intelligence Bureau (IB) in April, 1999, during the trial of Benazir Bhutto and her husband. Transcripts of the tapes published in the media established that the government itself dictated the judgment.[34] The tape scandal rendered the Lahore High Court's judgment controversial and put the country's entire judiciary on the defensive. Based on the tapes, appellant Bhutto established her case at the Bar that the judges who had convicted her were not independent and were coaxed by the government in power to oust her from the political arena. The Supreme Court, however, did not take serious notice of these tapes and instead accepted the appeal on other grounds that which spoke of "bias" of judges floating on the face of the Court record against Ms. Bhutto. While Ms. Bhutto and her political supporters greatly politicized the judgment, in its wake Justices Malik Muhammad Qayyum, and Rashid Aziz Khan were forced to quit the judiciary in disgrace.

PRESIDENT'S REFERENDUM, 2002

Petitions were filed under Article 184(3) of the Constitution in the Supreme Court, challenging the legality and vires of Referendum Order No. 12 of 2002, issued by the chief executive, wherein he decided to hold a referendum on April 30, 2002, "seeking the people's democratic mandate to serve the nation" as the president of Pakistan for a period of five years.[35] It was contended that despite the validation of the Proclamation of Emergency and the PCO by the Supreme Court, the 1973 Constitution was the supreme law of the land, as laid down in the *Syed Zafar Ali Shah* case. In constitutional petitions Nos. 12 and 15 of 2002, filed by the chief of Jamaat-i-Islami, Qazi Hussain Ahmed, and by Syed Zafar Ali Shah, a Pakistan Muslim League (Nawaz) (PML[N]) leader, a composite declaration was sought as to the illegality of the chief executive occupying the position of the president of Pakistan and that Muhammad Rafiq Tarar was still the president. On the status of the Referendum Order, the Supreme Court held that "it does not, in any manner, derogate from the parameters of the extra-constitutional measure validated by this Court in the *Syed Zafar Ali Shah* case, nor is it tantamount to converting the parliamentary system envisaged by the Constitution into presidential form of government, in view of the fact that elections to the National and Provincial Assemblies and the Senate of Pakistan would be held in October 2002, in accordance with the constitutional scheme and governments at the Federal and Provincial levels would be formed accordingly. The Referendum Order is intra vires the powers given to the Chief Executive by means of the judgment of this Court in Syed Zafar Ali Shah's case."[36]

The assumption of the office of the president was provided rationale by the Supreme Court judgment on the novel touchstone of the chief justice having administered the oath of office to the president, Musharraf was performing functions of the president, he swore in two chief justices of Pakistan, and he met foreign heads of the state as well as local politicians in his capacity as president. The judgment further asserted that no challenge was thrown to his assumption of office of president, and in these petitions it was collaterally challenged; hence the Supreme Court could not issue a writ of quo warranto, as prayed for. The 1973 Constitution stipulates under Article 41 that the president of Pakistan is to be elected, and his electoral college shall consist of the Parliament and the provincial assemblies. Nowhere in the Constitution is any such mechanism of electing president provided as the military regime adopted through the referendum, yet the Supreme Court sanctified it by its judicial stamp. It was vehemently argued on behalf of the petitioners that the provisions for referendum in the Constitution were general in nature. However, the Supreme Court, agreeing with the counsel of the respondent chief executive, that Article 41 be read with Article 48(6) of the Constitution for a harmonious construction thereon, held that the appeal (via the referendum) to the political and sovereign people of Pakistan could not be termed undemocratic and against the letter and spirit of the Constitution.[37]

Respectfully disagreeing with the worthy judges, suffice it to say that if Musharraf's referendum was democratic, then Article 41 of the Constitution was rendered nugatory, as it provided for a definite and different mode of electing the president. If the people of Pakistan were sovereign, then the same sovereign people had agreed upon a Constitution, which was being held in abeyance by Musharraf. Article 48(6) of the Constitution provides that if the president in his discretion, or on the advice of the prime minister, considers that if it is desirable that any matter of public importance should be referred to in a referendum, then the president may cause the matter to be referred to referendum in the form of a question that is capable of being answered either by "yes" or "no." However, there is a silver lining in paragraph 83 of the judgment, which could be employed to demolish Musharraf's self-serving device of making himself the president via the referendum. When the counsel representing the petitioners argued that the referendum would be a device for the military dictator to assume absolute powers, the Supreme Court held that "all these apprehensions, in our view, are purely imaginary, academic, presumptive, and hypothetical, and, in fact, such questions have been raised prematurely. We cannot anticipate, nor can the petitioners, as to the course of future events."[38] In fact, through such a conclusion the Supreme Court has left the issue of Musharraf becoming president for the next five years to be decided at a proper forum at the appropriate time!

While the judiciary hurriedly legalized the Referendum Order, the Election Commission manufactured its results up to 98 percent of voters supporting it, and that too, in the face of independent observers like the Human Rights Commission of Pakistan (HRCP) terming the voluntary participation as not more than three to five percent.[39] The referendum, which was conducted through the lopsided equation of the Election Commission and the army, further ridiculed the two institutions and the judiciary. The way the general and his commanders in uniform were hopping from city to city and addressing rent-a-crowd rallies, the exercise made a mockery of the office of the chief of army staff. The general—who otherwise euphemistically claimed himself "popular" among "the sovereign people of Pakistan"—spent billions of rupees on an image-building campaign. The overt partisan role of the provincial governors and top military brass could be visualized from the conduct of the commander, 4 Corps, in military outfit gracing the stage of Musharraf's Lahore rally on April 9, 2002.[40] Notwithstanding the fact of having chased out the two political leaders of the mainstream political parties through the biased accountability drive; the general's use of "objectionable language" against them at the rallies punctured his arrogant assertions of projecting himself as a holier-than-thou figure. The grossly contrived referendum campaign achieved little and the citizens' turnout was abysmally farcical, despite official claims to the contrary. It was in this context that the French foreign ministry spokesman on May 2, 2002, said that: "France has chosen officially to disregard the results of Tuesday's presidential referendum."[41] On the same day, the United States withheld praise for General Pervez Musharraf's much trumpeted "victory" in the referendum, saying Washington looked forward to "free and fair" elections in October 2002.[42] Terming his referendum as "free, fair, and transparent," the military general made a promise to his captive nation to hold the October 2002 general elections in "the same manner."[43] The "transparency" of the controversial referendum could be visualized from the order of the Election Commission to dispose of its complete record by December 31, 2002, possibly to save the Commission and its beneficiary from further ridicule.

LEGAL FRAMEWORK ORDER (LFO)

Nowhere in the world does the judicial organ of the state have the power to enable an individual to tamper with the law of the land. Such an act of Pakistan's judiciary is unprecedented, as neither the constitutional text nor its spirit allows the apex Court to assume the jurisdiction of conferring upon a general the sovereign right to legislate for the whole nation. However, while validating Musharraf's military coup in the *Zafar Ali Shah* case, the Supreme Court allowed him to resort to constitutional amendments only "if the Constitution fails to provide a solution for attainment of his declared objectives." This power was circumscribed by a declaration that "no amendment shall be made in the salient features of the Constitution, that is, independence of judiciary, federalism, parliamentary form of government blended with Islamic provision." Such limitations notwithstanding, Musharraf ab initio started with changing the entire complexion of the Constitution and ended up with the addition of his "commandments" into it. Seemingly, he also outclassed his preceding military dictator, General Zia, who had all his acts, orders, and ordinances validated and gained passage of the Eighth Amendment by the Parliament, though by means of blackmail, negotiation, or even coercion. Musharraf did not feel any need for that and asserted that by virtue of the powers assigned to him by the Supreme Court judgment, the LFO stood incorporated in the Constitution. He threatened that if the Parliament tried to reverse any of his amendments in the Constitution in general, and the one pertaining to the National Security Council (NSC) in particular, "they will have to quit or I will quit."[44]

The constitutional package titled "Establishment of Sustainable Federal Democracy" was made public in two installments; that is, Package I was released on June 26, 2002 and Package II on July 15, 2002. The constitutional package for the sake of "political stability" and "checks and balances in the power structure" of the country envisaged the following salient features: [45]

1. Voters's age reduced from 21 to 18 years.

2. Adoption of joint electorate system as originally contained in the 1973 Constitution. However, no reserved seats for the minorities were proposed.

3. President empowered to remove the prime minister and his cabinet, without dissolving the National Assembly.

4. President to appoint governors, in his discretion.

5. President can nominate any member of the National Assembly as prime minister.

6. Governor can nominate any member of the Provincial Assembly as chief minister.

7. Setting up of the National Security Council, and the president will be the chairman of the National Security Council.

8. Members of the Senate will be elected directly.

9. No independent candidate can take part in the Senate elections.

10. The minimum educational qualification of the bachelor's degree is prescribed for candidature to membership of legislatures.

11. An overall increase of 51 percent in the membership of the assemblies. Number of seats in National Assembly increased from 207 to 357.

12. Number of Senate seats increased from 87 to 100.

13. Number of seats of the Punjab Assembly increased from 240 to 390, Sindh Assembly up from 100 to 171, the NWFP Assembly from 80 to 130, and the Balochistan Assembly from 40 to 67.

14. Reserved seats for women, technocrats, and *ulema* in the Senate and assemblies increased.

15. Qualification for reserved seats in the Senate, National, and provincial assemblies for technocrats will be sixteen years of education, recognized by the University Grants Commission or a recognized statutory body, as well as at least twenty years of experience, including record of achievements at the national or international level.

16. The concept of caretaker government has been envisaged in case of general elections on the completion of the normal term of assemblies.

17. Election Commission to be converted into permanent and autonomous institution with four members. The tenure of the Chief Election Commission increased from three to five years.

18. Loan defaulters will not be able to contest elections.

19. Any political party securing less than 10 percent of the total votes cast in the election on general seats shall not be entitled to any seats.

20. Any party getting less than 5 percent of the votes will not get any seat in the Senate.

21. The amendments proposed disqualification of a convict from holding a political office, regardless of the lapse of time since his release. Similarly, another provision was added, debarring a person who had been proclaimed an absconder or convicted and sentenced to imprisonment for having absconded.

22. Local governments to have constitutional cover for their operation and existencece.

The constitutional package—doled out in two installments—was questioned by political forces of all shades, by constitutional experts, and by intellectuals belonging to various schools of thought. All of them were unanimous at least on one point, and that was the competency and bona fides of the chief executive to amend the Constitution. For creating checks and balances in the Constitution, the main thrust of the new grafting was enhancement of powers of the president, thus envisaging an all-powerful head of the state. On August 21, 2002, General Pervez Musharraf, with the stroke of his pen, made fundamental changes in the Constitution and felt no need to resort to the future Parliament even for their validation. He made himself the president for the next five years and revived Article 58(2)(b) for dismissing the government and dissolving the National Assembly. A new Article 152-A was inserted, creating the NSC. Several amendments, that is, the president's power to appoint anyone as prime minister, discretionary power to appoint governors, reducing the tenure of the assembly to four years, reservation of seats for technocrats in the National Assembly, amendments pertaining to the Council of Common Interests, National Finance Commission, and National Economic Council, etc., originally proposed in the constitutional package were withdrawn.

The controversial LFO incorporates strong features of the presidential form of government in the Constitution, and fully absolves the person holding the exalted office from any responsibility to the people or even being answerable to the Parliament. Musharraf is already considered to have been elected as the president via the referendum. In its actual operation, the LFO transforms the parliamentary status of the 1973 Constitution into a quasi-presidential–cum–quasi-military form of government, at least for the next five years when Musharraf shall be holding the office of the COAS as well. The LFO has axed the Parliament's supremacy, which amounts to the undoing of democracy in the country. The structural dynamics of the LFO make the case of the COAS president wanting a prime minister who works for, and is answerable to him, and not to the

National Assembly. How can the prime minister work when the NSC intervenes to decide whether the prime minister is competent or incompetent? The NSC would be derogating the constitutional system, itself.

The new constitutional and political engineering speaks of a system wherein civilian leaders would have to be ready to work within the parameters set out by the military regime.[46] These changes are not the solution of Pakistan's perennial political problems, yet they definitely reflect the mental makeup, psychological disposition, and political perspectives of the senior military commanders led by General Pervez Musharraf. The military ethos necessitates a hierarchical command and emphasizes centralization. Viewed from such a perspective, "the military rulers, despite their commitment to democracy, cannot overcome their psychological makeup that calls for establishing a focal point of authority at the top, and prefer control to participation and sharing of power."[47] The LFO inserted, at the will of the COAS president, in the Constitution without sanction from the Parliament, reflects the same ethos.

NATIONAL SECURITY COUNCIL (NSC)

The idea of the NSC has been perceived as an undemocratic and supra-constitutional exercise, with the ulterior motive to make the Parliament ineffective, and to reduce the role of the prime minister to zero. Initiatives of the NSC have always originated from the army, during the absence of an elected government. Notwithstanding its abject interventions in the democratic dispensation of the country, the military has a long-cherished desire of a constitutional role in the political permutations of Pakistan. General Zia, through his Presidential Order 14, had added Article 152-A to the Constitution, which pertained to the formulation of the NSC consisting of eleven power holders, of whom five were to be military men, including Zia himself. The initiative was declined by his carefully elected Parliament in December 1985, in the process of validating his orders and ordinances issued earlier. In the negotiation between the president/COAS, General Zia, and the Assembly members, a compromise was struck by what became Article 58(2)(b), providing for presidential discretion to dissolve the National Assembly and dismiss the government.

In 1989, the Benazir government set up a committee under Air Chief Marshal (Retd) Zulfiqar Ali Khan on revamping the intelligence agencies and their role in the unfolding circumstances. The Zulfiqar Committee recommended the setting up of the NSC under the prime minister, and its members included the ministers for defense, foreign affairs, interior and finance, the chairman of the Joint Chiefs Committee, and chairman of the proposed Joint Intelligence Committee. Although the three services chiefs were included in the committee as advisors, the recommendations and conclusions on their behalf were to be submitted by the chairman, Joint Chiefs Committee. In keeping with the democratic values and the supremacy of the Parliament, the recommendations seemed ideal, yet they were unacceptable to the military, which considers itself "the State, the so-called repository of 'collective wisdom,' and the messiah of the land."[48] After the dismissal of the Bhutto government in November 1996, the then president, Sardar Farooq Ahmed Leghari, on behest of the army, formed a Council of Defense and National Security (CDNS) by changing the Rules of Business of the Government. The CDNS consisted of the president, the prime minister, the three services chiefs, the chairman, Joint Chiefs of Staff Committee, and the secretaries of defense, interior, finance, and foreign affairs. The Sharif government undid the intense criticism of political parties notwithstanding, the CDNS, because it seemed an impediment to his version of governing the country.

The much-dreaded NSC, introduced by General Musharraf, agitates against democratic values and undermines the growth of representative institutions. Headed by the president, the NSC comprises four military personnel, that is, chairman, Joint Chiefs Staff Committee, the three services' chiefs, the prime minister, and the four chief ministers of the provinces. The NSC envisaged in the LFO would be an institution for checks on the prime minister, his government, and indeed, on the institution of democracy, itself. The composition of the NSC indicates that the army wants to run the state affairs from the back seat. The president in military uniform would head the NSC for the next five years. The chief ministers appointed by the governors (nominees of the president) would not be independent of the coercion and influence of the president and his governors. It is worth mentioning that not all of the chief ministers would belong to the political party of the prime minister, and a political scenario on the pattern of 1989 may well emerge once again, when the then Punjab chief minister, Mian Nawaz Sharif, confronted the then prime minister Benazir Bhutto, on the behest of the then president Ghulam Ishaq Khan. The naval and air force chiefs traditionally never play an independent role and always toe the army lines, whether it is coup-making or any other intervention in civil affairs. Besides the army chief, the three other chiefs would be present in the meetings, merely for decorative purposes and for increasing the military's vote in the Council. Through the NSC, the generals have succeeded in extracting a coercive constitutional role in the country's future governance. The main argument advanced in favor of the NSC is consultation on the "strategic situation" and "security of the state". The critics of the NSC consider the institution as an open-ended and all-embracing intrusive body. They contradict it with the arguments that such mechanisms for consultation are already in place in the form of the Defense Committee of the Cabinet (DCC), the Ministry of Defence, the Joint Chiefs Committee and, the ISI.[49]

JUNIOR JUDGES ELEVATION CASE

In December 2001, four judges (one from the Peshawar High Court and three from the Lahore High Court) were elevated as judges of the Supreme Court, and their appointments were challenged by various petitions, including petitions by the Supreme Court Bar Association (SCBA) and the Pakistan Bar Council (PBC) in a case styled as *Supreme Court Bar Association vs. Federation of Pakistan.*[50] The challenge was thrown to the appointment of three judges, namely, Justice Khalil-ur-Rehman Ramday, Justice Muhammad Nawaz Abbasi, and Justice Faqir Muhammad Khokhar, on the point of departure from the principle of seniority. It was contended that the appointment of junior judges, by passing over senior ones, militates against the doctrine of legitimate expectancy enunciated in *Al-Jihad Trust vs. Federation of Pakistan (PLD 1996 SC 324)* and *Malik Asad Ali vs. Federation of Pakistan (PLD 1998 SC 161)*, and is tantamount to an arbitrary practice of "pick and choose," which was fraught with disastrous consequences undermining the independence of the judiciary, that led to "public perceptions of the government having packed the Supreme Court with pliant and pliable judges of its own liking."[51] Interestingly, one of the judges, Justice Faqir Muhammad Khokhar, who was performing executive functions, being secretary of law to the government, was at No.13 in the list of seniority positions of the judges of the Lahore High Court on the day of his elevation. Whereas in his case ten senior judges were ignored, in the case of two other judges, two senior judges were overlooked in their elevation to the apex Court. The petitioners also demanded making available the record of the appointment of these judges in order to disclose why senior judges were ignored? Brushing aside the contentions and precedents set by the apex Court, itself, the petitions were dismissed on the plea that the rule of fitness and suitability had an edge over the principles of seniority and legitimate expectancy.[52] Justifying the impugned appointments as having been recommended by the chief justice, and as such, not justifiable, the Supreme Court held these were fresh appointments, not promotions, and secondly, supercession of senior judges of the High Court was not unprecedented.[53] The contention of making the record of appointments public was rejected on the plea that "apart from the element of confidentiality, making the record of the appointments public would not be in the interest of the institution, the judicial consultant, and the concerned judges for reasons which are too obvious to need elucidation."[54]

The SCBA and PBC (the two apex Bar Associations) filed a review petition against the above-referred judgment. Since taking oath under the PCO, the Supreme Court had not decided a single case in its constitutional jurisdiction against the military government, and through various petitions had validated all the major decisions, that is, imposition of emergency, referendum, appointment of junior judges, graduation bar for contesting of elections, etc. When the review petition was taken up for hearing on October 29, 2002, Hamid Khan, president of the SCBA, after submitting a written statement, completed his arguments with one sentence, saying, "since the judiciary is no more independent, we don't want to proceed with the case." The statement read:

> It has been resolved by the petitioner association and the Pakistan Bar Council that in view of the oath taken by the judges under the Provisional Constitutional Order, and in view of its recent verdicts upholding various orders and acts of the present military government, the judiciary has ceased to be independent, and that no substantial question of constitutional importance should be argued before this Honorable Court in its present composition.
>
> The general body of the petitioner association in its annual general meeting held on October 26, 2002 at Lahore, had unanimously condemned the enhancement of the retirement age of the judges through amendment in the Legal Framework Order, which, in the view of the lawyer's community, is an unconstitutional and invalid document. The petitioner association has also resolved that the enhancement of age is the last nail in the independence and credibility of judiciary.
>
> In view of the above, it is stated with a heavy heart that arguing the present review petition involving serious constitutional questions before this Honorable Court in its present composition, would be a futile exercise.[55]

In this statement of the petitioner association, the Supreme Court bench was left high and dry and had to leave for the chambers within five minutes of its arrival in the Court. On the following day, while dismissing the review petition as "having no merit in it," the bench termed the statement of the SCBA president as "contemptuous," and "reserved the right to take the proper action at an appropriate stage." The dismissal order further said: "Unfortunately, some members of the Bar motivated by malice, extraneous considerations and for political reasons or ill will, make irresponsible statements to tarnish the image of the judiciary, which is not at all in the supreme national interest."[56] Be that as it may be, the judiciary itself was the architect of tarnishing its own image. The five-member bench also defended the judges' oath under the PCO, and asserted that it had "saved the independence of the judiciary and preserved the Bar." The bench further opined that if the oath under the PCO had not been taken, the military would have "replaced the judicial system with an altogether new system unknown to a civilized society."[57] This was a far-fetched conclusion and against the actual appraisal of the circumstances under which the judges conceded in the ignominious act of taking oath under the PCO, and it could not be justified on any pretext whatsoever. A sacrifice on the model of the Fijian apex Court was most warranted by confronting the military regime and its agenda of stultification of the judicial institution, itself.[58] However, "the judiciary demurred, even though no military dictator could hope to send all the judges home, and survive. Judicial resoluteness could have provided the much needed deterrence against extra-constitutional adventures."[59]

The Supreme Court gave Hamid Khan the status of senior advocate when he was elected president of the SCBA a year earlier. In retaliation to his remarks while withdrawing the SCBA's review petition in the judges' case, the Supreme Court on November 5, 2002, withdrew that status. On this decision of the Supreme Court, the SCBA retaliated by condemning it as "personal malice and rage of judges against Hamid Khan, who was fighting the case of a collective nature to uphold the independence of the judiciary."[60] The SCBA was obliged to withdraw its review petition against the backdrop of acceptance by the higher judiciary of the benefits of tenure extension, and endorsing every extra-constitutional act of the military government. However, Hamid Khan was being penalized for acting in the larger public interest, while the higher courts always lent support to the military regimes and offered justifications for their misrule.

REVIEW OF THE *RIBA* CASE

In a case styled as *M. Aslam Khaki vs. Muhammad Hashim*,[61] the Shariat Appellate Bench of the Supreme Court had held that "any amount, big or small, over the principal, in a contract of loan or debt is *Riba* prohibited by the Holy Quran, regardless of whether the loan is taken for the purpose of consumption or for some productive activity."[62] On the touchstone of this definition, the Supreme Court held the prevailing financial system in Pakistan as against the injunctions of Islam, and directed the government to bring it in conformity with *Shariah,* by subjecting it to radical changes. The judgment was the affirmation of the decision of November 14, 1991, by the Federal Shariat Court, which had declared that *Riba* in all forms and manifestation was prohibited in Islam. This declaration contained in the judgment notwithstanding, the Shariat Appellate Bench of the Supreme Court suggested measures for the transformation of the existing banking and economic system in conformity with the Islamic ones, and decided to fix different dates for different phases of such transformation.[63] The multiphased transformation formula for the proposed interest-free financial and economic system notwithstanding, the Court declared that the Interest Act, various money lending laws, and Section 9 of the Banking Companies Ordinance, 1962, would cease to be effective on March 31, 2000.

Far from serving any meaningful purpose of its declarations, the judgment panicked the federal government, the country's financial institutions, and foreign investors. For assuaging the undercurrents of anxiety about the unfolding shape of the financial economic situation, the government reassured all concerned that nothing had changed and the court-designated bodies would analyze all such matters. Meanwhile, on the basis of miscellaneous applications, the Court had extended the period for implementation of its judgment in the *M. Aslam Khaki* case till June 30, 2002. The United Bank Ltd., along with others, had filed review petitions wherein the bank had contended that its following pleas were not answered either by the Federal Shariat Court or the Shariat Appellate Bench of the Supreme Court:

> 1. The banks in Pakistan are working within the framework of banking instruments prescribed by the State Bank, with the approval of the Council of Islamic Ideology, as valid Islamic instruments.
>
> 2. There is a considerable juristic opinion available to the fact that an increase to offset the inflation would have legal justification and would not be counted as *Riba*.
>
> 3. There is juristic opinion available to the fact that bank interest does not fall in the category of prohibited *Riba* (interest). According to his opinion, banks participate in the procedural processes of the society/community, make productive labor possible, increase social wealth, and take only a fraction of the profit that accrues to them, which is not *Riba*.[64]

On the contention that the Federal Shariat Court did not resolve these pertinent points, the Supreme Court held that a case for review of the impugned judgment was made out. Finding "errors floating on the surface of record," the Supreme Court remanded the matter to the Federal Shariat Court for redetermining the issue of *Riba* after thorough search and comparative study of the financial institutions working in the contemporary Muslim countries, and for giving definite findings on all issues raised in the petitions before it.

MILITARY AND THE CLERGY

In Pakistan, power vests in and is exercised by officers; even if and when it shared at certain interregnums, that was at the ministerial level, only. The self-nourishing and self-perpetuating institutions of the civil–military bureaucracy have monopolized all levels of executive authority, consequently making a mockery of the democratic, political, and election processes in the country. It has justified the dismissal of governments, dissolution of assemblies, and abrogation of constitutions on the peg of purging the holy precincts of politics from degraded, corrupt, and incompetent politicians and their misrules. The heroes of such missions were eulogized as "soldier–statesmen" and "saviors," who otherwise plunged the country in wars, economic disaster, abject poverty, ignorance, and the sociopolitical collapse.[65]

Pakistan's constitutional and institutional arrangements bestow powers on officers, without mentioning their responsibilities to the civil society. Even the fundamental rights mentioned in the Constitution are subject to laws enunciated and exercised by the officer class. The abject manipulations of the civil–military bureaucracy to assert its authority over the divided political parties, deny civil society the benefits of civil rule, grab resources, suppress dissent, thwart elections, and abrogate constitutions, have resulted in the instability of institutions, and generated intense feelings among masses of being grossly aggrieved at the hands of the crafty officers class. The military force in particular has never allowed the constitutional, democratic, electoral, and political values and processes to strike roots. This powerful institution has taken steps systematically to undermine the growth of popular legitimacy by "oppressing democratic movements."[66] Given the military's proclivity for interference in national affairs and guarding its own financial interests jealously, political analysts have tended to question the future of the democratic process, itself.[67]

In the present setup, over 150 serving and retired army officials are heading the government's major corporations, holding ministries, controlling education, leading police, subjecting Musharraf's opponents to accountability, running foreign missions, managing cricket, and so forth. This number is in addition to substantial regular inductions through the 10 percent quota fixed for military in the civil services. Musharraf, like his predecessors, has distributed the rewards of captured civil power among his military colleagues and juniors in an extensive manner. The army's hydra-headed financial and corporate stakes in civil affairs are awesome. Such interests could be visualized from the following opinion of a constitutional analyst:

> The army has such a large monetary stake in the country, that it will never allow a populist civilian government to interfere with the status quo. A civilian government may be permitted to continue only so far as it does not interfere with the financial interests of the army. Only a revolution may bring about a change in this state of affairs. Any civilian government brought into office by normal sedate democratic channels will neither have the strength, nor will it be permitted, to pursue a political or economic policy, which the military does not regard as conducive to its interests.[68]

For its persistent ascendancy in civil affairs, the military has bent or broken institutions like the Parliament, the Election Commission, and the judiciary. Notwithstanding the systematic excess and induction of army officers in all-important civil positions of the government, the force has its own politico–ideological agenda to fulfill. The Zia regime infused the doctrine of *jihad* in the army, which was "further developed and remained a driving force for well over two decades."[69] In the present circumstances, it is being wrapped up under the American pressure of its one-time supporter in the Soviet-Afghan context. The winding up of the *jihadi* doctrine has rendered a sizeable number of military officers redundant, who are ultimately landing in civil positions.[70] When this officer class loaded with its rigid theological orientations will interact with religious parties having the same bent of mind and trying to persuade the people to return to orthodoxy, the net result would be a tremendous pressure on liberal social values in the society.

Under foreign pressure, the Musharraf government often exhibited signs of purging the sociopolitical milieu of extremists, fanatics, and sectarian-minded terrorists, yet in reality this seems very difficult, if not impossible, altogether. The military and extremists in the country's clergy have several commonalties:

> On several occasions, they have practically demonstrated their ostensible opposition to constitutional democracy. The military and clergy do not believe in the supremacy of the constitution. If the military indulges in its abrogation, holding in abeyance or any other form of deviation from the constitution, the support from the clergy is readily available to it. In their mutual connivance, they derail the nation from treading the electoral, political, and democratic processes.
>
> The military rulers do not believe in sovereignty belonging to the people of Pakistan, and usurpation of power is justified on the peg of the country running risks of disintegration under civilian dispensations. Believing in rigged selection and not in fair elections, both silence the peoples' dissent by use of force and advancing lame excuses wrapped in dogmatic theology.
>
> Continuation of democracy and the political process, free and fair elections and the presence or emergence of an all-Pakistan leadership, is viewed as the death-knell to their ignominious vested interests. Both have prospered at the cost of the annihilation of democratic institutions, abrogation of constitutions, and unrestrained and untrammeled regimentation.
>
> Both played no role, whatsoever, in achieving an independent country, yet they claim themselves to be the sole guardians of its "ideological frontiers."
>
> The military–clergy alliance took its first shape in the 1971 East Pakistan crisis, when the Army let loose militant organizations such as *al Badar* and *al Shams,* affiliates of the Jamaat-i-Islami, against the people of eastern wing, who wreaked bloody havoc there. Emboldened on the ouster of Prime Minister Zulfikar Ali Bhutto, through the PNA's 1977 agitation, the clerics readily joined General Zia's "Islamization" project, which was sustained on social repression. The military–clergy holy alliance further cemented, when they joined and fought the American-led *jihad* against the godless Soviets in Afghanistan. Preceding the September 11, 2001, events, the military (including the period under Musharraf as the COAS, and later as the chief executive) and the *jihadi* militants were strategic partners in the Taliban's Afghanistan. In fact the extremist groups are the army's old buddies.
>
> Religious militancy in any case is the product of the U.S.-financed anti-Soviet campaign and ISI-orchestrated Afghan *jihad.* While Washington abandoned the *jihadis,* using them against the Soviets; the Army continued to embrace them as levers of its foreign policy in the Afghan and Kashmir context.
>
> Even in the October elections, the religious parties and *jihadi* groups were given freedom to propagate their versions of the Islamic ideology, while the regime adopted harsh perspectives against two mainstream parties, that is, PML(N) and the PPP. General Musharraf's tightening of the noose against the possible electoral victory of the mainstream parties, indirectly helped the clerics of MMA to get keys of power in the NWFP and Balochistan, and thereby backed the Jamali government at the Center.

ANTI-TERRORIST MEASURES

The preceding decade witnessed Pakistan hosting rabid gangs of religious zealots, preaching and resorting to violence, conveying messages of hate, and targeting rival sects and minorities. The display and use of automatic and sophisticated lethal weapons, particularly brandishing them at public rallies, had become a prestigious and routine exercise. *Jihad* was going on in the rugged mountains of Afghanistan and green valleys of Kashmir. *Jihadi* camps in the major cities of Punjab and the NWFP, and nexus between the *jihadi* outfits and intelligence agencies, despite official denials to the contrary, indicated the country's gradually unfolding slide in the abyss of anarchy. The highly motivated and armed fanatics had rendered the corrupt and incompetent police apparatus into an impotent force. Religious outfits such as the Lashkar-i-Toiba, Jaish-i-Muhammad, Sipah-i-Sahaba, and Tehrik-i-Jafaria, and a host of others, were not only involved in cross-border insurgencies, but were also shooting each other. The religious power of trained and armed activists exhibited alarming dimensions, and the country's entire social scene depicted a pathetic sense of helplessness.

Following the events of September 11, 2001, and General Musharraf's toeing the American line on the "freedom-fighters of yesterday turned into terrorists of today," this readily transformed him and his military dictatorship into the darling of the West. Be that as it may, initially the military government legitimized the activities of such armed groups by drawing a distinction between *jihad* and terrorism. On compulsions from abroad, Pakistan's decision to rein in religious extremist groups and banning their collection of funds was an appreciable step. The religious outfits were soliciting funds in the name of religion and its tradition of *jihad*, and the response was always impressive. The ban on such funds drew violent reactions from the beneficiaries, who were answerable to none, as the huge financial contributions were beyond the imagination of *jihadis,* mainly drawn from the *madrassas*, and even colleges.

The system of *madrassas* for spreading religious education had worked well in the past. However, its continuous pursuits of a puritanical world, and abject refusal to learn modern knowledge, outclassed it. The Afghan crisis transformed these *madrassas* into breeding nurseries for holy warriors. Mindless meddling in Afghan affairs, on behest of the shadowing intelligence organizations, encouraged religious students to flex their muscles in pursuit of the objectives of those who had reared them in military training. In the opinion of an analyst:

> The unrestricted and unchecked growth of [*madrassas*] had led to increased rivalry, tension and even bloody clashes among various sects. These clashes had created serious problems of law and order and threatened social harmony and national unity. Second, some of these [*madrassas*] were imparting military training to their students, who were later found involved in sectarian violence and terrorist activities. The religious parties running these [*madrassas*] were

following their own agenda on foreign policy; thus challenging the writ of the state.[71]

On June 19, 2002, the military government promulgated the *Madrassah Ordinance 2002* for setting in motion a legal mechanism for the removal of anomalies in the country's socioeducational system. The ordinance provides for the integration of Islamic education with general education in the *madrassas*. Under the ordinance, all the *madrassas* must be registered at the provincial or federal level to be eligible to receive financial assistance, grants, donations, *zakat* (religious gifts), or any benefit from the government. *Madrassas* refusing to register are to be disbanded or banned from operation. The religious schools are required to maintain accounts and to submit annual reports to their respective *madrassas* boards. To bring *madrassas* education in line with Pakistan's mainstream educational system, the religious schools courses in modern disciplines such as science, mathematics, English, and Urdu are compulsory and are incorporated into the teaching curricula.

To rope in rampaging terrorism, the military government reviewed and amended the Anti-Terrorism Act, making it more stringent. While seven militant and sectarian organizations were proscribed, a special monitoring mechanism was formulated for dealing with serious cases of sectarian terrorism in the courts. Under the U.S.-aided project, a Special Investigation Group was set up in the Federal Investigation Agency, which consisted of fifty experts in forensics, intelligence collection, cyber technology, and financial matters. The government also formed a National Crisis Management Cell in its Interior Division, for collecting, coordinating, analyzing, and disseminating vital information of terrorists to all the concerned law enforcing agencies. Besides upgrading the Anti-Terrorist Training School on modern lines, the military government embarked on a deweaponization drive to flush out illegal weapons, and partially succeeded in its efforts.

Within a day of the swearing-in of the National Assembly members, Musharraf promulgated Ordinance No. CXXV of 2002, amending the Anti-Terrorist Act, which expanded police powers to detain a suspect for a year, without charge or evidence, merely on casting of suspicion on him. No law including the harsh NAB Ordinance, authorized detainee's detention for such a lengthy period. This was giving virtually an unbridled license to the police to irremediably tie down persons falling in the suspicious net of the administration. It is still uncertain, that for depriving any person of his freedom for a year, and making life miserable for his family including parents, wife, and children, who will cast the suspicion on him? The new law also enables police to probe assets and bank accounts of the suspect and his family. Such an inhuman provision is directly in conflict with Article 10 of the Constitution, which provides safeguards against arrest and detention.

POLICE LAW

To revamp the police force and to make it accountable, Police Order 2002, was promulgated, replacing the antiquated Police Act of 1861, a colonial era law. The main thrust of the new law is to separate investigation work from the general watch and ward functions of police. A Public Safety Commission at the district, provincial, and national level is envisaged in the new law. For investigating cases of neglect, excesses, or misconduct by police officials, a Police Complaint Authority is being set up at the federal and provincial level to receive such complaints. A National Forensic Science Agency, equipped with a state-of-the-art laboratory and training school would be set up at Islamabad, and regional laboratories at the provincial level. No public representative will have any role in the appointment, promotion, and transfer of police officials, as there would be only regular appointments in the police department. Though the regime made loud claims that, on its promulgation, the law would transform the police from an admittedly repressive entity to an accountable, responsive, free from political pressure, and people friendly setup enjoying the confidence and trust of the citizens, its actual operation, and the subsequent police conduct would only confirm such exaggerated assertions. However, for its implementation, the federal government has provided the sum of Rs 1.52 billion for enhancing the operational capabilities of the police in the changing circumstances.

GRADUATE LEGISLATORS

In the Conduct of General Elections Order, 2002 (Chief Executive's Order No. 7 of 2002), vide Article 8-A, it was provided that only a graduate candidate would be eligible to contest the elections of assemblies. The provision was assailed before the Supreme Court in the case *Pakistan Muslim League (Q) vs. Chief Executive*[72] on the touchstone of being unreasonable and irrational in the light of the prevailing poor state of literacy in the country and violative of the fundamental rights enshrined in the Constitution and of the importance of political experience. And it militates against the universal definition of democracy that it is a government of the people, by the people, and for the people. The following was an interesting line of argument in favor of the petitions so filed:

> Wisdom has nothing to do with graduation. Most of the sages were illiterate. On the other hand, some of the highly qualified graduates are totally uneducated. In the past, the performance of graduate and nongraduate members of the Parliament was at par with each other. There is no substitute for experience. As a matter of fact, it is a question of representation. The elected members represent the people, 65 percent of whom are illiterate.[73]

The arguments against these petitions were equally cogent and substantial, that is, the condition being an incentive to education, the need for educated legislators, because uneducated or less educated ones could not participate in debates on the legislative work, and the Constitution provided for only the fundamental rights. The Court, while dismissing the petitions, provided rationale to its judgment that the educational qualification prescribed for the membership of assemblies will not only raise their level of competence and change the political culture, it will be an incentive to education as well. In the Court's view, "education related qualification is reasonable and not arbitrary or whimsical, because firstly, being a step toward transformation of political culture, it is not founded on unreasonable basis, and secondly, it equally applies to all the graduates and does not discriminate against any graduate or create a class within the graduates."[74] The graduation condition affected the political careers of many politicians and former legislators of different political parties.

OCTOBER 2002 ELECTIONS

Ab initio, the military ruler had the penchant of staying in power for a longer period. High sounding concepts, that is, accountability, transparency, devolution of power, genuine and grassroots democracy, cleanliness in politics, etc., were used as a façade to conceal his real intention of remaining a powerful executive chief, answerable to none. For that shabby project, the military junta adopted the strategy of keeping the leadership of two major political parties, PPP and PML(N), out, by beating drums of the charges of corruption and corrupt practices against them, by hoisting breakaway nonentities on the people via the uncertainty of the election process, and by inducting nonrepresentative handpicked cabinets of federal and provincial levels. On several occasions, Musharraf had stated that Nawaz Sharif and Benazir Bhutto would not be allowed to make a comeback in politics. The military regime did whatever it could possibly do to block a return by the two exiled leaders to Pakistan, thus:

1. On June 28, 2002, the regime promulgated the Political Parties (Amendment) Order 2002, and banned the holding of an office of a political party by a convicted person. The Special Court at Karachi convicted Nawaz Sharif in the plane hijacking case, and Benazir Bhutto was convicted for her absence from the Accountability Court at Rawalpindi. For that avowed mala fide end, an amendment to section 31 of the NAB Ordinance was effected, which provided that non-appearance of an accused before the Accountability Court was a convictable offense. This was in sharp contrast to the existing normal penal provision that if an accused person did not appear before any court trying a criminal offense, he would be declared an absconder, a legal status carrying with it, both presumptions of innocence and guilt.

2. The introduction of the condition of personal appearance before the returning officer for filing nomination papers in the October 2002, elections, was ostensibly introduced in the Representation of People Act, 1976, so that the exiled leaders could not personally file their election papers. The regime repeated its threats that if any of the two leaders landed in Pakistan, she or he would be driven straight to prison.

3. On July 6, 2002, the Chief Executive's Order No. 19 of 2002 titled *Qualification to Hold Public Offices Order, 2002*, was enunciated which read: "Notwithstanding anything contained in the Constitution or any other law for the time being in force, a person who has, at any time, held the office of the prime minister, or that of a chief minister of a province or a combination of such offices for two terms, irrespective of whether any one of the two or both the terms of office were completed or not, shall not be qualified to hold the office of the prime minister or that of a chief minister."[75] The regime justified the action on its much-trumpeted theme that "it was imperative to consolidate the measures taken by the president for the achievement of the objective of reconstruction of the institutions of state for establishing sustainable democracy, to ensure good governance, for an irreversible transfer of power to the people of Pakistan."[76] The two-term ban for the prime ministers and chief ministers was perceived as mala fide, ill conceived, and against all norms of democracy, by the media, constitutional experts, and major political parties whose leaders were affected through this device.[77] The introduction of such a law also reflected the mind-set of the military general, whose real intent was focused on the short-term personal interest of excluding the two politicians from the political arena, and seemed to be a self-serving device.

4. The constitutional engineering of the NRB, NAB, and ISI, and the abject bending and breaking of political stalwarts by coercive levers of the state, and the introduction of detesting plea bargain and deal culture by the military regime, indicated that the main political parties had lost in advance the October election battle that was yet to be fought.

The very appointment of the present Chief Election Commissioner (CEC), and his subsequent conduct in holding the president's referendum and general elections, was often portrayed as partial and controversial by the media and political parties, alike. Preceding his occupation of the CEC office, Justice (Retd) Irshad Hassan Khan was the chief justice of the Supreme Court. His elevation to that august position was controverted, criticized, and even maligned by the bar, media, and the political parties, inasmuch as the PBC and the SCBA, the two apex Bar bodies, were constrained to deny him the traditional farewell party in protest. There were consistent vociferous demands in the media, advising the military government to desist from appointing the said retired chief justice as the CEC.[78] The appointment of Justice Khan as the CEC notwithstanding, the military government brought about changes in the tenure and composition of the Election Commission itself. The tenure of office of the CEC was enhanced from three to five years, and its membership increased from two to four. In view of the substantial increase in the number of seats in the National Assembly and the four Provincial Assemblies pertaining to general members, women, and technocrats, the process of formulation and delimitation of constituencies was undertaken by the Election Commission, vide the Election Commission Order, 2002; Election Commission (Amendment Order), 2002; and the Conduct of General Election Order, 2002. The 1998 census in the country was made the basis of such delimitations.

In the wake of the referendum, public confidence and trust in holding a fair election was very low. Very high and credible standards of official neutrality were required to dispel public suspicion, and this was completely lacking in the given scenario. However, the unfolding developments tended to confirm the premises that the purpose of holding these elections was seemingly not to transfer power to civilian leadership, but to get legitimacy for one-man rule, hide the military junta behind a properly elected civilian setup, and to silence critics. As is sufficiently evident from the preceding analysis, the rules of the game were changed in a farcical manner to suit the general's political ambitions and the king's party. Enumerable amendments, and amendments to amendments were promulgated in rapid succession by the lawmakers of the regime, with the singular aim of decapitating the actual and potential opponents of the general. The front-ranking political leadership of the mainstream parties was either put at a great disadvantage, or replaced through the crude ordinances and misuse of official funds with insignificant ones. "Whichever party comes out on top," *The Times* of London wrote prior to the October 2002 elections, "in reality the vote will do no more than cloak continued military rule in democratic mufti,"[79]

The military regime cherished the desire that, the new and unfolding political setup should consist of and be controlled by legislators favoring Musharraf and his reforms agenda. This carted his coterie around to ensure the success of regime-backed candidates. Besides formation of the PML(Q), the military supported the creation of Sindh Democratic Alliance (SDA); Grand National Alliance (GDA), National Alliance, and the installation of PPP-Sherpao. The king's party was born on the day when chairman of the NAB, General Syed Amjad Ali, was made to quit commanding a military corps and politics of abject compromises, on behest of Musharraf, returned to rule the country. That event dashed even the weakest chances of the cleaning up of Pakistan from corruption and the degraded politicians. For the sake of enlisting such politicians in the PML(Q) the much-trumpeted rules of accountability were thrown out of the window, and the country faced the predicament of a shady deal culture. Consequently, the flawed electoral process stacked against the democratic norms.

In the case of *Elahi Bukhsh Soomro vs. The Federation of Pakistan,* the NAB submitted, before the Supreme Court, a list of 109 former legislators with their alleged financial bungling, including wrong declaration of assets with the Election Commission or the Income Tax Department, asserting that it was based on incontrovertible cogent evidence. The list included the names of present senior leaders, (i.e., Chaudhury Shujat Hussain, Chaudhury Pervez Elahi [now the Punjab chief minister], Abida Hussain, Humayun Akhtar [federal minister] and others of the king's party). In the regime's process of political reengineering, these leaders jumped on the bandwagon of the officially sponsored PML(Q), and were let off the NAB's hook. With the passage of time, the general's accountability drive was transformed into continuation of his parochial politics by other means, which definitely agitated against his moral stance of exhibiting unimpeachable integrity.

The military regime, despite claims of the CEC to the contrary, continued the postings and transfers of key civil officers for facilitating its strategy of poll rigging. For giving these deceitful transfers a legal cover, readily available No Objection Certificates were obtained from the CEC. The mighty civil and military bureaucracy continued to pursue winnable candidates aggressively to convince them to change party loyalties. Besides the intelligence agencies' covert pursuits of active workers of the PPP and PML(N), the police conducted raids on the offices of these parties for harassing their candidates. On such complaints, the CEC remained merely a spectator and issued formal statements warning the police not to harass the contesting candidate or political workers of the two parties. For propping up the PML(Q), and other regime-backed candidates, the governors of Sindh and Punjab addressed public meetings and announced development projects in the constituencies where the king's party needed an urgent helping hand to win.[80] The governors, the inspectors general of police, and other senior bureaucrats resorted to their frenzied behind-the-scenes politicking for manipulating the ballot on October 10, 2002, for the electoral triumph of the king's party.

The Election Commission was not lacking in its contribution to cough up a positive election outcome either. For instance, in its drive to educate the citizens on how to cast their votes, it ran advertisements on the PTV showing a ballot paper marked by only four party symbols. The symbols of major parties, that is, the PML(N), the PPP-P, or the MMA were not included, but it included "bicycle" of PML(Q). For this and similar other partisan acts, the CEC was accused of partiality.[81] The assertion that the October 10 elections were neither fair nor free, was corroborated by the National Democratic Institute, the European Union, and the Human Rights Commission of Pakistan and other similar groups monitoring the hustings, as quoted below:

> [I]t is an unfortunate fact that the October 10 elections have already been recorded in Pakistan's checkered political history as having been manipulated by seen and unseen forces for their narrow institutional interests. And, the spate of allegations is not the only basis of this strong perception. There are credible reports of result manipulations in some close contests, and in others the turnout

> was inexplicably far in excess of the national average. Tellingly, in all such cases, the winner was perceived as being officially sponsored.[82]

The final results of October elections, in most constituencies, did not tally with the results collected by the polling agents of candidates, and such results included results of ghost polling stations, as well. The shadows of night witnessed changing of results, whereby winners were declared losers, and the CEC rejecting demands of recounting the ballots. On account of such practice, the former prime minister Nawaz Sharif called the October electoral outcome a "farce," and opined that "the election results had been delayed for an inordinate period to enable tampering by the rigging experts of the military regime." and therefore, it was not "a public mandate."[83] On the confirmation of various observers, commentators and political parties, be that as it may, but who else knows the rigging mechanism better than Sharif himself, because he was the beneficiary of such a process in the 1990 and 1997 general elections. At that time, the military's rigging experts were on his side.

The verdict in the October 2002 elections did not result in the emergence of any party bagging the majority votes in the National Assembly. It was a split mandate and the party position was: PML(Q) 116; National Alliance 16; PML(F) 5; PML(J) 3; PPP-Sherpao 2; MQM 17; MMA 68; PPP(P) 81; PTI 1; and PML(N) 19. (See also chapter 5.) In view of such combinations and permutations, those vying for the prime ministerial slot had to struggle hard to hammer an out-of-the house arrangement to seek the support of the requisite number of members of the National Assembly (MNAs). The total strength of the National Assembly members, as provided in the LFO, was 342.

On October 9, 2002, the chief executive had amended the LFO, providing for independent candidates to join any political party within three days after the official publication of their names by the Election Commission. The move had its background in the manipulative election process, itself. Dozens of independent candidates had contested elections on a common symbol of "Crescent." They were suspected and charged by the opponent political parties as playing second fiddle to the king's party.[84] The majority of such candidates were returned elected to the National Assembly, and the ordinance was motivated to help the PML(Q), thus out of twenty-nine independent MNAs elected directly and indirectly, eighteen joined the king's party.[85]

WANT A PRIME MINISTER?

Despite rigged and grossly flawed elections, the political forces of all shades accepted it as a fait accompli. No political party seriously questioned the fairness of the electoral process. The military establishment got what it had wanted from the elections, a hung Parliament with no single political party bagging the majority votes to form a government on its own. The Musharraf government, though mused with the split mandate, found none of its potential or actual adversaries, that is, PPP-P and PML(N) in a position to form a government on their own, yet it also seemed difficult for the PML(Q) to form a government on its own either. The military government faced difficulty to get validation for its LFO, or all the acts performed and laws promulgated by it in the past, by the Parliament, where it required a two-thirds majority. At one stage it seemed that pro– and anti–LFO/Musharraf parties had emerged, which meant trouble inside the Parliament. As packs of various parties were struggling to be partners-in-power at the center, their lack of socio-economic, political, constitutional, and foreign policy vision was quite clear.

After the elections, the whole game of making the government or sharing power at the center revolved around the penchant of General Musharraf to have a prime minister who would work for him. The first session of the National Assembly was to be convened on November 8, 2002, but it was postponed mainly because the king's party was unable to show even a simple majority, though the civil bureaucracy, the NAB, and intelligence agencies were working hard to encourage desertions from the PPP-P and PML(N). The cajoling process, set in motion at the behest of Musharraf, defied his avowed stance of November 17, 1999, when the much-publicized seven-point agenda was announced on the electronic media. The announcement of a ten-member "forward block" in the PPP was seen as a result of inducements and intimidation by the military government. Besides facilitating the formation of government by the PML(Q) at the center, this was ostensibly done to break the tough stand of the PPP leadership for joining the government on its own terms. The act was condemned by the PPP as horse-trading for securing an easy endorsement of the military-enacted constitutional amendments.[86] The move also belittled the regime's boast that it wanted genuine democracy, and confirmed the widely held view that it was taking recourse to old pejorative practices, which its leader used to malign so vociferously. The act exposed the dark side of Pakistani politics and politicians shedding old loyalties and joining the government to share power.

The Muttahida Majlis-i-Amal (MMA) consisting of six religious parties, was seemingly the work and product of those generals, colonels, and brigadiers of the intelligence agencies who had been deprived of free wrestling fields in Afghanistan.[87] These parties, on behest of their mentors, had sidelined the sharp edges of mutual sectarian differences, and were ambitious to form the coalition government at the center as well as in the two provinces of the NWFP and Balochistan. The MMA and its collective leadership had apparently taken a tough stand on the LFO, NSC, and the COAS–president in the future Constitution and their role in the parliamentary form of government. The MMA, soon after the October 10 elections, was insisting on General Pervez Musharraf to seek his election through the new setup, taking oath under the 1973 Constitution, and the deletion of several amendments to the Constitution as provided in the LFO. The

MMA's clerics were quite competent in making loud noises in and outside the Parliament, but they were not averse to sharing of power and switching stables. They had won National Assembly and provincial assembly seats on an anti-Musharraf and anti-American platform, yet the religious combine had no qualms in negotiating partnership with the king's party.

The pro-Musharraf counterargument to scorning of the LFO by the MMA, PPP, and PML(N), was that if they were reluctant to accept those amendments, then why did they agree to contest elections under the law they were determined to avoid? The political compulsion to do so can be ascribed to the national interest and the need for restoration of democracy and it could be condoned on the touchstone of the infamous "doctrine of necessity." Contesting elections in itself did not validate the LFO. In the *Asma Jilani* case, the Supreme Court declared the regime of General Yahya Khan as usurper and unconstitutional, though validity of the 1970 elections held under the military-enacted PCO was accepted, and the same National Assembly formulated the 1973 Constitution.

On November 16, 2002, the general took the oath for entering the constitutional presidency, with the COAS cap and powers to dissolve the Parliament and sack governments. The swearing-in of COAS president, General Pervez Musharraf, bypassing the constitutional procedure (through the Parliament and provincial assemblies being the electoral college, as provided in Article 41 of the Constitution), was justified on winning the referendum. The Supreme Court chief justice, who along with his fellow judges had abandoned the 1973 Constitution through their oath of office under the PCO, administered constitutional oath to the general, as the president of Pakistan for the next five years. Ironically, the Supreme Court itself, in the case of *Hussain Ahmed,* had left the legality of referendum to be decided at a proper forum, that is, by the Parliament. The oath to Musharraf was administered when the Senate was not in place and the members of the National Assembly and four provincial assemblies had not yet taken the oath. On the same day, 324 out of 342 members of the National Assembly took the oath under the 1973 Constitution. The constitutional provisions pertaining to the Senate, the provincial assemblies and floor-crossing, remained suspended. Under Section 3(2) of the LFO, the general had acquired the power to further amend the Constitution if "there is any necessity" for it, or "any difficulty arises in giving effect to any of the provisions of this Order." Coupled with this intriguing provision was Section 4 of the LFO, which empowered the chief executive to fix the day on which the Constitution would stand revived. Musharraf followed General Zia and opted for partial revival of the Constitution on November 16, 2002. The notification for restoring the Constitution stipulated that Musharraf would remain the chief executive till the prime minister's election, and this was ostensibly done to exercise the powers of amending the Constitution further for making it compatible to the general's future objectives.

Having got the speaker of the National Assembly elected, the PML(Q) and its allies succeeded in securing the premiership on November 21, 2002, when

Mir Zafarullah Khan Jamali of Balochistan got 172 votes, out of 342. On November 22, Jamali was sworn in as prime minister along with a twenty-one–member cabinet, by the COAS president. It appeared from the panoply of unfolding events that the COAS president and the establishment got the kind of National Assembly and the prime minister for which they had meticulously worked for the last three years. If left to himself, Jamali had as remote a chance of becoming the country's prime minister as the sun to rise from the west. The choice in catapulting Jamali to the premiership cloaked the wish of the general to establish a patron–client relation with the civilian leadership and to baby it the way the General Headquarters (GHQ) wanted. With the GHQ's standard guidelines, Mir Zafarullah Khan Jamali and his cabinet would be expected to serve the general obediently, or, as a critic tauntingly alludes: "Ask not what Musharraf can do for you, but what you can do for Musharraf."[88]

Of late, through an amendment in the NAB Ordinance, Musharraf has transferred the control of NAB from the chief executive (now the prime minister) to the president. Notwithstanding the intense criticism that he had no power to legislate in the presence of the National Assembly, Musharraf seemingly brought the NAB under him to whip the members through it if they tried to be righteous by betraying the king's party. Besides the constitutional provisions relating to floor-crossing was restored, yet its operation was made dependent on the day when the Senate would be convened. This meant that until that time, the members could be induced in changing loyalties in favor of "the king's party" and afterwards the constitutional provision would be employed to restrain them to do so.

The Minorities

The separate electorate system introduced by the Zia regime had virtually ousted the minorities from mainstream politics. Firstly, the issue, dyed in religious hues, was employed by Zia to court the extremists to his side, and secondly, it was used by his regime to create cleavages among the Muslims and non-Muslims in the country. The system of joint electorate was provided in the 1973 Constitution, but the Zia regime, in its enthusiastic drive for Islamization, opted for the separate electorate system. The pertinent question was that, if the non-Muslim voters could jointly elect the president and the prime minister, how could they be debarred from jointly electing the members of Parliament? The minorities had never demanded a system of separate electorate, yet the military government of Zia, to appease the religious elite, foisted it on them.[89] The abject alienation of minorities, an anathema to national integration notwithstanding, the separate electorate system had proven a gigantic problem for the Election Commission, particularly in the following context:

1. While delimiting constituencies, the non-Muslim voters were listed with the Muslim population. The Muslim voters exercised their right for electing the members of the National and Provincial Assembly from that constituency, the non-Muslims could not do that because they, as voters, were not divided into constituencies, and they voted for candidates whose constituencies were spread almost all over the country. If a Christian voter from Rawalpindi wished to contact his elected representative, he might have to go to Lahore or Multan, and similarly a Parsi voter in Karachi could have his representative somewhere in the distant part of the NWFP.[90]

2. The Election Commission also faced multifarious problems in the preparation of electoral rolls for four categories of non-Muslims, that is, (1) Christians, (2) Hindus and persons belonging to the scheduled castes; (3) Sikhs, Buddhists, Parsis and other non-Muslims; and (4) persons belonging to the Qadiani group or the Lahori group (who call themselves Ahmadis).

3. The candidates faced immense problems in campaigning for their votes throughout the country.

The apartheidlike system of a separate electorate was replaced by the joint electorate system by the Musharraf government; vide Section 7 of the Conduct of General Elections Order, 2002 (Order 7 of 2002). The system of joint electorate provided that the non-Muslims could vote for any candidate for a general seat that they wished to support, and there was no bar to their contesting any general seat, a seat reserved for women or technocrats in election to the Senate, National Assembly, or a provincial assembly. Initially, the minorities were denied the advantage of ten reserved seats, but the military government subsequently amended the Conduct of General Election Order 2002, restored these seats in the National Assembly and provided for twenty-three reserved seats in four provincial assemblies. However, the method provided for the election of minority members was the proportional representation system based on the election of the National Assembly members and party position therein. The candidates to be elected to non-Muslim reserved seats in the National Assembly were to be picked from lists given by political parties in proportion to the number of the general seats in the National Assembly won by these parties. Similarly, in each provincial assembly, a political party would win these seats in proportion to the number of general seats won by that party in that assembly. This system provided for the ascertainment of the non-Muslim electorate's will, indirectly. The proportional representation system violated and negated the spirit of joint electorate system, inasmuch as no minority member, whatsoever his voters' strength and popularity among the community, was made dependent on the political parties and their electoral success. In the joint electorate system, it was for the minorities to select their own candidates, as against giving the right to the political parties to select the candidates of their choice. On the basis of proportional representation, the Election Commission (EC) announced on November 1, 2002, the election of ten minority members to the National Assembly. The election of the minority members was announced at a time when some citizens from the Christian community had moved the Supreme Court and the Federal Shariat Court against their representatives' selection in that way.

WOMEN PARLIAMENTARIANS

The founding fathers of the 1973 Constitution had reserved twenty seats for women in the National Assembly for ensuring their representation in national affairs. The constitutional provision for reserved seats lapsed in 1990 during the government of Mian Nawaz Sharif. During the second government of Benazir Bhutto, a bill for the restoration of women's seats in the assemblies was presented, but it could not get through because of her government's subsequent dismissal. In the three elections of 1990, 1993, 1997, though there were no reserved seats for women, some women candidates contested these general elections. Taking away the reserved seats for women in the assemblies notwithstanding, their fundamental right to vote in general elections was often curtailed at the unscrupulous hands of male members in some areas of the country. This prejudiced practice of keeping women voters away from the polling stations through restrictive jirgas (tribal councils) and the consequent deliberate neglect on the part of the EC to take legal action against those responsible, has continued unabated. It is in the knowledge of the Election Commission and all those bodies associated with it that in most tribal parts of the NWFP, Balochistan, and some other backward areas of the country, women voters are not allowed by their menfolk to come to the polling stations for voting. The practice was revived in the 2000 local government elections, as well as in the October 2002 general elections, when women were openly disenfranchised. The tribal *jirgas* in NWFP unanimously decided and threatened that men who would allow their women to cast votes in the October elections would have their house demolished. In the local body elections, women candidates were not available in such areas because of this illegal practice.

The Conduct of Election Order 2002 revived and restored the provision of reserved seats for women, increasing their strength from twenty to sixty seats in the National Assembly. About twenty women contested for general National Assembly seats, and nine succeeded in reaching the Parliament. The contemporary composition of the National Assembly indicated that women legislators constitute about 22 percent of its total strength. The putting up of a relatively increased number of women candidates on the general seats was mainly ascribed to the graduation provision, which knocked many traditional candidates out of the electoral race. This challenging situation had compelled traditional political families to bring out their wives, daughters, daughters-in-law, and sisters to compete for a share in the political pie of the assemblies.

Barring a few, all shades of political parties placed the names of women closely related to or belonging to traditional political families on their lists before the Election Commission. Such lists were generally devoid of women belonging to diverse segments of society, especially the poor and middle classes. Going by the traditional custom of keeping ancestral property within the family, the party heads brought women who were their kith and kin in the assemblies. On such a practice, there was no difference between secular and religious parties, and all entered the race for the enhancement of their personal political clout in the assemblies.[91]

The origins, mode, and manner of such women legislators notwithstanding, their very presence in the Parliament along with the Muttahida Majlis-Amal (MMA, a collection of religious parties) members vehemently demanding complete imposition of the *Shariah,* would be an interesting scenario that never happened in the whole history of the country. Believing in the spirit of *Shariah* (as understood by it), the MMA has denounced the women's rights lobbies demanding the winding up of the *Hudood* laws, discrimination against the weaker sex and equal opportunities for work and workplace. Toeing the line of the Council of Islamic Ideology (CII, a constitutional recommendatory body for bringing the country's laws in conformity with Islam), the MMA would be engaged in heated debates of issues concerning women, with the female legislators who possess degrees from modern colleges and universities at home and abroad. The CCI's 1999 to 2000 annual report stresses mandatory observance of the veil by every woman, and the MMA has taken upon itself to implement this and other such recommendations in toto.[92] An instance of the CCI's observations pertaining to women is hereunder:

> The use of women's pictures in advertisements should be banned. Purdah observing women seeking employment should not be forced to submit photographs to employers. Pakistani women should not be obliged to receive foreigners at airports, men should not be allowed entry in female wards (especially gynecology) at hospitals and women should not go to male doctors nor have their clothing stitched by male tailors.[93]

Conscious of their rights and strengthened by the recommendation of the government-constituted National Commission on the Status of Women (NCSW), the women legislators (barring the pro-MMA) would definitely press for an equitable social order empowering the women through their rights. Against the conservative perspectives of the MMA, the NCSW has already recommended to the president for complete reviewing of the *Hudood* laws and for curtailing the misuse of laws against women.[94] Even otherwise, reserving and increasing women representation in the local bodies and in the October elections was a part of Musharraf government's policy to improve the country's image abroad and dispel the impression of the Pakistani society being shadowed by the medieval Taliban image. It would be a far-fetched conclusion to depict an overwhelming majority of women parliamentarians being silenced by the clerics in the assembly debates or submitting to the CCI's recommendation.

THE PRESS LAWS

After the end of its three years' Supreme Court sanctioned tenure on October 12, 2002, the military regime continued promulgating ordinances, without any inhibition. These ordinances included four laws pertaining to the press, namely, Press Council of Pakistan Ordinance, 2002; The Press, Newspapers, News Agencies and Books Registration Ordinance, 2002; Freedom of Information Ordinance, 2002; and The Defamation Ordinance, 2002. Media persons felt uneasy, as these military-enacted laws placed constraints on their functioning. These laws provide for jail terms for offending editors, journalists, and publishers. The associations of journalists, including All Pakistan Newspapers Society (APNS), the Council of Pakistan Newspaper Editors (CPNE), and the Pakistan Federal Union of Journalists, have rejected them, as being "black press laws."[95]

NATIONAL RECONSTRUCTION BUREAU (NRB) AND THE DEVOLUTION PLAN

The establishment of the NRB by the Musharraf government would be remembered as one of the most controversial and self-serving decisions. Lacking any mandate or settled framework of its operation, the NRB ab initio charted itself on a questionable course of introducing novel innovations and demolishing the old administrative and political system of the country. One of such decisions was the introduction of a local government system, which the chief executive always exhorted, was his most solid achievement. In his October 17, 1999 speech, the General pledged to devolve power to the grassroots level in the country. Consequently, the Local Government Plan 2000 was launched on August 14, 2000, wherein a three-tier local government system in every district across the country was installed on August 14, 2001. It envisaged the integration of the rural with urban local governments, on the one hand, and the civilian bureaucracy with the local governments, on the other, all into one coherent structure in which the district administration and police were answerable to the elected chief executive of the district, known as Zilla Nazim. Under the plan, local governments were formed at three levels: district, tehsil, and union, each headed by its Nazim and Naib Nazim. The former apex administrative divisions were abolished. On the promise of involving the people in community development, grassroots organizations like village councils and citizen community boards were envisaged in the system. The new system replaced the one and a half century old system of commissionerate in the country, whereby the offices of commissioner and deputy commissioner were dispensed with, for allowing the local representatives to run their affairs themselves. In the new system, women, peasants, workers, and minorities were provided representation in the councils of the three-tier system.

Despite its loud claims on the devolution of power to the grassroots level, the NRB's scheme took the districts out of the provincial domain, and placed them under the center's supervision. A pointer to such assertion could be the political manipulations, through the Nazim system of the president's referendum and leveling the grounds for the king's party's electoral victory in the October elections. Through hundreds of amendments in the local government law, the military regime has already whittled down its operation and effectiveness. The NRB, the regime's premier thinktank, formulated the Press Laws, the Police Ordinance, the Constitutional Package, the LFO, the PPO, and the election plan, with the singular aim of keeping Musharraf and the military perpetually in power. The NSC and Article 58(2)(b), the NRB's two brainchildren, would be a constant source of friction between the political parties and the praetorian establishment. Indeed, the NRB's diverse engineering caused more harm than good to the country's system it wanted to reform. And precisely, these controversial reforms and their questionable continuity are the military general's raison d'etre of hanging onto power. With the NRB chief, Lt. General Tanvir Hussain Naqvi gone, leaving behind his half-baked reconstructions, the future of devolution faces uncertainty.

CONSTITUTIONAL MORTALITY: CONCLUSIONS

The Musharraf regime often claimed that the changes in the Constitution were designed to block any military takeover in the future. However, they are aimed at stalling the return to power of the two condemned former prime ministers with a mass following, to solve the long-standing cherished demand of a constitutional role of the armed forces in politics and to change the configuration of the political system, with power passing from the prime minister to the president, even though the fiction of the parliamentary system is maintained, ensuring effective government by the anointed president for the rule of man as opposed to the rule of law. Evidently the checks and balances in the Constitution have been placed not for the sake of running a democratic government, but for the person of an exerciser of power only. Its merits and success would be tested in situations where the extraconstitutional powers available in the unique institution of the COAS president in office will not be enjoyed by a future successor in the presidency.

Such constitutional engineering is not new for Pakistan and its citizens, as they have been through the arbitrary legal and constitutional deviations in the past. The military government of General Muhammad Ayub Khan created a steel frame of the Basic Democracy System and the 1962 Constitution, for the sake of keeping him and the military in power, presumably forever. General Agha Muhammad Yahya Khan and his military government opted for the LFO through which the civilian leadership and legislators had to pass as a qualification for entitlement to an eventual civilian setup. General Muhammad Zia-ul-Haq endeavored to incarcerate his captive nation initially in a prolonged martial law and then by saddling it with the Eighth Amendment to the Constitution, a Constitution unto itself. Interestingly, having even changed the complexion of the Constitution for keeping all the levers of power in his hands, Zia could not dare to take off the cap of the chief of the army staff.

The military government's constitutional amendments, without sanction from the Parliament, have made the COAS president the most powerful player in power permutations through his discretionary powers, and the prime minister losing his constitutional and executive authority in favor of the former. All these legal devices are aimed at ensuring that the military and its leader, General Pervez Musharraf, retain their hold on the state power. With such constitutional engineering, the locus of state power has shifted to the president and NSC, an unelected body dominated by the armed forces answerable to none. However, experience of all the past military rulers indicates that devious political structures so raised fell apart after the exit of the ruler, yet in the process they plunged the country into grave crises, that is, physical attrition with neighbors, political and constitutional chaos, social repression, and economic disaster for the whole society. General Pervez Musharraf is not the first military dictator, but the fourth one, who ascended the pinnacles of power in Pakistan, for saving the nation from within. Notwithstanding the saga of past military interventions in general, and the disastrous systemic crises of state in 1971, in particular, the generals have failed to learn the hard lesson that they cannot solve the country's perennial problems, but instead, with their overbearing blatant interferences, they have contributed to and multiplied them.

The higher courts in Pakistan have seldom enjoyed a reputation for averting the scuttling of the democratic process, abrogation of the Constitution and routing the electoral mechanism. Instead, they readily provided a blanket cover to such situations contrived by military dictators. By judging military interventions as phases of constitutional deviations, and making individuals the sole lawmakers, the courts have diminished their distinction and dignity in the society. By validating the extra-constitutional moves of the Musharraf regime, the superior judiciary has strengthened the military in national politics. This has led to a significant distortion of the 1973 constitution.

Pakistan has experimented with various constitutional formulae in the hope that every new Constitution would be an everlasting sacred national document. However, no Constitution or high treason clause appended therein could discourage military's strongmen to abrogate or hold it in abeyance. The patience of those who are living at the unacceptable cost of sociopolitical enslavement, tyrannical whims of despots, and abject exploitation is appreciable. If the civil–military bureaucracy is the chief malcontent in uprooting constitutional democracy through the electoral process, political parties are equally responsible for it; some sided with the dictators and others sat on the fence and waited for opportune moments. Political parties must put an end to such organized hypocrisy and keep the political and electoral process growing and in their hands, instead of inviting the military to meddle in civil matters for personal, partisan or parochial ends.

A political system, in which the unelected president simultaneously holds the post of COAS, cannot be a democracy but a military dictatorship. A Constitution, which is amended at-will by the COAS, is a military-enacted law, not the legislative will of the Parliament. The country has an elected prime minister, yet the powerful head of the state is an unelected one. There is the Parliament to legislate future laws, but there is the NSC, headed by the COAS president, as was the case in the decade of democracy preceding Musharraf. It too has the power to dissolve the Parliament. Legislation belongs to the domain of the sovereign, and in all democratic dispensations, the people and their elected parliament are sovereign. In Pakistan, with the staging in of his military coup, all electoral and constitutional laws have been reconstructed mainly for, and enacted by the COAS, General Pervez Musharraf to arrogate sovereign rights unto himself.

NOTES

1. At some stage, in the first week of October 1999, the corps commanders must have decided that enough was enough and were seemingly determined to take the prime minister on.

2. Abdul Hafeez Pirzada's interview with the *Newsline* (Karachi), October 1999, pp 27-28.

3. Based on extracts from FIR No. 201-1999, registered with the police station, Karachi Airport, registered against Mian Nawaz Sharif and others.

4. "Amendments with a View," *Newsline* (Karachi), October 1999, p 22.

5. Ibid., p 23.

6. Ibid.

7. PLD (*Pakistan Legal Decisions*) 1998 SC 1445.

8. PLD 1999 SC 504.

9. Ibid.

10. *Dawn* (Islamabad), December 11, 2000.

11. *Newsline* (Karachi), January 2001, p 29.

12. Ibid.

13. Major General Rashid Qureshi's statement quoted in Ibid.

14. The statement released by the PPP said: "They have one standard for a prime minister from Larkana (Sindh) and another for a prime minister from Lahore (Punjab)," quoted in *The News* (Islamabad), December 11, 2000.

15. See Mubashir Zaidi, "The Case of the Missing Constitution," *The Herald* (Karachi), February 2001, p 22. See also Hamid Khan, *Constitutional and Political History of Pakistan* (Karachi: Oxford University Press, 2002), pp 934-935.

16. See Zaidi. Among these key figures was Sharifuddin Pirzada, main legal author of the military governments who had picked up row with Mushtaq Menon of the Sindh High Court who had declined to allow him to appear as *amicus curiae* in one of the cases being heard in his Court.

17. PLD 2000 SC 869.

18. *Dawn* (Islamabad), June 8, 2001.

19. PLD 1972 SC 139.

20. PLD 1977 SC 675.

21. In an interview, former president Muhammad Rafique Tarar complained: "I was told in harsh words by Musharraf in June 2001 that he has decided to relieve me, therefore, I should just write two-line resignation." *The News* (Islamabad), July 4, 2002.

22. PLD 2000 SC 869.

23. Justice Siddiqui's interview published in *Newsline* (Karachi), July 2001, p 42.

24. PLD 2001 SC 607.

25. "NAB's New Role," editorial, *The News* (Islamabad), October 26, 2002.

26. "NAB Law" *The News* (Islamabad), September 20, 2002.

27. M. Ilyas Khan, "Narrowing the Net," *The Herald* (Karachi), March 2002, pp 44-45.

28. Ibid.

29. "NAB Law," *The News* (Islamabad), September 20, 2002.

30. Amir Mir, "See No Evil," *Newsline* (Karachi), October 2000, p 45.

31. PLD 2001 SC 568, 572-573.

32. Ibid., p 599.

33. *Asif Ali Zardari vs. The State*, PLD 2001 SC 568, 595.

34. "*Caught with the Tapes On,*" *Newsline* (Karachi), March 2001, pp 23-36.

35. *Hussain Ahmad vs. Pervez Musharraf, Chief Executive*, PLD 2002 SC 853.

36. Ibid., p 870.

37. Ibid., p 938.

38. Ibid., p 937.

39. Kunwar Idris, "An Unnecessary Referendum," *Dawn* (Islamabad), May 5, 2002.

40. M. Ilyas Khan, "Manufacturing a Mandate," *The Herald* (Karachi), May 2002, p 31.

41. Farrukh Saleem, "Is the US media changing direction?" *The News* (Islamabad), May 5, 2002.

42. Ibid.

43. See *The News* (Islamabad), May 4, 2002.

44. "Another Leap in the Darkness," editorial, *Dawn* (Islamabad), August 23, 2002.

45. The author drew for the summary of these packages from *Dawn* (Islamabad), June 27, 2002.

46. Dr. Hasan-Askari Rizvi, "Rationale Behind Package," *Dawn* (Islamabad), July 3, 2002.

47. Ibid.

48. Farhatullah Babar, "NSC Revisited," *The Nation* (Islamabad), June 20, 2002.

49. Ibid., "National Security System," *The News* (Islamabad), June 13, 2002.

50. PLD 2002 SC 939.
51. Ibid., p 949.
52. Ibid., p 983.
53. Ibid., p 983.
54. Ibid., p 992.
55. Quoted in *The News* (Islamabad), October 29, 2002.
56. *The News* (Islamabad), October 31, 2002.
57. Ibid.
58. The judges of the Fijian apex Court raised tents outside the court complex, which was sealed by the military coup-makers. The judgment of the Fijian court rallied the political and democratic forces, which rolled back the military coup and restored the constitutional rule in the tiny island country. See "Bar vs. Bench," *The News* (Islamabad), November 7, 2002.
59. Ibid.
60. *The News* (Islamabad), November 6, 2002.
61. PLD 2000 SC 225.
62. PLD 2000 SC 225, 302.
63. *United Bank Ltd. vs. Messers Farooq Brothers and Others*, PLD 2002 SC 800, pp 803-804.
64. These points were raised in his interim written reply by eminent jurist and senior counsel, namely M. Khalid Ishaque, appearing on behalf of the United Bank Ltd. before the Federal Shariat Court, PLD 2002 SC 800, pp 814-815.
65. Zulfikar Khalid Maluka, *The Myth of Constitutionalism in Pakistan* (Karachi: Oxford University Press, 1995), p 317.
66. Rasul Bakhsh Rais, ed., *State, Society and Democratic Change in Pakistan* (Karachi: Oxford University Press, 1997), p 255.
67. Maluka, p 8.
68. Makhdoom Ali Khan, "1973 Constitution—The Founding of the Federation," an unpubished paper read at a seminar: "The Heritage of Prime Minister Bhutto," in Karachi, April 3-5, 1989, note 10.
69. Shahwar Junaid, "Public, Politics and Economic Management," *The Nation* (Islamabad), May 2, 2002.
70. Ibid.
71. Anjam Khan Qadwani, "Basis of a Seminary," *The Nation* (Islamabad), June 29, 2002.
72. PLD 2002 SC 994.
73. Ibid., 1003.
74. Ibid., 1032.
75. *The News* (Islamabad), July 7, 2002.
76. Ibid.
77. "Two-Term Ban," editorial, *The Nation* (Islamabad), July 8, 2002.
78. See, *The News* (Islamabad), May 5, 2002.
79. Quoted in *Dawn* (Islamabad), October 19, 2002.
80. "Reality and Perception," *Dawn* (Islamabad), October 5, 2002. The PML(N) issued a fact sheet wherein over a dozen public meetings attended by the governor of Punjab were pointed out, where plots and development funds were distributed.
81. Ibid.

82. "Priority No. 1," editorial, *The News* (Islamabad), October 24, 2002.

83. "Nawaz Sharif Calls Poll Results a 'Farce,'" *Dawn* (Islamabad), October 12, 2002.

84. Ahmad Hassan, "Parties Shocked by 'Crescent,'" *Dawn* (Islamabad), October 3, 2002.

85. Rafaqat Ali, "Laws Being Made in SC Ruling Violation," *Dawn* (Islamabad), October 30, 2002.

86. *The News* (Islamabad), November 15, 2002.

87. H. K. Burki, "Two Cheers for Musharraf," *The News* (Islamabad), December 1, 2002.

88. Faisal Rahman, "Is Jamali Playing Offside?" *The News* (Islamabad), November 23, 2002.

89. I. A. Rahman, "The Worse Off Non-Muslim Voters," *Dawn* (Karachi), January 28, 1997.

90. Ibid.

91. Two nieces of the former president and head of the Millat Party Farooq Ahmed Khan Leghari; a daughter of Qazi Hussain Ahmed, head of Jamaat-i-Islami; Maulana Shah Ahmed Noorani'sister: wife of a former deputy speaker; and a number of other cases can be stretched up to about 90 percent of women legislators.

92. See Nadeem Iqbal, "Opposite Ends," *The News* (Islamabad), November 10, 2002.

93. Quoted in Ibid.

94. Ibid., and "The Religious Writ," *Newsline* (Karachi), November 2000, pp 43-44.

95. "Steps to Curb Press Freedom Slammed," *Dawn* (Islamabad), October 7, 2002.

5

Elections 2002: Legitimizing the Status Quo

Andrew R. Wilder

On October 10, 2002, nearly 30 million Pakistani voters went to the polls to elect representatives to the National Assembly as well as to the four Provincial Assemblies. The elections marked the formal restoration of democracy in Pakistan following three years of military rule by General Pervez Musharraf. The resulting hung Parliament had been widely predicted before the elections, but the dramatic success of a coalition of religious parties—the Muttahida Majlis-i-Amal (MMA), particularly in the Northwest Frontier Province (NWFP) and Balochistan—caught nearly all political observers by surprise.

The elections were followed by six weeks of unseemly horse trading, backroom deal making, and considerable arm twisting on the part of the military before a shaky coalition government could be formed at the national level. On November 16 the National Assembly was finally convened, and the newly elected members took their oaths of office. On the same day in a separate ceremony of dubious constitutional validity General Pervez Musharraf took the oath of office for a five-year term as president of Pakistan. But it was not until November 21, following the generous use of carrots and sticks, that the military was able to cobble together the bare minimum of 172 votes in the 342-seat National Assembly to get Mir Zafarullah Khan Jamali of the pro-Musharraf Pakistan Muslim League (Quaid-i-Azam) (PML-Q) elected as the prime minister of Pakistan. It took several more weeks of coercing and cajoling before governments were finally formed in Pakistan's four provinces.

While on the surface the elections represented a return to democracy and civilian rule, the holding of elections in Pakistan should not necessarily be equated with democratization. This chapter will argue that both the April 2002 presidential referendum and the October Provincial and National Assembly elections form the latest chapter in a long history of elections intended more to legitimize the power of the unelected institutions of the state than to transfer power to elected institutions.

Preserving the Status Quo: The Historical Context

Representative institutions were introduced into colonial South Asia following the mutiny of 1857 not to promote a democratic process that would transfer power to elected representatives, but, rather to strengthen the colonial state. The "representative"—rather than "democratic"—institutions were formed to co-opt local elites, to deal with local administrative issues rather than substantive issues, and to serve as advisory rather than policy-making bodies.[1] While the scope of elections and representative institutions expanded during the late colonial period, elections did not fundamentally alter the power imbalance between powerful unelected bureaucrats and weak elected representatives.[2]

In the fifty-five years since independence, Pakistan has had seven national party-based elections based on universal suffrage, as well as various forms of indirect and nonparty elections, local government elections, and presidential referendums. Despite their variations in style and format, the consistent theme running through nearly all of these electoral exercises was that their primary purpose was to legitimize the retention of power by the unelected institutions of the state rather than to transfer power to elected institutions.[3] This is not to say that elections have not been important in Pakistan or that the unelected institutions of the state have always been successful in ensuring that elections did not alter the status quo. Despite the weakness in Pakistan of the legacy of constitutionalism and rule by public representatives, the unelected institutions have felt compelled to hold elections periodically to seek political legitimacy. The fundamental electoral dilemma confronting Pakistan's ruling elites has been, therefore, how to accommodate the legacy of rule by elected representatives and to accommodate the growing international pressure to govern through democratic institutions without threatening the legacy of rule by unelected institutions—namely, the military. To a considerable extent, Pakistan's electoral and political history has been shaped by the various strategies that have been devised to achieve this objective, which are summarized in Table 5.1.[4]

PRESERVING THE STATUS QUO: MUSHARRAF'S STRATEGIES

During his three years as the military ruler of Pakistan, General Musharraf was able to skillfully employ many of the strategies outlined above to seek legitimacy for his regime without having to resort to holding elections. But Musharraf recognized that he could not avoid holding elections indefinitely, especially since the Supreme Court had ruled that elections would have to be held no later than three years after his military coup on October 12, 1999. The following sections describe in greater detail some of the strategies adopted by Musharraf to ensure that holding elections would not fundamentally alter the power imbalance in Pakistan, where real power resides with the military and not with democratically elected public representatives.

Taming the Judiciary: The Oath of Office (Judges) Order, 2000

All of Pakistan's military rulers—as well as most of its civilian leaders—have used various methods to compromise the independence of the judiciary in

Table 5.1: Electoral Strategies to Preserve the Status Quo

Strategy	Examples
Rigging elections	—1951 Punjab Assembly Elections —1977 National and Provincial Assembly Elections —1984 and 2002 presidential referendums
Pre-poll and post-poll manipulations to achieve desired results	—All elections, but particularly the 1990 and 2002 elections
Holding presidential referendums to bypass Constitution and Parliament	—General Ayub Khan, 1960 —General Zia-ul Haq, 1984 —General Pervez Musharraf, 2002
Holding local rather than provincial and national elections to gain the legitimizing effect of elections, deflect attention from national politics, and create local constituencies dependent on military for survival	—Basic Democracies, 1959–1960 and 1964 —Local Bodies, 1979, 1983, 1987, 1991 —Local government, 2001
Using Pakistan's geopolitical importance to get Western powers to turn a blind eye to the abuse of democratic norms	—Ayub's pro–United States stance in the Cold War politics of the 1960s —Zia's "front line" against the Soviets in Afghanistan during the 1980s —Musharraf's support for the U.S.-backed "war against terror" in 2001–2002
Creating a malleable judiciary that will sanction unconstitutional military actions, as well as the writing and amending of constitutions in order to strengthen presidential powers at the expense of those elected	—Ayub's coup and 1962 Constitution —Zia's coup and eighth Amendment to the 1973 Constitution —Musharraf's coup and Legal Framework Order of 2002
Weakening political parties by holding nonparty- rather than party-based elections	—Basic Democracy 1959–1960 and 1964 —National and West Pakistan Assembly, 1962 —Local Bodies 1979, 1983, 1987, and 1991 —National and Provincial Assembly elections, 1985 —Local government, 2001
Weakening political parties and facilitating the manipulation of results by holding indirect rather than direct elections	—Using "Basic Democrats" as an electoral college in the presidential referendum 1960 and 1965 —National and West Pakistan Assembly elections in 1962 and 1965
Promising but postponing and/or canceling elections	—1947–1958 —1977–1979

order to ensure that their unconstitutional actions and ordinances were not overturned in the courts. Two days after taking power in a military coup General Musharraf passed the Provisional Constitutional Order (PCO), No. 1 of 1999, which stated that presidential ordinances would override all other legislation, including the Constitution, and that these ordinances could not be challenged in a court of law.[5] This order was soon challenged in the Supreme Court by Syed Zafar Ali Shah, a Pakistan Muslim League politician. Soon thereafter, in January 2000, Musharraf passed the Oath of Office (Judges) Order, 2000, which required all judges of the Supreme Court and the Provincial High Courts to swear an oath to uphold the PCO (as opposed to the Constitution which they had all previously sworn to uphold), and to "not call in question or permit to be called in question the validity of any of the provisions" of the Proclamation of Emergency of October 14, 1999, the Provisional Constitutional Order No. 1 of 1999, or the Oath of Office (Judges) Order, 2000.[6] The chief Justice and five other members of the Supreme Court, and seven judges of the High Courts were subsequently removed for either not taking the oath or not being invited to take the oath.[7] Not surprisingly, when the verdict in the *Syed Zafar Ali Shah* case on the constitutionality of the Musharraf's coup was announced in May 2000, the accommodating Supreme Court ruled that the military takeover was justified by the "doctrine of necessity," and that Musharraf could amend the Constitution as long as the amendment did not "change the basic features—independence of judiciary, federalism, and parliamentary form of government, blended with Islamic provisions—of the Constitution."[8] Musharraf was subsequently to take a very liberal interpretation of what this permitted him to do with the Constitution on the assumption that the judiciary was unlikely to stand up to him.

Localizing Politics: Nonparty Local Government Elections, 2001

Learning from the example of General Ayub's Basic Democracies in the 1960s, and General Zia's Local Bodies in the 1980s (see Table 5.1), Musharraf launched a local government scheme to devolve certain functions of the state to the district level. The stated objective of devolution, which undoubtedly had some merit, was to help strengthen and improve service delivery and accountability of government departments by giving some decision-making authority to district level officials. However, local government elections had also helped Ayub and Zia legitimize their military regimes by deflecting criticism that national elections were not being held. They also helped to shift the attention of politicians to local issues, leaving national issues to be dealt with by the military. Furthermore, they had the effect of creating a grassroots political constituency dependent on the military for its survival as no local government system has survived long once party-based national politics have been restored. In the April 2002 referendum campaign, the recently elected local government officials were pressured to campaign in their districts on behalf of a "yes" vote. It was made clear to them that the continuation of the local government system was contingent on Musharraf's tenure as president being extended because only he would be in a position to defend the devolution scheme and the powers it gave local officials at the expense of the newly elected parliamentarians.[9] The inevitable tensions that will emerge at the district level between the local government politicians and institutions, and the newly elected members of the Provincial and National Assemblies, will undoubtedly provide the military opportunities to play divide and rule politics.

Geopolitics: The War against Terror

Pakistan's geopolitical importance has often been a lifesaver for the country's military dictators. In the 1960s General Ayub Khan benefited from large levels of U.S. military and economic assistance in exchange for being an anti-Communist ally in the Cold War and for providing the United States with air-base facilities for its U2 spy planes flying over the Soviet Union. The Soviet invasion of Afghanistan in December 1979 transformed General Zia-ul Haq from being an unsavory military dictator into the United States's ally in the war against the expanding "evil empire." In exchange for allowing Pakistan to be used as a "frontline state," the fact that General Zia was a military dictator was conveniently overlooked and Pakistan soon became one of the largest recipients of U.S. economic and military assistance.

The terrorist attacks on September 11, 2001, were General Musharraf's equivalent to the Soviet invasion of Afghanistan. Overnight, Pakistan regained its geopolitical importance in the eyes of the United States, and Musharraf's speedy decision to join the war against terror ended his international isolation as a military dictator. The sanctions imposed on Pakistan both for its nuclear program as well as for military rule began to unravel and pressures for Musharraf to restore democracy eased. One example of this was the statement of the U.S. Assistant Secretary of State, Christina Rocca, following Musharraf's rigged presidential referendum, that "It is up to Pakistani institutions to determine what is constitutional and legal."[10] Ironically, at the same time that Musharraf was giving the impression to the West that he was curtailing the activities of militant Islamic parties, his intelligence agencies were widely suspected of supporting the election campaign of the MMA, a coalition of religious parties led by the pro-Taliban Jamiat-i-Ulema Islam (JUI) and the Jamaat-i-Islami (JI).[11]

The Rigged Presidential Referendum, April 2002

Following in the footsteps of General Ayub Khan in 1960, and General Zia-ul Haq in 1984, on April 9, 2002, General Pervez Musharraf issued Chief Executive's Order No. 12 of 2002, known as the "Referendum Order." According to Article 4 of the Referendum Order, the consequence of the result of the referendum would be as follows:

> Notwithstanding anything contained in the Constitution or any law for the time being in force, if the majority of the votes cast in the referendum are in the affirmative, the people of Pakistan shall be deemed to have given the democratic mandate to General Pervez Musharraf to serve the nation as President of Pakistan for a period of five years to enable him, inter alia, to consolidate the reforms and the reconstruction of institutions of State for the establishment of genuine and sustainable democracy, including the entrenchment of the local government system, to ensure continued good governance for the welfare of the people, and to combat extremism and sectarianism for the security of the State and the tranquility of society.[12]

No stone was left unturned to ensure that Musharraf received an overwhelming "yes" vote.[13] In order to increase the number of voters, the requirement of having electoral rolls was waived along with the requirement that voters could only vote in the constituency where they were registered. Furthermore, the National Identity Card voting requirement was also waived and anyone with a valid photo ID was permitted to vote. The government administration was put fully at the disposal of Musharraf's election campaign, not to mention the exchequer, which had to foot the estimated bill of Rs 2.5 billion.[14] It was also widely reported that intelligence agencies used carrot and stick tactics, for example releasing jailed Muttahida Qaumi Movement (MQM) party activists and threats to launch corruption investigations to get politically influential parties and individuals to support the referendum.[15] In a much criticized and unprecedented move for a military officer, Musharraf launched a whirlwind three-week election campaign where he addressed political gatherings in every province of the country.[16] Many argued that by "stooping to the level of politicians," Musharraf's greatest comparative advantage in the eyes of many Pakistanis—of not being a politician—was lost.

On April 30, 2002, Pakistani voters were asked to answer "yes" or "no" in the referendum to the following question: "Do you want to elect President General Pervez Musharraf as president of Pakistan for the next five years for: survival of local government system; restoration of democracy; continuity and stability of reforms; eradication of extremism and sectarianism, and for the accomplishment of Quaid-i-Azam's concept?"[17]

While both questions were designed to ensure a positive answer, the reformist or modernist theme to the Musharraf referendum question, not to mention that a specific reference was made to extending his tenure as president by five years, stood in marked contrast to the Islamic theme of General Zia-ul Haq's 1984 referendum question:

> Do you endorse the process initiated by General Zia-ul Haq for bringing the laws of Pakistan in conformity with the injunctions of Islam as laid down in the Holy Quran and Sunnah of the Holy Prophet and for the preservation of the ide-

> ology of Pakistan, the continuation and consolidation of that process, and for the smooth and orderly transfer of power to elected representatives of the people?[18]

Once the ballots had been counted it was clear that Musharraf had been overwhelmingly successful—farcically so. The government claimed that nearly 44 million voters cast their ballot, and 97.5 percent of these had voted "yes."[19] This represented a voter turnout rate of nearly 71 percent, 30 percent higher than the 41 percent who voted in the national elections in October, and 10 percent higher than in the previous highest turnout rate recorded in the 1970 elections. With the exception of the military-backed PML(Q), the major political parties boycotted the referendum; so these figures were clearly fabricated. Many independent observers noted that the polling stations were virtually empty most of the day and estimated that turnout was between 10 to 15 percent; (opposition parties claimed a turnout rate of 6 percent). Reports of irregularities abounded, including blatant stuffing of ballot boxes. According to Ayaz Amir, a respected newspaper columnist:

> A young friend of mine proudly told me that in front of the Municipal Library he had stamped 135 ballots as a mark of his love for General Musharraf. His mother, an active lady, had stamped another hundred, his sister, all of fourteen years old, 150. Only fatigue rather than anything else had cut short their exertions.[20]

The extent of the rigging evidently embarrassed even General Musharraf, and he was forced to issue a half-hearted apology in a televised address to the nation on May 22, in which he attributed the referendum malpractices to the "overenthusiasm" and "incompetence" of a few government officials, but claimed that his victory was still beyond doubt.[21] In a subsequent interview with the BBC he mentioned that the low point of his three years in power was the referendum that, "unbeknownst" to him, had been conducted in a "dubious manner" and had "cast aspersions on his own credibility."[22]

Prior to the referendum, Musharraf's personal popularity in Pakistan had been quite high. But the extraconstitutional use of a referendum to extend his tenure in power, the blatant rigging that took place, and the perception that he was engaging in the very "sham" politics for which he was so fond of criticizing the politicians, seriously undermined Musharraf's reputation as a straight-talking and honest general. Increasingly—and much to Musharraf's annoyance—parallels were drawn to previous military dictators.[23]

The farcical nature of the referendum and the political cost Musharraf was willing to pay to hold it was an indication of the seriousness of the predicament with which he was faced. With less than six months to go until the expiration of his Supreme Court–mandated three-year term as chief executive, and national elections scheduled, Musharraf was running out of creative options to extend his tenure in power. He could have followed in General Zia's footsteps in having the newly elected National Assembly pass a constitutional amendment indemnifying his acts as chief executive. But by the spring of 2002, Musharraf was isolated politically. Musharraf's official support for the U.S.-backed war on terror had alienated the religious parties that had traditionally been allies of the military. He had alienated the members of Pakistan's two major political parties—the PML(N) and PPP—through his concerted efforts to divide and weaken them. The army's attempts to create a "king's party," the PML(Q), were not proceeding very smoothly (primarily due to disputes between competitors for the throne). Having alienated most of the major political parties in Pakistan, it was extremely unlikely that after being democratically elected these party members would agree to indemnify the constitutional amendments that Musharraf was proposing to strengthen the hands of the president at the expense of Parliament.

Musharraf was therefore left with little choice but to hold a referendum that would bypass Parliament and the Constitution and go directly to voters to seek legitimacy for his plan to stay on in power. This was a clear violation of the 1973 Constitution on two counts: first, because the president has to be elected by the members of the National Assembly, the Senate, and the four provincial assemblies; and, second, because the president cannot also hold the position of chief of army staff.[24] The unconstitutional nature of the presidential referendum will inevitably be a bone of contention between the president and the newly elected Parliament and will likely lead to legal challenges to Musharraf's claim to be president. Undoubtedly, the military will have to resort to its well-tested strategy of using the carrot and stick to insure a pliant judiciary that will rule in favor of these unconstitutional measures.

Tampering with the Constitution: The Legal Framework Order (LFO), 2002

If any doubts existed after the presidential referendum that Musharraf had any intention of letting the national elections transfer power out of his hands, these were removed by the LFO, 2002,[25] announced on August 21. The twenty-nine constitutional amendments contained in the order include several key measures to ensure Musharraf's hold on power:

1. Restoring the powers of the president to dissolve the National Assembly. General Zia had introduced these powers in 1985 in Article 58(2)(b) of the Eighth Amendment to the Constitution, and it was subsequently used by Pakistani presidents to dismiss four elected governments between 1988 and 1997. One of Nawaz Sharif's first actions after winning a two-thirds majority in the 1997 elections was to pass the thirteenth Amendment to the Constitution, which repealed this clause.

2. Creating a National Security Council (NSC), chaired by the president,[26] with a far-reaching mandate to examine "strategic matters pertaining to the sovereignty, integrity, and security of the state; and matters relating to democracy, governance, and inter-provincial harmony." The NSC would essentially be a

supraparliamentary cabinet that would legalize the role of the military in the political affairs of the state and undermine the authority of the Parliament. The idea of an NSC is not a new one—General Zia-ul Haq tried to create one, but the newly elected parliament in 1985 refused to give it constitutional cover. When General Jehangir Karamat, then chief of army staff, proposed the concept of a NSC again in 1998, Prime Minister Nawaz Sharif promptly fired him.

3. Giving the president the power to appoint provincial governors, whereas previously the president appointed on the advice of the prime minister. An additional amendment then gives governors the power to dismiss provincial assemblies with the prior approval of the president.

4. Giving the president authority to appoint the chairman, the joint chiefs of staff, and the chiefs of the army, navy and air Force and to approve appointments of judges to the superior courts.

5. Extending Musharraf's term as both president and chief of army staff for five years.

6. Indemnifying and validating all the chief executive and president's orders and ordinances since October 14, 1999.

It should be noted that the LFO also proposed some positive constitutional amendments, including reducing the voting age from twenty-one to eighteen, increasing the number of reserved seats for women from twenty to sixty, and increasing the overall size of the National Assembly from 217 to 342 and the Senate from 87 to 100. To his credit, Musharraf risked the wrath of the religious parties and removed the system of separate electorates for religious minorities.[27] This system, introduced by General Zia-ul Haq at the behest of the religious parties, had marginalized religious minorities from mainstream politics by stipulating that they could only vote for candidates for the limited number of reserved minority seats in the assemblies.

Despite these positive features, they did little to redeem the overall extremely negative implications and potential consequences of the LFO. This was particularly true given Musharraf's claim that based on the Supreme Court ruling in the *Syed Zafar Ali Shah* case, the constitutional amendments contained in the LFO did not need parliamentary approval.[28] Even General Zia had the newly elected Parliament in 1985 debate and then pass his controversial Eighth Amendment to the Constitution. Opposition politicians and most constitutional lawyers argue vehemently that the LFO amendments so fundamentally alter the "salient features of the Constitution" that they would need to be approved by the newly elected Parliament.[29] This argument is hard to dispute as the LFO essentially transforms the parliamentary form of government provided for in the 1973 Constitution into a presidential form of government controlled by the military with few checks and balances. According to a prominent Pakistani human rights activist, I. A. Rehman, "The LFO is the instrument of legitimizing Pakistan's transformation into a praetorian state."[30] The accumulation of power by the president, in turn, undermines the federal nature of the Pakistani state as provided for in the 1973 Constitution.[31]

Not surprisingly, the major topic of debate on the very first day that Mir Zafarullah Khan Jamali was elected prime minister was the need for Parliament to review and approve the constitutional amendments contained in the LFO.[32] It is clear that the LFO, which symbolizes the tension between the elected and unelected institutions of the state, will be a major source of political instability and tension between the president and the Parliament.

THE NATIONAL ASSEMBLY ELECTIONS

On October 10, 2002, Pakistan held its seventh direct franchise party based elections since independence. The result of the election most discussed by the press was the success of the coalition of religious parties. A more significant feature of the election, however, was the extent to which the military was unabashedly willing to go in order to achieve the result it desired—namely a pliant Parliament that would not challenge the status quo. The following sections provide a brief overview of the major political parties contesting the election, illustrations of the pre- and post-poll manipulations of the electoral process, and an analysis of the National and Provincial Assembly election results.

Overview of Major Political Parties

Of the approximately 100 political parties that registered to contest the 2002 elections, only sixteen ended up winning one or more seats in the National Assembly. The following section gives an overview of the five top vote winners in the 2002 elections, which together won nearly 80 percent of the vote and 211 of the 269 seats won. The relationship of these parties to the military establishment can be categorized as shown in Table 5.2.

Pakistan Muslim League—Nawaz Group and Quaid-i-Azam Group

The PML traces its ancestry back to the All-India Muslim League of Mohammad Ali Jinnah, which then became the Pakistan Muslim League after independence. Because of its legitimizing link to Jinnah and the traditionally strong base of support for the PML in Pakistan's politically most important province, Punjab, the party name has been a favorite for subsequent generations of politicians to fight over, use, and abuse. The traditionally strong links of the PML to the civil and military establishments along with the reputation of many Leaguers as "men of easy political virtue" easily enticed to switch their allegiances[34] has always made the PML the military's party of choice out of which to carve a loyal king's party.[35] Numerous factions of the PML have emerged over the years, either created either by the establishment or emerging due to power struggles and differences between party leaders.[36]

Table 5.2. Party–Military Establishment Relationships

Party	Relationship to Establishment[33]
Pakistan Muslim League—Nawaz Group (PML-N)	Anti-establishment, pro-status quo
Pakistan Muslim League—Quaid-i-Azam (PML-Q)	Pro-establishment, pro-status quo
Pakistan People's Party—Parliamentarians (PPP-P)	Anti-establishment, pro-status quo
Muttahida Majlis-i-Amal (MMA)	Pro-establishment, anti-status quo
National Alliance (NA)	Pro-establishment, pro-status quo

PML(N)

Mian Nawaz Sharif, the leader of the PML(N), was a political creation of General Zia-ul Haq's rule from 1977 to 1988. Sharif started his political career in the Local Body elections in 1979, served as the finance minister in the Punjab Provincial Cabinet from 1981 to 1985, and then rose to political prominence as the chief minister of Punjab from 1985 to 1990. In 1990 he became the prime minister following the success of the Islami Jamhoori Ittihad (IJI), a coalition of anti-PPP parties created and backed by the military, which won the 1990 elections. Through nearly twelve years of providing patronage and controlling the bureaucracy at the Punjab level, as well as through populist measures while serving as prime minister, Nawaz Sharif was able to transform himself from being a creature of the establishment into a popular national leader with a considerable following of his own. Not surprisingly, this increasingly led to clashes with the establishment represented by President Ghulam Ishaq Khan, and the subsequent dismissal of Nawaz Sharif's government in 1993.

As a political party the PML(N) emerged as a major political force in Pakistani politics in the 1993 National and the Punjab Provincial Assembly elections. Although the elections were won by the PPP and the PML(Junejo) faction, the PML(N) won an impressive 39.9 percent of the vote. In the 1997 elections, the PML(N) won a landslide victory, winning 134 of the 204 National Assembly seats contested on election day. Its two-thirds majority made it the most powerful elected government (in terms of National Assembly seats) ever in Pakistan. Nawaz Sharif's abuse of this power, and the inevitable tension his power created with the military, culminated in his overthrow in General Musharraf's military coup d'etat on October 12, 1999. He and his family were subsequently banished to Saudi Arabia, and barred from contesting in the 2002 elections.[37] The PML(N) nevertheless contested the 2002 elections, but with the serious disadvantages of having its popular leader in exile and with the military enticing and pressuring the party's politicians and supporters away to the PML(Q). In 2002 the party's main base of support remained in northern Punjab and the urban areas of central Punjab, most notably Nawaz Sharif's hometown of Lahore.

PML(Q)

The PML(Q) was initially formed by discontented members of the PML(N), unhappy with Nawaz Sharif's accumulation of power at their expense between 1997 to 1999. Following Sharif's dismissal from power in 1999, the party formally came into existence,[38] headed by Mian Azhar, a former governor of Punjab and leader of the Arain *biradari*.[39] Azhar's leadership was constantly undermined and challenged by the powerful Chaudhuris of Gujrat—Chaudhury Shujaat Hussain and Chaudhury Pervez Elahi—who were viewed by many to be the real powers behind the throne.

The PML(Q)'s anti-Nawaz Sharif credentials made it the military's natural ally to weaken the PML(N) and the logical choice to be developed into a pro-Musharraf king's party.[40] It was the patronage of the military that breathed life into the PML(Q). In Punjab, in particular, the perception of who will win the election and be in a position to provide patronage is one of the most important determinants of voting behavior.[41] The presidential referendum sent a very clear message that Musharraf was going to stay on in power and that the party that he supported would be the most likely to end up in power. With both the covert and overt support of the military many prominent politicians from the PML(N), as well as other parties, read the writing on the wall and joined the PML(Q) after the referendum and in the runup to the elections.[42] According to one press report, two-thirds of the PML(Q) candidates in the 2002 elections were either former PPP or PML(N) legislators.[43] Like the PML(N), the PML(Q)'s main base of support was in Punjab.

Pakistan People's Party–Parliamentarians

The Pakistan People's Party (PPP) was founded in 1967 by Zulfiqar Ali Bhutto—who served as prime minister of Pakistan from 1972 until he was overthrown in a 1977 military coup by General Zia-ul Haq and was later executed. Leadership of the party passed on to his daughter, Benazir Bhutto, who returned from exile in 1986 following the partial restoration of democracy by General Zia in 1985. In the 1988 National Assembly elections the PPP won 38.5 percent of the vote (the same percentage as the party won in the 1970 elections), and with the support of some smaller parties and independent members formed a government headed by Benazir Bhutto. In 1990, President Ghulam Ishaq Khan dissolved the PPP government on charges of corruption and incompetence. In the 1990 elections, the PPP won a respectable 36.9 percent of the vote but lost the elections to the military-backed coalition, the IJI. The PPP and its coalition partner, the PML(J), won the 1993 elections with 41.8 percent of the vote, and Benazir served her second term as prime minister until her government was again dismissed in 1996 on charges similar to those in 1990. The PPP suffered a crushing defeat in the 1997 elections at the hands of the PML(N), winning only 21.8 percent of the vote, and no seats outside of Sindh province.

As with the PML(N), the PPP contested the 2002 elections with the serious disadvantage of having the party leader in exile. Furthermore, in order to avoid disqualification, it had to change its name to the Pakistan People's Party–Parliamentarians (PPP-P) headed by the PPP leader, Makhdoom Amin Fahim. In its favor, however, was the fact that its main political rival, the PML, was split into two major factions, and the conservative vote was further divided between the PML factions and the MMA. The PPP's main base of political support is rural Sindh and southern and central Punjab.

Muttahida Majlis-i-Amal (MMA)

The MMA (United Council for Action) was formed as an electoral alliance of six religious parties—the Jamaat-i-Islami, the Jamiat-ul-Ulema-i-Islam (Fazlur Rahman), the Jamiat-ul-Ulema-i-Islam (Sami-ul Haq), the Jamiat-ul-Ulema-i-Pakistan (Noorani), the Jamiat-i-Ahle-i-Hadith, and the Tehrik-i-Islami. In reality, it was more of a two-party alliance with the JI headed by Qazi Hussain Ahmad and the pro-Taliban JUI faction headed by Fazlur Rahman being the driving force behind the alliance.[44]

Pakistan's religious parties have rarely fared well in electoral politics and the alliance was largely motivated by the need to improve on their dismal past performances. Much of the preelection analysis in the press focused on the internal divisions within the MMA that would undermine its effectiveness. Indeed, soon after the formation of the MMA, one of the six members, the Jamiat-i-Ahle-i-Hadith headed by Professor Sajid Mir, left reducing it to a five-party alliance.[45] The major factor in the MMA's favor, however, was the sharp rise in anti-American sentiment, especially in the ethnic Pashtun belt of the NWFP and Balochistan, following the U.S.-led war against terror in neighboring Afghanistan. The MMA was also widely believed to be receiving support from the military, especially in the NWFP, as part of the strategy to weaken Pakistan's two major political parties, the PPP and the PML(N). The establishment strategy in Pakistan had always been to use the religious parties against leftist and ethnic parties who were viewed to be the major threat. But with the virtual elimination of significant leftist and ethnic parties (the Muttahida Qaumi Movement [MQM] being the only exception), and with the MMA now becoming a mainstream party and therefore a possible threat to the establishment, it will be interesting to observe the evolving relationship between the military and the religious parties.

The National Alliance

The National Alliance (NA) was an alliance of six relatively insignificant proestablishment parties led by former President Farooq Leghari and his Millat Party. After the PML(Q), it was the largest beneficiary of the military's strategy to patronize parties most likely to split the PML(N) and PPP vote. For example, one member of the National Alliance was the Sindh Democratic Alliance (SDA), a party of anti-PPP politicians from Sindh created with the military's assistance in August 2002 to help split the PPP vote in Sindh.[46] To unite the proestablishment parties and votes, the National Alliance entered into an electoral agreement with the PML(Q), forming what became known as the Grand National Alliance.[47]

Pre-Poll Manipulations

The massive rigging of the presidential referendum did not augur well for the fairness of the National and Provincial Assembly elections. Neither did the appointment of a chief election commissioner who had been the chief justice of the Supreme Court when it legitimized Musharraf's military takeover, and subsequently gave his stamp of approval to the rigged presidential referendum.[48] The stakes were high for General Musharraf who needed elections that would legitimize the continuation of his rule but would not produce a Parliament that could place checks on his power. It therefore came as no surprise when the government engaged in extensive pre-poll manipulations to achieve the desired result.

The government's blatantly partial election strategy was to do everything possible to weaken Pakistan's two major political parties, the PPP and the PML(N), while doing everything possible to create viable pro-Musharraf parties and alliances, notably the PML(Q) and the NA. One of the first steps taken was to ensure that the leaders of the two major parties would remain in exile and not be in a position to contest the elections. Legislation deliberately targeting Benazir Bhutto was passed, which barred "absconders" who failed to appear before courts from contesting the elections or from heading political parties.[49] On July 6, Musharraf passed Executive Order No. 19, specifically targeting Sharif and Bhutto, as it barred anyone from holding the position of prime minister or chief minister more than twice.

Another tactic was to use corruption cases to disqualify candidates or to pressure them to join the PML(Q) or other pro-Musharraf parties or alliances.[50] During the campaign Imran Khan, leader of the Pakistan Tehrik-i-Insaf, demanded that two of the most powerful PML(Q) politicians, Chaudhury Shujaat Hussain and his cousin, Chaudhury Pervez Elahi, be disqualified for getting loans written off. As leaders in the PML(Q) and linchpins in the military's strategy to win Punjab, no action was taken.[51] On the other hand, the former PPP Speaker of the National Assembly, Yousaf Raza Gillani, was jailed and barred from contesting the elections for not paying his phone bills when he was the Speaker. Perhaps most disturbing was the government's release of the notorious head of the extremist Sunni sectarian party Sipah-e-Sahaba, Azam Tariq, who was being held on murder charges, in order to enable him to contest the elections.[52]

In another controversial move, Musharraf amended the Conduct of General Elections Order 2002, and inserted a clause requiring that members of the National Assembly possess the equivalent of a bachelors degree. This amendment single handedly disqualified around 100 former members of the National Assembly and the Senate. Not only was this an undemocratic action in that it disqualified approximately 96 percent of Pakistan's population from contesting, it was also used as a deliberate strategy to eliminate many of the "old guard" of Pakistani politics. In a televised address to the nation on the eve of the elections, President Musharraf took credit for the fact that "almost 96 percent of the traditional faces have vanished due to the graduation condition."[53]

Some of the concerns about the conduct of the elections raised in the Preliminary Statement of the European Union Election Observation Mission (EUEOM) to Pakistan, issued on October 12, were as follows:[54]

1. Failure of the Election Commission of Pakistan (ECP) to curb the authorities' misuse of state resources in favor of political parties, in particular, but not exclusively, for the PML(Q).

2. The inappropriate use of actual election symbols—the most prominent being that of the PML(Q)—on mock ballot papers in the ECP's public information video broadcast on national television.

3. Solid evidence to believe that public authorities from the local administrations (Nazims) up to senior levels of governance were actively involved in partisan electioneering.

4. The requirement for candidates to have B.A. degrees deprives some 96 percent of Pakistan's citizens of the right to run for office.

5. The enforcement of the provision that loan defaulters and convicts could not contest the election was marked by a lack of uniformity.

6. Many indications that the disqualification of prominent politicians from the elections came about as a result of a government strategy.

In the lead-up to the elections numerous other complaints appeared in the press about pre-poll rigging and manipulation aimed at "tailoring democracy and stitching together a government that will obediently toe the army's line."[55] These included the use of local government officials to influence election results, the time-honored tradition of transferring and posting accommodating government officials in key constituencies and districts, and the active use of Pakistan's intelligence agencies to help run the election campaigns of the progovernment parties.[56]

Despite all the evidence of pre-poll manipulations, there was no serious discussion of boycotting the polls by any of the major political parties in Pakistan. This played a major role in helping to legitimize the elections. Furthermore, on Election Day there were relatively few complaints of massive rigging which had a further legitimizing effect.

Analysis of Election Results

Soon after the election results started coming in it was clear that Pakistan was going to have a hung Parliament. The party with the largest number of votes was the PPP, with 25.9 percent of the vote, followed closely by the PML(Q) with 25.6 percent. The MMA and the PML(N) won 11.5 and 11.3 percent of the vote, respectively. Nevertheless, seats won rather than votes won are what count in Pakistan's first-past-the-post electoral system, and here the PML(Q) secured seventy-seven seats, the PPP sixty-two seats, the MMA fourty-five seats, the PML(N) fourteen seats, and the NA thirteen seats. Other parties won 10.7 percent of the vote and twenty-eight seats, and independent candidates won 10.2 percent of the vote and thirty seats.[57] These results pertain to the directly elected seats. Additional seats were filled by special constituencies by indirect voting.

Electoral Success of the Religious Parties

The most widely commented on result of the 2002 elections in Pakistan was the success of the MMA, especially in the NWFP and Balochistan. The only other time when religious parties have done well in elections was in 1970, when the collective votes of four religious parties contesting independently totaled 21.7 percent in West Pakistan. To put the MMA's 2002 vote in perspective it is worth noting that the 3.4 million votes (21.7 percent) won by the Islamic parties in 1970 exceeds the 3.3 million votes (11.5 percent) won by the MMA in 2002.[58]

Nevertheless, the MMA's electoral success was a major development in Pakistani politics, especially in light of the very poor performance of religious parties since the 1970 elections. Because they rarely fared well in electoral politics, it is common for political commentators to conclude that this reflects their lack of popular support. Popularity, however, is difficult to determine from Pakistani election results. In Pakistan's first-past-the-post electoral system Islamic parties, like most other third parties, rarely fare well. Especially in the patronage-based political environment that exists in Pakistan, few voters are willing to "waste" their votes on candidates who are not expected to win.[59] What is therefore interesting about the 2002 election result of the MMA was not just that it represented an increase in the popularity of Islamic parties, but that a third party had emerged that voters were willing to vote for.

Most commentators interpreted the MMA's success in the NWFP and Balochistan as a protest vote against the U.S.-led war against terror, especially in the Pashtun areas in neighboring Afghanistan, and the government of Pakistan's support for that war. This raises the question of the extent to which the vote was an Islamic vote or a Pashtun nationalist vote. A closer look at the data supports the perception that there was an ethnic dimension to the support for the MMA. A comparison of the percentage of votes the MMA received in the five National Assembly constituencies in the Hazara Division of the NWFP, which contains the only districts[60] that are not predominately Pashtun, shows that the MMA received only 22.8 percent of the vote in contrast to its overall NWFP result of 46.7 percent. Similarly, in the fourteen Provincial Assembly constituencies in the Hazara Division where the MMA contested, it received only 12.3 percent of the vote compared to its NWFP Provincial Assembly result of 26.7 percent.[61]

In addition to the ethnic dimension of the vote, the MMA benefited from the military's divide and rule strategy in the NWFP. Not only was the PML split between the "Q" and "N" groups, but the PPP was also split into two factions. Prior to the elections the military dropped all charges against the former PPP provincial leader, Aftab Amed Khan Sherpao, who had earlier been convicted on corruption charges and fled to London. He was encouraged to return so that his splinter faction of the PPP, known as the PPP (Sherpao), would help split the PPP vote in the NWFP. The PPP(S) created an electoral understanding with the MMA and won two National Assembly seats, the only two in the entire province (excluding the Federally Administered Tribal Areas) where the MMA did not put up a candidate. The PPP(S), however, focused its attention on the Provincial Assembly elections where it won more votes and seats (9.8 percent and 9 seats) than the main faction of the PPP (9.0 percent and 8 seats).

Religious parties in general—and the Jamaat-i-Islami in particular—have received most of their support from the conservative urban middle classes. The findings of an exit poll conducted by Gallup Pakistan and released by the Pakistan Institute of Legislative Development and Transparency (PILDAT)[62] indicate that the electoral support for the MMA was highest from the educated middle and upper classes, compared to the PPP and PML(Q) who did better amongst illiterate and very poor voters. The poll also showed that the MMA did particularly well with new voters in the eighteen to twenty-one age range who were given the franchise for the first time in 2002. A separate study of the election results from Pakistan's ten largest cities reveals that the MMA received a higher percentage of urban votes (21.7 percent) than any other party.[63]

Weakening of the Two-Party System

Table 5.3 illustrates one of the most important aspects of the 2002 election results—a move away from what had been an evolving two-party political system. In 1988, 1990, and 1993 the percentages of the vote won by the top two parties increased from 68.7 to 74.2 to 77.8 percent, which represented 72, 72, and 79 percent of the total number of National Assembly seats, respectively. This dropped in 1997 to 67.7 percent, primarily due to the dismal performance of the PPP, although this still accounted for 75 percent of the total number of seats. In 2002, however, the top two parties received only 51.5 percent of the vote and the same percentage of seats, which paved the way for the rise of a third party, the MMA.

Ironically, after the MMA, the PPP was the biggest beneficiary of the "tripartite" election result, since it meant that it could still be the second largest party while winning only 25.9 percent of the vote.[64] The inability of the PPP to bounce back to the 37 to 39 percent of the vote that it consistently won between 1970 and 1993 does not bode well for its future electoral prospects, especially if there is a return to the earlier evolving pattern of two parties dominating electoral politics. Prior to the elections, most political commentators had expected the PPP to do better, since the conservative vote was split between the PML factions and the MMA. And yet the PPP was still only able to increase its vote numbers by 4.1 percent from the 21.8 percent of the vote it received in its crushing defeat by the PML(N) in 1997, indicating that the voters who deserted the party in 1997 did not return in large numbers in 2002. The various factions of the PML, on the other hand, have been able to maintain a respectable 39.1 percent of the vote, down only 6.8 percent from the PML(N)'s landslide 45.9 percent in 1997.

Provincial Results

The 2002 election results illustrate that there are very few political parties in Pakistan with strong support in more than one province. In the National Assembly elections only the PML(Q) and the MMA won seats in all four provinces, the PPP only in Punjab and Sindh, and the PML(N) only in Punjab. In the Provincial Assembly elections only the PML(Q), the PPP, and the MMA won seats in all four provinces.

Table 5.4 summarizes the results of the 2002 Provincial Assembly elections. In the Punjab, the PML(Q) won 33.5 percent of the vote, nearly the exact same percentage (34 percent) of the Punjab vote it won in the National Assembly election. The PPP, however, received only 22.8 percent of the Punjab Provincial Assembly vote compared to 26.1 percent of the vote in Punjab constituencies of the National Assembly. As with the PPP's national election results, the PPP results do not bode well for the party in Punjab if there is a return to the pattern of

Table 5.3. Comparison of 1970, 1988, 1990, 1993, 1997, and 2002 Election Results

PARTY	2002		1997		1993		1990		1988		1970
	%	Seats	%	Seats	%	Seats	%	Seats	%	Seats	%
PPP	25.9	62	21.8	18	37.9	86	36.9	45	38.5	93	38.9
PML(N)	11.3	14	45.9	134	39.9	73	—	—	—	—	—
IJI	—	—	—	—	—	—	37.3	105	30.2	54	—
PML(Q)	25.6	77	—	—	—	—	—	—	—	—	—
PML(F, J, Z)	2.2	7	—	—	3.9	6	—	—	—	—	—
PML/IJI Total	39.1	98	45.9	134	43.8	79	37.3	105	30.2	54	22.8
MMA	11.5	45	—	—	—	—	—	—	—	—	—
JI	—	—	—	—	3.3	3	—	—	—	—	6.0
JUI (F)	—	—	1.8	2	2.4	4	3.0	6	1.8	7	7.3
JUP	—	—	—	—	—	—	1.5	3	—	—	8.2
Other Islamic	1.4	3	—	—	1.1	2	1.1	0	0.4	1	0.2
Total Islamic	12.9	48	1.8	2	6.8	9	5.6	9	2.2	8	21.7
Other Parties	11.9	31	15.5	29	4.2	13	9.9	26	9.4	9	5.7
Independents	10.2	30	15.0	21	7.3	16	10.3	22	19.5	40	10.9
TOTAL	100	269	100	204	100	203	100	207	100	204	100

Source: Compiled by author using Election Commission of Pakistan data

two parties dominating elections in the future. The PML(N) came in third in the Provincial Assembly elections, winning 16.5 percent of the vote and 39 seats.In the unlikely event that the PML factions are ever able to unite in future elections, the 52.3 percent of the vote that they collectively won in 2002 is an indication that their strong support in Punjab could sweep them into power at both the provincial and national levels.

Table 5.4. 2002 Provincial Assembly Results (Directly Elected Seats)

PARTIES	Punjab		Sindh		NWFP		Balochistan	
	%	Seats	%	Seats	%	Seats	%	Seats
PML(Q)	33.5	129	7.7	11	14.5	6	19.7	10
PPP	22.8	63	28.1	50	9.0	8	6.6	2
MMA	5.7	9	8.1	9	26.3	48	16.6	13
PML(N)	16.5	39	—	—	9.2	4	—	—
PML(F, J, Z)	2.3	6	5.2	10	—	—	—	—
NA	3.1	12	10.7	13	—	—	8.4	5
MQM	—	—	12.0	32	—	—	—	—
ANP	—	—	—	—	11.1	7	—	—
PPP-S	—	—	—	—	9.8	9	—	—
JWP	—	—	—	—	—	—	9.7	3
BNM	—	—	—	—	—	—	6.8	3
BNP, BNDP	—	—	—	—	—	—	6.9	3
PKMAP	—	—	—	—	—	—	5.0	2
Other Parties	2.3	0	20.0	1	5.3	1	4.9	0
Independents	13.8	38	8.3	5	14.9	14	15.3	7
TOTAL	100.00	296	100.00	131	100.00	97	100.00	48

Source: Compiled by author from data provided by Election Commission of Pakistan.

A closer look at the National Assembly election results for Punjab, broken down by region, reveal that the PPP received much more support (34.2 percent) from southern Punjab, followed by central (27.3 percent), northern (20.6 percent), and western Punjab (16.1 percent). The PML(Q) did well in southern (36.0 percent), central (34.1 percent), and western Punjab (34.0 percent), and worse in northern Punjab (28.8 percent). The PML(N) received most support in northern Punjab (24.2 percent), followed by central (18.1 percent), southern (12.8 percent), and western Punjab (11.4 percent). The MMA received its strongest support (9.7 percent) from northern Punjab. The strongest parties in urban Punjab constituencies were the PPP (27.5 percent) and the PML(N) (26.9 percent), followed by the PML(Q) (17.5 percent) and by the MMA (12.7 percent).[65]

In Sindh, the main electoral contest was, as usual, between the PPP—which won 28.1 percent of the Provincial Assembly vote and fifty seats—and the MQM[66]—which won 12.0 percent of the vote and thirty-two seats. The PPP received most of its support in Sindh from rural constituencies and won only 15.0 percent of the vote in National Assembly urban constituencies. The MQM and MMA, on the other hand, received nearly all of their National Assembly votes from urban constituencies, the MQM winning 39.3 percent of the urban vote and the MMA 27.4 percent.[67] While the PPP's 2002 National Assembly result of 36.7 percent was up from the 32.1 percent they received in 1997, it was considerably lower than the 51.7 percent and 46.5 percent that the PPP won in the 1993 and 1988 elections, respectively.[68] An interesting development in urban Sindh in the 2002 elections was the considerable increase in support for religious parties and the considerable decline in support for the MQM. The MQM's support has declined from a high of 64.9 percent of the urban Sindh vote in the 1990 National Assembly elections to 47.8 percent in 1997 and to 37.6 percent in 2002.[69]

In the NWFP the main story was the dramatic and unexpected victory of the MMA, which won 26.3 percent of the vote and half of the Provincial Assembly seats. The MMA received a much higher percentage of the vote in the National Assembly, where it won 46.7 percent of the vote and twenty-nine seats, in comparison to the Provincial Assembly. The PPP won only 9.0 percent of the vote and eight seats, while the splinter party headed by Aftab Sherpao (PPP-S) won 9.8 percent of the vote and nine seats. Perhaps the second most significant election result in the NWFP after the rise of the MMA was the sharp decline in support for the Awami National Party (ANP), which won only 11.1 percent of the Provincial Assembly vote and 9.4 percent of the National Assembly vote in the NWFP. This was a dramatic decrease from the 19.1, 14.2, 15.0, and 18.4 percent of the vote the ANP had respectively won in the 1997, 1993, 1990, and 1988 elections.[70] The Hazara Division has traditionally been a Muslim League stronghold, and this continued in 2002 with the PML(Q) winning 34.1 percent of the National Assembly vote and the PML(N) an additional 14.2 percent of the vote.[71] As discussed previously, the MMA received a much higher percentage of the vote (over 50 percent) in Pashtun areas of the NWFP than in non-Pashtun areas, notably the Hazara Division.

The PML(Q) secured the highest percentage of the vote (19.7 percent) in Balochistan in the Provincial Assembly election, followed by the MMA (16.6 percent). The ethnic and regionally based parties generally did not fare well, with the four major Baloch and Pashtun nationalist parties,[72] collectively only winning about 28.4 percent of the Provincial Assembly vote. In general, the Baloch ethnic parties appeared to have lost votes to the PML(Q) and the Pashtun ethnic parties to the MMA.[73] The MMA won the highest vote percentage and seats (19.9 percent and 6 seats) in the National Assembly results in Balochistan, followed by the PML(Q) (17.4 percent and 2 seats). The combined National Assembly result of the Baloch and Pashtun nationalist parties was 32.9 percent and 3 seats.

Positive Results

There were a number of positive features of this election, the most important of which was that these were amongst Pakistan's most peaceful elections. Another positive development in the 2002 elections was the lowering of the voting age from twenty-one to eighteen, giving Pakistani youth their first opportunity to participate in National and Provincial Assembly elections. Other positive features are discussed below.

Increase in Women's Representation

Women won 13 of the general seats of the National Assembly, the largest number ever in Pakistani elections. One reason for this was that the election clauses requiring candidates to be BA graduates, and disqualifying candidates convicted on corruption charges, had the unintended side effect of increasing the number of female candidates whose fathers and brothers did not meet these conditions. Thus, while women's representation increased, many of the female candidates were simply running as proxy candidates for their male family members.[74] The women who won the thirteen general seats, combined with the increase in reserved seats for women from twenty to sixty, means that more than 20 percent of Pakistan's new Parliament will be women.

Minorities Brought Back into the Political Mainstream

An important feature of the 2002 elections was that religious minorities, with the unfortunate exception of the Ahmadis, were brought back into the mainstream of Pakistani politics as a result of the removal of the system of separate electorates, described earlier in the chapter. In 2002, for the first time since the 1977 elections, political parties and candidates actively campaigned to win the votes of the religious minorities. The PPP was widely believed to be the favored party of religious minorities and, therefore, the party that would benefit the most from the removal of separate electorates. Owing to factional politics, however, it is unlikely that the religious minorities all favored one party.

Increase in Voter Turnout

Another positive feature of the 2002 elections was that voter turnout increased by 6 percent to 41.4 percent from a low of 35.4 percent in the 1997 elections, although it was lower than in 1990 (47.1 percent) and 1988 (43.1 percent) (see Table 5.5). Turnout would have been higher if everyone who had wanted to vote had been able to.[75] New lists of registered voters and new locations for many polling stations led to considerable confusion on election day. Many other voters did not have the new ID cards necessary to vote. Furthermore, it is likely that many women who wanted to vote were prevented from doing so, especially in the more conservative districts of NWFP and Balochistan. As usual, there was considerable variation in turnout rates between provinces, with the highest being 46.3 percent in Punjab and the lowest being 27.2 percent in Balochistan.

Table 5.5. Voter Turnout, 1970–2002 (Directly Elected Seats)

Province	2002	1997	1993	1990	1988	1985	1970
Punjab	46.3	39.8	47.1	49.6	46.5	60.1	66.5
Sindh	36.8	31.3	28.2	43.3	42.4	44.4	58.4
NWFP	33.2	27.8	34.6	35.7	33.9	40.6	46.8
Balochistan	27.2	23.2	24.9	29.2	25.7	37.4	39.0
All Pakistan	41.4	35.4	40.3	45.5	43.1	53.7	61.5

Source: 2002 figures from Gallup Pakistan. All other figures compiled from Election Commission of Pakistan reports.

Post-Poll Manipulation

As widely predicted before the election, the military succeeded in its overall objective of achieving a hung Parliament. What was not so clear in the aftermath of the election, however, was whether the resulting weak and divided Parliament will be as pliant and easily manipulated as the military desires. The six-week post-poll confusion over who would form the next government was an indication that General Musharraf's job of keeping the political parties in line would not be an easy one. Despite blatant military interference in the form of threats and incentives to get the newly elected legislators to support the PML(Q)'s candidate for prime minister, Mir Zafarullah Khan Jamali, it proved a formidable challenge to get a majority of 172 legislators to finally vote on November 21 for the military's man in the 342 seat National Assembly. Maulana Fazlur Rahman, the MMA candidate for prime minister, won eighty-six votes and Shah Mehmood Qureshi, the PPP candidate, seventy.

One of the government's first actions to manipulate the results, taken on the eve of the elections, was to amend the LFO 2002 to permit independent candidates to join political parties after the elections.[76] This was clearly designed to facilitate their move to the king's party.

The next slightly embarrassing task was to amend the clause specifically designed for Nawaz Sharif and Benazir Bhutto in the recently promulgated LFO, preventing those who had twice held the position of prime minister or chief minister from again holding either of these offices. This clause inadvertently would have prevented the military's choice for prime minister, Jamali, from becoming prime minister as he had served as a chief minister of Balochistan on three occasions, twice as a caretaker chief minister. The LFO was therefore amended to exclude from this provision those who had served as a caretaker prime minister or caretaker chief minister.[77]

In order to get the critical support of the MQM and its seventeen votes, the military agreed to crackdown on the MQM's rival in Karachi, the Haqiqi faction of the MQM. The MQM also demanded the removal of cases against its activists as well as the position of chief minister of Sindh province. In a possible sign of the troubles ahead for Jamali's new government, only a few days after voting for him, the MQM withdrew their support from Jamali's government alleging that the military had reneged on its commitment to crackdown on the MQM-Haqiqi.[78] Shortly thereafter they renewed their support, but they had succeeded in illustrating the shaky foundation on which Jamali's government is based.

In another cynical move, the government kept the antidefection clause of the Constitution and Musharraf's own LFO in abeyance when most other sections were restored following the elections. This permitted the military to use its influence to convince candidates from other parties to defect to the PML(Q). This is what ultimately enabled the PML(Q) to win a one vote majority as ten members of the PPP were induced to create a "forward block" and vote against their party in support of Jamali as prime minister.[79] Those who defected from their parties to vote for PML(Q) were richly rewarded. Of the ten members of the PPP who defected, six were given ministerial portfolios in the government, including the powerful defense, interior, and petroleum ministries.[80]

On November 29, provincial governments were formed in the NWFP and Punjab. The MMA's landslide victory in the NWFP enabled its candidate for chief minister, Akram Khan Durrani, to defeat the opposition candidate, Haji Qalandar Khan Lodhi, by 78 votes to 41 in the House of 124 members. In Punjab, the PML(Q)'s Chaudhury Pervaiz Elahi defeated the joint PPP-PML(N) candidate, Qasim Zia, by 235 votes to 102.[81] On December 1, the PML(Q)'s Jam Muhammad Yousuf, supported by the MMA, the Balochistan National Democratic Party and the Jamhoori Watan Party, defeated Muhammad Akbar Mengal of the Balochistan National Party by 47 votes to 12 to become the chief minister of Balochistan.[82] Two months after the elections, the Sindh Provincial Assembly had still not been called into session as the military wanted to give more time for the PML(Q) to try to form a government that would exclude the PPP from power in the province. Finally, on December 16, their efforts succeeded, and the PML(Q) candidate, Ali Mohammad Maher, supported by the NA, MQM, and PML(Functional), won eighty-nine of the 162 seats in the Sindh Assembly.[83]

In the short term, at least, Musharraf's efforts to manipulate the election results to get friendly governments at the center and in the provinces was very successful. Not only was a PML(Q) candidate elected prime minister, but in three out of four provinces PML(Q) candidates were elected as chief ministers.

CONCLUSION

This chapter has argued that the primary purpose of elections in Pakistan has not been to promote democratization and civilian rule, but to create a veneer of democracy to legitimize the continued domination of power by the military establishment. This veneer, however, has become increasingly thin. General Musharraf has pursued the various strategies outlined in this chapter to maintain the status quo in an unabashedly transparent manner, probably best summed up by himself at a press conference in Washington prior to the election, when he stated that "I will put a label of democracy on the existing system."[84]

Musharraf frequently maintains his commitment to democracy, but like the generals who ruled Pakistan before him, he believes that Western democracy does not suit Pakistan, and that "We should have a system of government that suits our environment."[85] He wanted to do away with sham democracy and promote sustainable democracy, but he did not hide the fact that for him this meant giving as little power to elected representatives as possible. Referring to his proposed constitutional amendments to strengthen the powers of the president at the expense of Parliament, Musharraf was clear that "What we are aiming at is not a balance of power or sharing of power" but "checks on the exercise of authority."[86] Using Orwellian language, Musharraf made clear that the "democracy" he was pursuing through these constitutional amendments was "meant to ensure unity of command and a sustainable democracy. . . . Unless there is a unity of command, unless there is one man in charge at the top, the government will never function."[87]

But what many Pakistanis were asking after the blatant pre-poll manipulations by the military, and their open role in coercing, bribing, and promoting horse-trading to form proestablishment governments at the center and in the provinces in the aftermath of the elections, was how Musharraf's sustainable democracy differed from the sham democracy of the past that he was so fond of criticizing.[88] The unprecedented degree to which the military establishment played an overt role in manipulating the elections and forming the subsequent national and provincial governments, and the extent to which they have set the politicians up to fail, will make it unconvincing for the military to blame the politicians if the current experiment with "democracy" fails.

And the chances of failure are high. Not only does Prime Minister Jamali's government have only a razor thin majority in Parliament, but it also faces a strong opposition that is unanimous in its opposition to the constitutional amendments contained in the LFO. Musharraf's efforts to create constitutional cover for the power imbalance between the president and Parliament is, therefore, bound to have a destabilizing effect. The unconstitutional nature of his appointment as president and the fact that, despite all the establishment's efforts, pro-Musharraf parties won only 30 percent of the vote mean Musharraf is left with a rather shaky mandate to pursue his consolidation of presidential power. It is unlikely that this will deter him, however, and, with the help of a pliant judiciary and the usual inability of Pakistani politicians to rise above their own narrow self-interests, he could still succeed. But this would indeed be a sad day for Pakistan, since a veneer of democracy, however thin, has played an important role in ensuring the continuation of elected institutions in Pakistan. While such elected institutions exist there is always hope that they will grow and mature and gain ground relative to the powerful unelected institutions of the state that have played such a destructive role in Pakistan's history. In their absence, the transformation of Pakistan into a praetorian state will be complete.

APPENDIX

ACRONYMS USED FOR PARTY NAMES

ANP	Awami National Party
BNDP	Balochistan National Democratic Party
BNM	Balochistan National Movement
BNP	Balochistan National Party
JWP	Jamhoori Watan Party
MMA	Muttahida Majlis-Amal
MQM	Mutahida Qaumi Movement
NA	National Alliance
PKMAP	Pakhtunkhwa Milli Awami Party
PLM(F)	Pakistan Muslim League (Functional)
PML(J)	Pakistan Muslim League (Junejo)
PML(N)	Pakistan Muslim League (Nawaz)
PML(Q)	Pakistan Muslim League (Quaid-i-Azam)
PML(Z)	Pakistan Muslim League (Zia)
PPP	Pakistan People's Party
PPP(S)	Pakistan People's Party (Sherpao)

NOTES

1. See David Washbrook, "The Rhetoric of Democracy and Development on Late Colonial India," in Sugata Bose and Ayesha Jalal, *Nationalism, Democracy and Development: State and Politics in India* (New Delhi, India: Oxford University Press, 1997). See also the discussion of the traditions of South Asia of "formal democracy" or "democratic authoritarianism" as opposed to "substantive democracy" in chapter 2 of Ayesha Jalal, *Democracy and Authoritarianism in South Asia: A Comparative and Historical Perspective* (Cambridge, England: Cambridge University Press, 1995), pp 29–65.

2. For a more detailed discussion of the meaning of elections in Pakistan, see chapters 1 and 2 in Andrew R. Wilder, *The Pakistani Voter: Electoral Politics and Voting Behaviour in the Punjab* (Karachi, Pakistan: Oxford University Press, 1999), pp 1–33.

3. For a more detailed discussion of elections for their "legitimacy function" as opposed to their "participation function," see Mohammad Waseem, *The 1993 Elections in Pakistan* (Lahore, Pakistan: Vanguard Press, 1994), pp 6–57.

4. Wilder, *The Pakistani Voter*, p 17.

5. Text of PLO in Muhammad Yasin, "Assemblies, Senate Suspended: Constitution in Abeyance," *Dawn*, October 15, 1999.

6. For text of the Oath of Office (Judges) Order, see *The Herald*, February 2000.

7. For a more detailed discussion of the Oath of Office (Judges) Order, see I. A. Rahman, "It's Just Not On," *Newsline*, February 2000, pp 37–39. See also Mubashir Zaidi, "The Case of the Missing Constitution," *The Herald*, February 2000, pp 22–25.

8. Rafaqat Ali, "Government Given Three Years to Hold Polls," *Dawn*, May 30, 2000.

9. See Zafar Abbas, "Games Dictators Play," *The Herald*, April 2002, p 30. See also Massoud Ansari, "How the Referendum Was Won," *Newsline*, May 2002, p 18.

10. Farhan Bokhari, "The Dangers of Miscalculation," *The News*, April 11, 2002.

11. M. Ilyas Khan, "Inside the MMA," *The Herald*, November 2002, pp 44b–47. See also Zahid Hussain, "The General's Selection," *Newsline*, October 2002, pp 25–26.

12. "Referendum on April 30," *Dawn*, April 10, 2002.

13. Ansari, "How the Referendum Was Won," *Dawn*, April 10, 2002.

14. Ibid., p 19.

15. Ibid.

16. See Zahid Hussain, "The Great Gamble," *Newsline*, April 2002, p 18.

17. "Referendum on April 30," *Dawn*, April 10, 2002.

18. As summarized by Afzal Iqbal, *Islamization of Pakistan* (Lahore, Pakistan: Vanguard Books, 1986), p 122.

19. http://www.pak.gov.pk/public/referendum/return_of_referendum.htm

20. As reported in Ansari, "How the Referendum Was Won," p 22.

21. See Idrees Bakhtiar, "Anyone Responsible?" *The Herald*, June 2002, pp 48–49.

22. Rehana Hakim, Editor's Note, *Newsline*, September 2002, p 11.

23. "General Musharraf has often emphasized that he is neither another Ayub nor a Zia-ul-Haq, but appears to be following their script to the letter. Not only is he holding a referendum in an attempt to legitimize his rule but is also engaged in trying to establish a 'king's party' using local government as his political base." Zahid Hussain, "The Great Gamble," *Newsline*, April 2002, p 18.

24. Article 41(2) requires that the president be qualified to be elected to the National Assembly, which a serving Army would not meet. Article 43 debars the president from holding any office of profit in the service Pakistan. Article 63 (k) stipulates that a two-year period must elapse before government officials can contest National Assembly elections. For more details see I. A. Rahman, "Crisis of Legitimacy," *Newsline*, April 2002, pp 32–33.

25. The Gazette of Pakistan, "Legal Framework Order, 2002," August 21, 2002.

26. The other members would be the prime minister, the chairman of the Senate, the speaker of the National Assembly, the leader of the opposition in the National Assembly, the chief ministers of the provinces, the chairman of the Joint Chiefs of Staff Committee, and the chiefs of the army, navy, and air force.

27. In a highly discriminatory move, however, the LFO maintained the system of separate electorates for the Ahmadi minority community.

28. In a press conference following the promulgation of the LFO, Musharraf dismissed a question as to whether or not the Parliament would need to ratify his amendments, stating, "I don't need any approval." He went on to warn that any attempt to overturn these amendments by parliamentarians would " bring them into conflict with me and the National Security Council. Then I will decide whether I should quit or they should go." Zahid Hussain, "How to Steal an Election," *Newsline*, September 2002, p 20.

29. Ibid., pp 20–21.

30. I. A. Rahman, "Law of Contention," *Newsline*, December 2002, p 23.

31. See Sairah Irshan Khan's interview with constitutional expert and former Supreme Court judge, Fahkruddin G. Ebrahim, "Changing the Constitution Will Endanger the Unity of Pakistan," *Newsline*, July 2002, p 25.

32. Following the newly elected Speaker of the National Assembly's statement that the LFO was part of the Constitution, the leaders of every major party other than the PML(Q) spoke out against the LFO and criticized the Speaker for not acting in an impartial manner. See Muhammad Anis, "Opposition Questions Speaker's Impartiality," *The News*, November 22, 2002.

33. These categorizations for the PML(Q), PPP, and MMA were originally used by Professor Mohammad Waseem, "Election Analysis", a presentation at the Sustainable Development Institute, Islamabad, October 17, 2002.

34. As one commentator noted, "The party is much like a free-size garment. It simply assumes the shape of its wearer." Aziz Siddiqui, "Whose League Is It Anyway?" *Newsline*, September 1993, p 49.

35. For example, in 1965 General Ayub Khan created the PML (Convention) faction of the PML to serve as the "king's party" in the elections held that year. It proved a successful strategy and the pro-Ayub party won 54.8 percent of the vote and 120 of 150 seats in the National Assembly. For further details see Sharif al-Mujahid, "The Assembly Elections in Pakistan," *Asian Survey*, 5 (1965), pp 538–51.

36. In the 2002 elections, no fewer than seven factions of the PML contested:. They were: PML(Functional), PML(Junejo), PML(Jinnah), PML(Nawaz), PML(Qasim), PML(Quaid-i-Azam) and PML(Zia).

37. Saudi Arabia reportedly brokered a deal such that in exchange for Musharraf releasing Nawaz Sharif, he and his family would go into exile and not participate in Pakistani politics for ten years. See Aamer Ahmed Khan, "Turning on the Heat," *The Herald*, September 2002, p 24.

38. Initially, the PML(N) dissidents formed a "Like-Minded" faction of the PML, known as the PML(LM), which, prior to the local government elections in 2001, changed its name to the PML(Quaid-i-Azam Group). Azmat Abbas, "Party Profiles," *The Herald*, October 2002, p 31.

39. *Biradaris* are patrilineal kinship systems that play an influential role in central Punjab politics. For more details on the role of *biradaris* in electoral politics in Pakistan, see Wilder, *The Pakistani Voter*, pp 177–187.

40. In the two months leading up to the elections the press was full of reports of Musharraf's closest advisors as well as the Interservices Intelligence (ISI) officers trying to create a king's party as well as other promilitary electoral alliances. See Zahid Hussain, "How to Steal an Election," *Newsline*, September 2002, pp 17–22, and Zaffar Abbas, "Tailoring Democracy," *The Herald*, October 2002, pp 17–21.

41. For a more detailed discussion of the major determinants of voting behavior in the Punjab, see chapter eight of Wilder, *The Pakistani Voter*, pp 188–214.

42. The military's patronage, however, made many PML(Q) candidates complacent, since they felt that with the military campaigning on their behalf there was little need for them to campaign. The head of the PML(Q), Mian Azhar, hardly campaigned at all, and, much to his and the military's embarrassment, he lost from both the National Assembly constituencies he contested. Author's interview with Zaffar Abbas, Islamabad, November 5, 2002.

43. Hasan Akbar, "The Rise of the King's Party," *Newsline*, October 2002, pp 52–53.

44. It was common to hear the JI referred to as "the brains" and the JUI(F) as "the brawn."

45. Tensions between the Brelvi JUP and the two Deobandi factions of the JUI, as well as tensions between some of the Sunni parties and the Shia Tehrik-i-Islam headed by

Syed Sajid Naqvi, did not bode well for the smooth functioning of the alliance. Rahimullah Yusufzai, "The Mullahs Fight Back," *Newsline*, October 2002, p 77.

46. See Azmat Abbas, "Party Profiles," *The Herald*, October 2002, p 34. See also Massoud Ansari, "Motley Crew," *Newsline*, October 2002, p 35.

47. Ibid., p 35.

48. See concerns raised in the European Union Election Observers Mission, "Interim Report," September 2002.

49. See Article 63 of the Legal Framework Order.

50. Mubashir Zaidi, "Winning Ways," *The Herald,* October 2002, pp 24–27.

51. See Nadeem Iqbal, "Still Going Strong," *Newsline*, October 2002, pp 84–85.

52. See Zahid Hussain, "The General's Selection," *Newsline*, October 2002, pp 19–20.

53. European Union Election Observers Mission, Parliamentary Elections, Pakistan 2002, "Preliminary Statement," October 12, 2002, p 3.

54. Ibid.

55. Zaffar Abbas, "Tailoring Democracy," *The Herald*, October 2002, p 18.

56. Mubashir Zaidi, "Winning Ways," *The Herald*, October 2002, p 25.

57. Figures were compiled by the author based on Election Commission of Pakistan data. Results from three constituencies, NA 111, 262, and 263 were withheld for repolling and are not included in these figures.

58. Ibid.

59. Wilder, *The Pakistani Voter*, pp 170–171.

60. The Abbottabad, Haripur, and Mansehra districts.

61. Statistics compiled by the author from constituency results provided by the Election Commission of Pakistan.

62. Gallup Pakistan and PILDAR, "Who Voted for Whom on October 10, 2002: Findings from an Exit Poll Survey, October 19, 2002."

63. Election Commission of Pakistan data compiled by the author from forty-three urban constituencies of Karachi, Lahore, Faisalabad, Hyderabad, Multan, Gujranwaka, Rawalpindi, Peshawar, Quetta, and Sialkot. Party results were as follows: MMA, 21.7 percent; PPP, 20.6 percent; MQM, 19.2 percent; PML(N), 13.6 percent; and PML(Q), 9.8 percent.

64. Author's interview with Dr. Ijaz Gillani, Gallup Pakistan, Islamabad, November 4, 2002.

65. All statistics in this paragraph are compiled by the author based on data provided by the Election Commission of Pakistan.

66. The MQM, a party whose base of support is in the Urdu-speaking *muhajir* (refugees from India) communities of Karachi and Hyderabad, has swept the polls in urban Sindh since the 1988 elections.

67. Statistics compiled by the author based on data provided by the Election Commission of Pakistan.

68. Statistics compiled by Gallup Pakistan based on data provided by the Election Commission of Pakistan. "Changing Fortunes: Vote Banks of Political Parties in Pakistan," December 2002, p 7.

69. Ibid., p 8.

70. Ibid., p 10.

71. Ibid., p 11.

72. The Jamhoori Watan Party, Balochistan National Movement, Balochistan National Party, and the Pakhtunkhwa Milli Awami Party.

73. Author's interview with Dr. Ijaz Gillani, Gallup Pakistan, November 4, 2002.

74. Aisha Aqeel, "I'm Every Woman," *Newsline*, November 2002, p 71.

75. A survey conducted by an NGO, Pattan, a week before the elections indicated 85.5 percent of men and 74 percent of women planned to vote in the elections. Aziz Jan, "Majority Wants Benazir, Nawaz to Contest Polls, Study." *Dawn*, October 4, 2002.

76. European Union Election Observers Mission, "Preliminary Statement," p 3.

77. See Faraz Hashmi, "Caretakers Can Contest for the Third Time," *Dawn*, October 27, 2002.

78. Mazhar Abbas, "Here Today, Gone Tomorrow," *Newsline*, December 2002, pp 31–33.

79. In a feat of alliteration, the dissident group has reportedly created a new political party named Pakistan People's Party Parliamentarians Patriots (PPPPP), Jalilur Rehman, "Dissidents Add Another 'P' to PPPP," *The News*, November 25, 2002.

80. At the oath-taking ceremony, one military officer was overheard saying, "We are proud of you," to Faisal Saleh Hayat who led the PPP defectors. Staff reporter, "Forward Bloc Bags Six of 21 Cabinet slots," *The News*, November 25, 2002.

81. Syed Bukhar Shahm, "Durrani, Pervaiz NWFP, Punjab CMs," *The News*, November 30, 2002.

82. Muahmmad Ejaz Khan, "Yousaf Sworn in as Balochistan CM," *The News*, December 2, 2002.

83. Tahir Hasan Khan, "Maher Elected Chief Minister," *The News*, December 17, 2002.

84. Quoted by Nasim Zehra in "Power Politics: Old Challenges in the New Phase," *The News*, December 17, 2002.

85. Zahid Hussain, "The Great Gamble," *Newsline*, April 2002, p 18.

86. Tariq Butt, "Amendments Seek Checks on Authority—Musharraf," *The News*, July 4, 2002.

87. See Zahid Hussain, "Of the General, By the General, For the General," *Newsline*, p 20. According to Musharraf, the elections would lead to "a transition from democratic dictatorship to an elected essence of democracy." Zahid Hussain, "How to Steal an Election," *Newsline*, September 2002, p 21.

88. "All that the King's men, with all their wheeling and dealing, coercion and cajoling, and bribing and bamboozling have not been able to deliver is a one-vote majority that is in danger of coming down like a house of cards with the slightest hint of turbulence in the air." Rehana Hakim, Editor's Note, *Newsline*, December 2002, p 13.

6

Pakistan: Economic Challenges for a New Millennium

Bashir Ahmad Khan and Faisal Bari

This chapter examines the genesis of the Musharraf regime in Pakistan in terms of its influence on the economic and financial situation of the country. The chapter attempts to show the interlinkage between past political events and the subsequent military takeover, as well as how the economic and financial situation prevailing in the country today largely stems from a series of actions initiated in the earlier part of the 1990s. In October 1999, when General Pervez Musharraf took over power in Pakistan, through a bloodless coup, he inadvertently set the seal on a decade of political turbulence and economic opportunism in the country. The 1990s had been marked by a political setup that had seen no fewer than four changes of government instigated through executive action, while important progress had been made in the economy. However, since the changes in government were primarily the result of a concern over financial and political overcentralization, economic progress during the 1990s had only gone so far as a consistent stated policy for a return to market forces.

This chapter argues that there has been some institutional change for the better in the country despite the generally uneven economic performance and the overwhelming reliance on financial support from the multilateral donors. It is important to remember that Pakistan's precarious economic situation is closely tied up with its political upheavals. Matters had come to a head in May 1998, when Pakistan undertook a tit-for-tat response to India's nuclear tests in May 1998. In the immediate aftermath of this event, the country suffered from a political isolation never experienced before: suspension from the Commonwealth, the immediate cessation of economic assistance from the G7, and strong pressure from the United States to sign the Nuclear Nonproliferation Treaty. Economically, the country had to adopt draconian measures to shore up its reserves, while renegotiating loans with both domestic and foreign lenders.

The current economic crisis, as well as past crises, has largely been survived owing to the support of the multilateral donors. Following the political crisis stemming from the Kargil operation, in which Pakistani-inspired Kashmiri fighters had occupied strategic hills denying India the ability to resupply its forces in the region, the country had become a pariah.[1] India's response was disproportionate, and although it eventually succeeded in dislodging the relatively small numbers of occupiers of the strategic hills, its operational capabilities were badly exposed. On the other hand, its political response was far more effective. A concerted diplomatic campaign not only succeeded in labeling Pakistan as the culprit, but it raised doubts about who was in control in the country, the civilians or the military. The civilian government's attempt to replace the military planners of the operation was followed by an immediate countercoup, bringing General Pervez Musharraf to power. This chapter examines the economic and financial consequences of this political change and, in particular, looks at how the post–September 11 political climate has permitted Pakistan to take advantage of shifting international priorities.

THE MUSHARRAF TAKEOVER

General Pervez Musharraf took over the government in October 1999. One of the reasons that the general cited for his takeover was the poor economic condition of the country, and he also mentioned that economic betterment would be one of the top priorities of this government. After the takeover, the Supreme Court of Pakistan gave General Musharraf three years (till October 2002) to affect any changes that were necessary before he would have to go back to civilian rule and a democratic system of government, in accordance with the Constitution of Pakistan. Three years were deemed to be enough by the esteemed court, to bring about fundamental institutional and economic changes that the military regime wanted to implement before the introduction of the democratic system.

When the military took over the reins of the country, the economic situation was indeed quite grim. GDP growth rate for 1998 to 1999 was only 4.2 percent.[2] Given that the trend GDP growth rates in Pakistan, till the early 1990s, had been well above 5 percent per annum, the economy was not performing well at all. In fact, economic growth had been much slower throughout the 1990s, compared to the 1980s. The nonspectacular growth performance was true of all sectors of the economy: agriculture grew by only 2 percent, manufacturing by 4.1 percent, and the service sector by 5 percent in 1998 to 99. Total investment declined by 3.6 percent in 1998 to 1999. This was driven largely by a -11.4 percent growth in private investment. Accumulated debt had grown to the point that Pakistan was perpetually on the brink of default on its international debt obligations. Foreign exchange reserves were down to a few hundred million U.S. dollars, and the exchange rate was continually under significant downward pressure.

Part of the poor performance could be attributed to the sanctions that had been placed on Pakistan in the wake of its decision to conduct nuclear fission tests in May 1998, in response to the April 1998 Indian nuclear tests. Whereas the Indian economy, with its larger size, less open nature, stronger reserves, and less accumulated debt, was able to withstand the sanctions more easily, Pakistan was brought to the brink of disaster by the tests. The government was desperately looking for ways of raising foreign currency. It had already confiscated $11 billion held by the Pakistani public, had restricted foreign capital convertibility, was negotiating with lenders for rescheduling and reprofiling, and was even raising very expensive short-term debt from commercial markets. The situation was clearly not sustainable. Hence, the contention of General Musharraf when he took over, that the economy was in a very poor state and needed fundamental reforms to ensure sustainability and a return to decent growth performance, was not unfounded.[3]

By October 2002,[4] the government was claiming that it had delivered on its promise of putting the economy on a much firmer footing and on the path to sustainable growth. In what follows, we will take a detailed look at that claim. We will start with the macroeconomic picture prevailing in October 2002, and then evaluate the performance of the more important sectors of the economy. This will not only allow us to evaluate the condition of the economy and the contributions of the Musharraf government over the last three years, but it will also facilitate our understanding of what the incoming civilian government will be faced with.

MACROECONOMIC PICTURE

The economy grew at about 3.6 percent in 2001 to 2002. Government sources have argued that the slower growth was largely due to two reasons. Firstly, manufacturing grew slower than expected due to the direct and indirect effects of the September 11 attacks in the United States and what has happened since. Apart from the global slowdown induced by the attacks, Pakistan's manufacturing and exports also took a hit due to the "war on terror" conducted in Afghanistan and its fallout on Pakistan. Regular orders were cancelled or got delayed, financial and shipping channels were disrupted, travel to and from Pakistan became difficult, and risk-averse investors became much more cautious about investing overseas.

Where there was indeed some effect of September 11, 2001, on Pakistan's manufacturing sector, we think that attributing the continued slower performance wholly to the event and its fallout is incorrect. We will argue, in the section on manufacturing, that poor manufacturing sector performance is in line with the trend over the last few years, and that there are better explanations of this performance than the events of September 11. These have to do with the collapse in domestic private and public investments, the lack of success in initiating and managing institutional reforms, and the high level of transaction costs that Pakistani businesses have to incur to conduct business in Pakistan.

Secondly, the slower growth of agriculture has been attributed to the effects of the drought that most agricultural areas in Pakistan had to contend with over the last three years. The rains in summer of 2002 have finally ended the drought in most parts of Pakistan. Again, we will show that the drought did have some effect, but there are other reasons for the slower growth in agriculture as well.

These have to do with the significant changes that the government has introduced in the agricultural input and output markets.

The slower growth of the economy has resulted in substantial problems for the population at large. Wages, for unskilled and low skilled, have not kept up with the inflation rates.[5] Unemployment has increased from 5.37 percent in 1996 to 7.82 percent in 2002. Poverty, which was at 17.32 percent (headcount) in 1987 to 1988, has increased to about 32 percent.[6] There is a significant population that subsists around the poverty line and could swell the ranks of the poor significantly if slow growth continues. Inequality, over the same period, has increased substantially. The Gini Coefficient has increased, and the relative share in national income, of the lowest 20 percent of the population compared to the top 20 percent, has declined.[7] Microsurveys[8] show school enrollment rates have declined due to increases in poverty and lack of assurance about rates of return to education. The middle class in Pakistan, apart from the low-income groups, has come under increasing economic pressure in the last decade, and the last three years have not been able to arrest this trend of the 1990s.[9]

GDP growth for 2001 to 2002 was in line with the growth that we have witnessed in the last few years (see Table 6.1). GDP growth rate was much higher in the 1980s, and since then we have had a sustained slowdown. The 1995 to 2000 average, at 4 percent, was slower than the 1990 to 1995 average at 4.9 percent. As Table 6.1 shows, the main reason for the slowdown in GDP growth rate has been the slowdown in the manufacturing sector and especially the very significant slowdown in the large scale manufacturing (LSM) sector. Agriculture, though it has slowed down a bit, and has had a more erratic year-to-year performance, does not explain the slowdown of GDP. Neither does the small slowdown in the services sector. By breaking down the growth contribution to GDP, Bari et. al. (2002) show more rigorously, too, that the slowdown in GDP has largely been due to the slowdown in the manufacturing sector over the 1990s. We will study the trends in manufacturing in more detail below, but clearly the Musharraf government has been unable to reverse the trend of the 1990s, and the 2001 to 2002 performance is not solely due to the international events.

Table 6.1 also sheds some light on the macroeconomic reason for the poor performance of LSM. Total investment, as a percentage of a slow growing GDP, has declined over the 1990s. And the trend has not been reversed in the last three years. From 19.5 percent of GDP in the early 1990s, total investment has come down to only 13.9 percent by 2001 to 2002. Fixed investment also shows a similar trend. It is also important to bear in mind that these figures are for gross investment. If one allowed for replacement investment (depreciation) the relative effect of the slowdown becomes clearer. With 13.9 percent of GDP as total investment, and a depreciation allowance of say 7 percent, we have only about 7 percent of net investment. If conversion rates from investment to growth are about 0.3,[10] with this level of investment, we could only expect growth rates of GDP in the 2 to 3 percent range.

Table 6.1
Growth Performance of Real Sector

Item	Unit	1980s	1990–1995	1995–2000	2000–2001	2001–2002
A. GDP Growth Rate	%	6.1	4.9	4.0	2.5	3.6
a. Agriculture	%	4.1	4.2	4.9	-2.6	1.4
b. Manufacturing	%	8.2	4.8	3.2	7.6	4.4
c. Large-scale Manufacturing	%	8.2	4.7	2.4	8.6	4.0
d. Services	%	6.6	5.1	4.0	4.8	5.1
B. Total Investment	As % of GDP	18.6	19.5	17.1	15.9	13.9
a. Fixed Investment		16.8	18.0	15.3	14.3	12.3
b. Public Investment		9.1	8.6	6.4	6.3	4.7
c. Private Investment		7.8	9.4	8.9	8.0	7.6
C. National Saving	As % of GDP	14.7	14.9	12.7	15.1	15.4
a. Domestic Saving		7.7	13.9	13.8	16.5	14.7

Source: Economic Survey 2001–2002.

The decline in investment is very pronounced for the public sector. Public investments have dropped from 9.1 percent of GDP in the 1980s to 4.7 percent by 2001 to 2002. This has been a deliberate government policy. Given the large and increasing burden of debt servicing, and the significant fiscal deficits that the state had been running, state expenditures had to be slashed from somewhere.[11] Development expenditure and public investments have borne the brunt of public sector expenditure reduction.

Over the same period, private sector investment has not increased to compensate for the reduction in public investment. In fact, private investment has also declined, as a percentage of GDP, over the same period. Initially it was argued that public investment was crowding out private investment. Reductions in public investment were, therefore, expected to be matched by increases in private investment, but this did not transpire. Recent literature has instead talked about the phenomena of the "crowding in" effect of public investment. Public investments, in infrastructure and utility provision (transport, electricity, ports, railway, gas, electricity, water, and sewage), allow more extensive and efficient investments by the private sector. Evidence from Pakistan[12] strongly suggests that poor infrastructure and utility provision is seen as a very binding constraint by potential and existing investors in Pakistan. The decline in public investment might have caused lower private investment in Pakistan. This might also partially explain why substantial reductions in interest rates over the last three years, despite expectations, have not been able to revive private investment in Pakistan.

The last three years have seen substantial changes on the monetary side of the economy. From the brink of default Pakistan has been able to move to a situation where the State Bank of Pakistan (SBP) has foreign currency reserves of over $8.5 billion.[13] These reserves have been built over the period of only about two years. Furthermore, Pakistan has been able to pay off some of the more expensive short-term international debts, was planning to pay off another $3 billion worth of debts in the next year, and was servicing its existing debt without any problems. Over the same period, it has been able to reduce the total debt burden from about $38 billion to $36 billion, has been able to have most of its debt rescheduled to get relief of a decade or more, has been able to renegotiate the terms on many debt contracts, and has also been able to convince the World Bank, the IMF, and the Asian Development Bank (ADB) as well as other lenders and donors to lend generously to Pakistan again.[14]

The stability on the monetary side, discussed in more detail in the section on capital markets below, has led to several desirable outcomes. With the buildup of reserves the pressure of imminent or possible default has receded. This has allowed the government the space to negotiate and renegotiate better terms with lenders. The reserves have also made lenders more willing to lend as the risk of default has reduced substantially.

Foreign exchange market stability has removed the pressure from the exchange rate and the rupee has remained stable for more than a year now. In fact, the SBP has had to intervene in the market a number of times to ensure that the rupee does not appreciate against the dollar. Exchange rate stability has also allowed Pakistan to reduce the effect of imported inflation.

The GDP slowdown as well as tighter monetary policy had brought down the inflation rate in the economy in the 6 to 7 percent per annum range even before General Musharraf had taken over. In fact, inflation, apart from a few years in the early to middle 1990s, has never been a significant problem in Pakistan and has usually been in single digits. The Musharraf years have seen the continuation of the same trend. Inflation has remained low in the 3 to 6 percent range, and has not been a major problem for the government. Even with significant reductions in prime lending rates, inflation is still in the 3 to 4 percent per annum range.

We agree with the numerous other commentators who have argued that the better performance of the economy, on the monetary side, had a lot to do with the impact of the events of September 11 and the "war on terror." Pakistan has so far received $900 million in budgetary support and aid directly from the United States. The United States has also committed some support for the education sector in Pakistan, it has supplied ammunition and other support to strengthen Pakistan's military capability, and it has paid for the logistic support that Pakistan has provided for its forces in Afghanistan. The United States has used its influence to convince the international agencies and other donors and lenders to lend to Pakistan, and it has used its significant powers of persuasion to convince countries not only to give Pakistan some debt relief, but also to contribute to the development of Pakistan through aid. The United States and the European Union have also given Pakistani textile exporters easier access to their domestic markets. All of the above have not only allowed the government to negotiate its outstanding debt, but also have allowed the government to borrow on better terms and to build up its reserves to an extent. After September 11, the United States has also cracked down on money laundering and informal money transfer markets. This has forced Pakistanis working abroad to switch to remitting dollars through the official channels. According to the SBP this alone has allowed the bank to buy or mop up $3 to 4 billion from the markets to build up its reserves. To the extent that September 11 has helped Pakistan improve its condition on the monetary side, Musharraf government's economic policies cannot be seen as a break from the past.

POLICY CONTEXT

In the preceding section we have argued that the economic performance during the Musharraf years does not exhibit any significant deviation from the years leading up to it to allow us to say that the economic policy of the Musharraf years has been able to address the economic issues facing Pakistan. Before we study the important sectors of the economy in detail, to establish the trends more succinctly, we would also like to show that the economic policies followed in the last three years were also not different from what had been followed until then. This makes our case for seeing the Musharraf years as a continuation of the trend of the 1990s even stronger.

By the late 1980s, the continued twin fiscal and foreign exchange deficits, the collapse of textile industry—which was the mainstay of industry and the main foreign exchange earner—, and the decline in foreign aid led the government of Pakistan to seek help and advice from the World Bank and the IMF on an emergency basis. This led to the acceptance of and the implementation of the Structural Adjustment Programs (SAP). These programs, despite their various guises,[15] have had a very high degree of similarity.

On the fiscal side the conditionalities that have accompanied the programs have included target levels for deficits. The agencies have insisted that the government of Pakistan reduce the fiscal deficit by reducing public expenditures and increasing tax revenue. Since the expenditure on debt servicing and defense could not be reduced, and these two expenditures have formed the bulk of public expenditure through most of the 1990s, and there was limited scope for reducing nonproductive expenditure, the conditionality on fiscal deficit has implied significant cuts in development expenditure and expenditure on various subsidies. Table 6.2 shows that development expenditure was reduced from 7.6 percent of total expenditure in 1991 to 1992 to 2.7 percent in 2000 to 2001.

Table 6.2
Fiscal Indicators as Percent of GDP (Market Prices)

Year	Fiscal Deficit	Expenditure			Revenue			
		Total	Current	Dev	Total	Tax	Dir. Tax	Indir. Tax
1990–1991	8.8	25.7	19.3	6.4	16.9	12.7	2.0	10.7
1991–1992	7.5	26.7	19.1	7.6	19.2	13.7	2.5	11.2
1992–1993	8.1	26.2	20.5	5.7	18.1	13.4	2.8	10.6
1993–1994	5.9	23.4	18.8	4.6	17.5	13.4	2.9	10.5
1994–1995	5.6	22.9	18.5	4.4	17.3	13.8	3.4	10.4
1995–1996	6.5	24.4	20.0	4.4	17.9	14.4	3.8	10.6
1996–1997	6.4	22.3	18.8	3.5	15.8	13.4	3.6	9.8
1997–1998	7.7	23.7	19.8	3.9	16.0	13.2	3.9	9.3
1998–1999	6.1	22.0	18.6	3.4	15.9	13.3	3.6	9.7
1999–2000	6.5	23.6	20.4	3.0	17.1	12.9	3.6	9.3
2000–2001	5.3	21.3	19.0	2.7	16.0	13.0	3.9	10.9
2001–2002	5.7	22.5	18.9	3.4	16.8	13.0	4.3	11.3

Source: Economic Survey 2001–2002.

On the revenue side the government of Pakistan has found raising tax revenue to be quite hard. The state has been unable to develop the capacity to levy a broad income-based direct tax. Instead, to raise revenue, it has repeatedly resorted to easy to levy, usually regressive, indirect taxes like excise levies and flat levies on consumption of utilities. Direct taxes tend to be more targeted, progressive, and less distortional. The inability of the state to institute well-designed direct taxes has led to the development of a fairly distortional tax system that has a very high compliance cost and a significant space for rent-seeking activity (corruption). Even where direct taxes have been levied, the state has relied mostly on withholding to ensure compliance. The 1990s also saw the introduction of the General Sales Tax (GST). But the problems mentioned above have also plagued the institutionalization of GST as well. Though its ambit has been broadened to include the sale of most goods, and it has become the largest revenue earner for Pakistan, it has introduced a horde of distortions in the economy, and has created substantial opportunities for corruption. The Musharraf government continued exactly the same policies as the previous governments.

For the last three years the government has not been able to change the expenditure priorities and for the first two years development expenditure had taken the worst hit. It has only been since the change of September 11 that the government has been able to increase development expenditure on the basis of the monetary dividends detailed in Table 6.2.

SAP conditionalities have also included conditions for liberalization of markets. Liberalization of trade markets has been achieved by removing all quotas and quantitative restrictions on trade, lowering of import duties, and removing barriers and taxes from export. Government monopolies on export of agricultural commodities have also been phased out. Standard import duty has been brought down to 25 percent, and the numbers of duty bands have been reduced. These have resulted in substantial reductions in average tariff rates as well as the dispersion in tariff rates.

Capital markets have also been substantially liberalized. The government moved to managed float for Pakistani currency in the late 1980s. Limited capital convertibility was introduced in the early 1990s, and credit markets were liberalized progressively through the 1990s. Banks, financial institutions, leasing and insurance markets, foreign exchange markets, and capital markets had all gone through significant liberalization in the 1990s. The private sector has been allowed a much larger role in most of these markets. The Musharraf government has continued these reforms in the 1999 to 2002 period.

The private sector has been allowed to enter almost all sectors of the economy. Even banking, infrastructure, and utility provision, which were thought to be the preserve of the public sector, have been opened up to the private sector. The private sector now also plays a very important role in social sectors like health and education as well.

Privatization of State Owned Enterprises (SOEs) has been a part of the SAPs as well. Over the years the government of Pakistan has sold most of its holdings in industries like cement, edible oil, textiles, and agro-industry. It has sold three public sector banks and a number of Development Finance Institutions (DFIs), and has plans to sell almost all of the others too. The airline and the telecommunication providers have been corporatized and some of their equity has been sold through the stock markets. The government has plans to sell electricity distribution companies and electricity generation units. The Musharraf government did not only continue the privatization policy, it made it a major priority. A privatization ministry was set up at the federal level in addition to the existing Privatization Commission to facilitate quicker decision making.

We can conclude the discussion up to here by saying that though the Musharraf government made the revival of the economy a major priority, macroeconomic performance over the last three years does not allow us to distinguish this government from the previous ones. The economy faces the same issues it was facing in 1999. There has been some improvement on the monetary side, but this, as we have shown, can be attributed to the international conditions and not the government's economic policies. Furthermore, we have also argued that the policies that the Musharraf government followed have been more or less the same as followed by the previous regimes. They have emanated from the SAPs that the governments had negotiated with the World Bank and the IMF.[16]

To strengthen the case further, we need to study the performance of the important sectors of the economy over the last few years. Performance in the areas of manufacturing, agriculture, and capital markets is detailed below. Apart from allowing us an informed analysis and judgment of the Musharraf years, this will also allow us to identify some of the institutional and policy shortcomings of the previous regimes. These will be important in identifying some of the crucial tasks that the incoming government will have to face.

MANUFACTURING

One of the most established empirical observations about the development process is regarding the structural transformation of the economy as it moves from low income to middle and high income per capita. For low income countries, the share of agriculture to GDP is the largest, while industry contributes little owing to its underdeveloped state.[17] With the increase in income the sectoral share of agriculture to GDP decreases substantially, while the share of industry increases till the economy reaches high-income status and then the share of industry also decreases a bit. The share of the services sector increases steadily and it becomes the largest contributor to the GDP for the high-income countries. For the highest income countries, the service sector contributes the largest, while industry comes in second, and the share of agriculture tends to be very small.[18] Sectoral shares are taken as an indicator of the stage of development as well. Sectoral shares over the 1990s show that the Pakistani economy has been more or less stagnating or changing very slowly (see Table 6.3). This has continued to hold for the last few years as well. In 1990 to 1991 manufacturing contributed 17.4 percent of the GDP, and in 2001 to 2002, it contributed 17.7 percent to GDP. The share of agriculture went down a little over the period, but it was the service sector that saw relative expansion to take up the share of agriculture. Industry's share, through the decade has been more or less stagnant, and the trend was no different over the Musharraf years.

Table 6.1 shows the slowdown in manufacturing—large-scale manufacturing in particular—over the decade. The relative decline in public and private investment, also shown in Table 6.1, explains the slowdown. The government of Pakistan does not report primary statistics for growth rates of small- and medium-scale industries. Instead it relies on imputed figures, and though it also acknowledged that Small and Medium Enterprises (SMEs) grew at 5.31 percent instead of 8 percent that had been reported earlier; this figure is thought to be an overestimate as well. Majid (2000) estimated growth rates of SMEs to be in the range of 2 to 4 percent over the last decade and a half, and he also reported that SME growth has slowed down over the period, though the slowdown is not as

Table 6.3

Sectoral Shares in Real GDP

	1990–1991	1991–1992	1992–1993	1993–1994	1994–1995	1995–1996	1996–1997	1997–1998	1998–1999	1999–2000	2000–2001	2001–2002
Commodity Producing Sectors	51.3	51.7	50.5	50.6	50.7	51.5	50.6	51.4	51.1	50.9	49.8	49.1
a. Agriculture	25.8	26.3	24.4	24.6	24.9	26.1	25.7	26.0	25.4	25.9	24.6	24.1
b. Manufacturing	17.4	17.3	17.7	17.7	17.3	16.8	16.6	17.1	17.1	16.7	17.5	17.7
Services Sector	48.7	48.3	49.5	49.4	49.3	48.5	49.5	48.6	49.0	49.1	50.2	50.9

Source: Economic Survey 2001–2002.

Table 6.4

Agricultural Growth (Percent)

Year	Agriculture	Major Crops	Minor Crops
1991–1992	9.50	15.50	2.40
1992–1993	-5.30	-15.60	3.60
1993–1994	5.20	1.20	12.60
1994–1995	6.60	8.70	6.90
1995–1996	11.70	6.00	4.90
1996–1997	0.10	-4.30	0.90
1997–1998	3.80	8.30	3.30
1998–1999	2.00	-0.02	4.20
1999–2000	6.10	15.10	-9.10
2000–2001	-2.60	-9.80	0.10
2001–2002(P)	1.40	-0.50	1.00
Average	3.50	2.30	2.80

Source: Economic Survey 2001–2002.

pronounced as the slowdown in LSM. Since SMEs depend on the large-scale for demand, it would have been surprising had SMEs not slowed down in the wake of the slowdown in LSM.

The slowdown in the manufacturing sector has occurred concurrently with the government of Pakistan following the SAP programs. With liberalization of most markets it was expected that the growth rate in industry would pick up, and not the opposite. This slowdown thus needs an explanation.

There is little doubt that substantial liberalization has happened in the manufacturing sector. Most licensing requirements were removed in the early 1990s. The government of Pakistan opened almost all sectors in manufacturing to private sector investment. The regulatory framework has been substantially toned down. The government of Pakistan has even allowed foreign investors to own 100 percent equity in most sectors of the economy, has allowed full repatriation of profits, and has a "no questions asked" policy regarding the sources of funds utilized for investment. In addition, there are generous incentives, in terms of lower import duties on machinery import and export finance for exporters, to encourage industrial activity.

The World Bank (2002) attributes the slowdown in manufacturing to deteriorating governance and political stability in the country. "What was new was the way that an accelerating, corrosive deterioration in the governance of public institutions weakened economic management and created an increasingly unfavorable investment climate." But World Bank (2002) does not give convincing evidence of this reading. We think there are other more convincing explanations.

Berry (1998) argued that LSMs are likely to show very little growth in Pakistan for another few years as they are going through a process of adjustment given the liberalization of international trade and capital markets of the last decade. Import tariffs have been decreased substantially, and local industry has had to cope with the new competitive environment. LSM has not had sufficient time to deal with this adjustment. Over the last decade and the next few years, as import duties continue to come down, LSM will go through a major shake up. Industries that cannot be internationally competitive will have to be phased out, while investments will have to move to potentially competitive sectors. The government of Pakistan started reducing import duties in the late 1980s and the slowdown in manufacturing followed shortly afterward. The government has been criticized for not following a rational and phased approach to reduction in duty, which has, according to critics, exacerbated the problems for LSM.

The World Bank (2001) and Bari et al. (2002) show, through primary qualitative, quantitative, and interview data, that businesses in Pakistan consider distortions in financial markets and regulatory framework, poor provision of infrastructure and lacunae in the legal/judicial framework to be binding constraints on expansion of business activities. Most of these distortions have to do with incomplete markets, lack of proper regulatory framework, lack of implementation of the legal framework, and distortions introduced due to the lack of information and implementation. The cost of doing business in Pakistan is much higher, due to these distortions, than in other developing countries and even the countries in the region. Bari et al. (2002) show that Pakistani entrepreneurs spend more time complying with the regulatory framework than do their counterparts in other countries; they pay more for infrastructure facilities, have much less reliable utility and infrastructure service provision, and have to deal with a higher level of rent-seeking activity.

The issue is not lack of regulation. The issue is a transparent and fair regulatory environment that is unambiguously implemented. Some commentators have highlighted the issue by arguing for the need now to have a "second generation of reforms" that focuses on these micro, institutional, legal, and market aspects of reform. SMEs complain of over regulation and list fifty plus regulations that they have to comply with. On the other hand, privatization and entry of the private sector in newly opened sectors have led to complaints of unchecked monopoly power and creation of illegal cartels. This issue of institutionalization and institutional reform will be picked up again in the later section on institutional reforms.

AGRICULTURE

Despite the structural transformation that Pakistan has been undergoing,[19] as it has been "developing," the contribution of agriculture still remains very important for the economy. Nearly 25 percent of total output (GDP) and 44 percent of total employment is generated by agriculture.[20] Agriculture provides for the food requirements of the country, contributes substantially to Pakistani exports, and contributes to growth as the major supplier of raw materials to industry. What happens in agriculture, therefore, is bound to affect not only the country's growth performance, it is likely to affect a large majority of the population directly as well. Any strategy for reviving growth and fighting poverty will depend substantially on robust and sustainable agricultural performance.

Agriculture has grown at an average of 3.5 percent per annum since 1991 to 1992 (Table 6.4). If population growth is taken to be at about 2.5 percent per annum over the decade,[21] agricultural growth has remained above the population growth rate. But the growth rates of major crops at 2.3 percent per annum have not kept up, while the minor crops with 2.8 percent per annum have performed better. Agricultural output has varied significantly over the decade showing growth rates of -5.3 percent in 1992 to 1993 to 11.7 percent in 1995 to 1996. The fluctuations in agriculture are driven largely by variations in output from major crops. While agriculture contracted by 5.3 percent, it was the major crops that had contracted by 15.6 percent. When agriculture grew by 9.5 percent, major crops had grown by 15.5 percent. Agricultural output fluctuates more owing to its dependence on weather and pest attacks, but in Pakistan the fluctuations also have to do with the availability of canal water, electricity to pump groundwater, and the timely availability of seeds, fertilizer, and pesticides. In the last two to three years drought-like conditions have also been a source of disruption for agriculture.

Experts have also pointed out that Pakistan had thus far been enjoying increasing output largely due to increases in area under cultivation. In addition, inputs like water, electricity, and even seed, fertilizer, and pesticides used to be subsidized. Over the last decade the availability of fertile land has become limited, and the government of Pakistan, due to fiscal pressures, as well as the structural adjustment agreements that have been negotiated with the World Bank and the IMF, has removed almost all of the subsidies.[22] On the output side too, the government has reduced its role significantly. Procurement prices are set for the very important crops only, and these too are no longer binding. The government allocates a fixed sum to procure a crop like wheat, and supports the procurement price only as long as the funding lasts. The farmers and the market are on their own afterward. The government is also moving out of the area of crop storage and handling. While export trade has also been opened up, this has ensured, for most of the crops, parity between international and local prices.

The government has argued that the slower growth in agriculture has been the result of the drought that has been plaguing most agricultural areas of Pakistan for the last few years. But this does not come through very clearly from Table 6.5. The availability of water did not decrease for 1998 to 1999 or for 1999 to 2000, and it was only in 2000 to 2001 that water availability went down by more than 30 percent. But agriculture had posted a growth rate of 2 percent in 1998 to 1999 as well. It is also interesting to note that the drought has not had any appreciable effect on the number of tube wells (Table 6.5). Furthermore, it is important to note that credit disbursement started declining from 1999 to 2000, and there was a very large dip in 2000 to 2001. Though the table does not clarify if it was the demand that decreased or the supply, but since the supply of funds to agriculture are determined by government policy, the lower disbursement is likely to be a supply issue. The explanation for lower output and slower performance of agriculture might thus have to do with the decrease in agricultural credit availability.

During the 1990 to 2002 period, the prices of agricultural commodities, food, and beverages increased in the range of 85 to 180 percent, the prices of fertilizer (agricultural input) increased by 100 to 400 percent. The prices of other inputs like electricity, oil, seeds, water, and pesticides also increased substantially over the same period. Again, some explanation for the poor performance of agriculture might be culled from these changes in prices.

REFORM IN THE FINANCIAL SECTOR[23]

The country's financial sector largely reflected the trend and direction of government policy in terms of its growth, structure, size, and operations during the decade of the 1990s, and the period after as well. Throughout the 1990s, the keyword was reform, characterized by both liberalization and deregulation, as well as by specific institutional and structural changes to support the financial services industry. As a result, the services sector as a whole had taken second place to agriculture in terms of contribution to GDP growth over the decade.

Table 6.5
Basic Data on Agriculture

Years	Water Availability (MAF)	Credit Disbursed (Rs Million)	Tubewells (Nos.)
1995–1996	130.85	19,187.31	485,050
1996–1997	132.05	19,547.67	489,601
1997–1998	122.15	33,392.30	531,259
1998–1999	133.78	43,683.65	531,298
1999–2000	133.28	40,188.63	531,344
2000–2001	97.01	29,101.41	531,390
2001–2002	—	32,599.65	—

Source: Economic Survey, 2001–2002.

The 1990s were characterized by a series of reform measures in the financial sector, as it emerged from the straightjacket of twenty years of nationalization (see Table 6.6). The stated objectives of the reform measures included the creation of a level playing field for financial markets and institutions, greater competition, a more positive investor response, improved governance, and a move toward a market-based system of monetary, exchange, and credit management. These objectives were translated by a series of policy measures on the ground, in the form of liberalization, institutional development, debt and monetary management, banking operations, and the foreign exchange and capital markets. Their impact was partly reflected in greater financial deepening and improved efficiency.

First, there was wholesale liberalization of the financial sector, particularly the all-important banking sector. This involved granting licenses to private companies to operate commercial banks, in an obvious reversal of policy over the previous two decades, and the sale of two large, well-known state-owned banks, Muslim Commercial Bank and Allied Bank to private groups. It also involved sanctioning the entry and operations of a range of financial intermediaries operating at the margins of banking, including asset management companies, discount houses, and investment banks.[24] Finally, the decade also saw asset restructuring in the state-owned development banks, and their subsequent sale to the private sector (Table 6.7).

Table 6.6
Financial Sector Summary, 1990–2000

	Amount (Rs. Billion)		CAGR (%)	Shares (%)		As % of GDP	
	1990	2000		1990	2000	1990	2000
Assets							
Private	43	856	34.9	5.3	30.0	5.0	26.9
Public	649	1,771	10.6	94.7	70.0	75.8	55.6
Total	692	2,627	14.3	100.0	100.0	80.8	82.5
Deposits							
Private	27	614	36.7	6.2	32.6	3.2	19.3
Public	482	1,436	11.5	93.8	67.4	56.3	45.1
Total	509	2,050	15.0	100.0	100.0	59.5	64.4

Source: State Bank of Pakistan.

Table 6.7
Banking Sector in the 1990s

	Amount (Rs Billion)		CAGR (%)	Shares (%)		As % of GDP	
	1990	2000		1990	2000	1990	2000
Assets							
Private	33	755	36.6	7.8	46.0	3.9	23.7
Public	392	885	8.5	92.2	54.0	45.8	27.8
Total	425	1,640	14.4	100.0	100.0	49.7	51.5
Deposits							
Private	25	579	37.0	7.0	43.8	2.9	18.2
Public	330	744	8.5	93.0	56.2	38.5	23.4
Total	355	1,323	14.1	100.0	100.0	41.4	41.6

Source: State Bank of Pakistan

Second, debt management was subject to major reform during the 1990s. During the 1990s, the total debt of the country increased from Rs 381.3 billion (1990) to Rs 1,800 billion (2001). The domestic debt component of this amount increased from 44.5 percent of GDP to 51.6 percent.[25] This was comprised of permanent debt composed of market loans and government issue bonds, floating debt composed of treasury bills and money market instruments, and the unfunded debt made up of certificates of deposit (CODs) issued by the government-owned National Savings Organisation. As a percentage of GDP, all the components of debt increased during the period 1980 to 2001. However, in the period 1990 to 2001, the permanent debt declined, while the floating debt and unfunded component increased.

Many of the high-cost COD schemes of the National Savings Organisation were withdrawn and rates were reduced. At the same time, the government shifted toward a system of auctions on tap for treasury bills (as opposed to ad hoc auctions), as well as introducing a three-day repo facility at the central bank. Institutionally, a system of primary market dealers was established to bring greater depth to the auction market. The major impact of this change was the rationalization of short-term rates in the money market, which together with the rate in the call money market, reflected market conditions. Consequently, there was an across the board decline in the expansion of domestic debt during the 1990s, and especially during the period 1995 to 2000, as the annual rate of expansion fell by five percentage points.

Third, successive governments accepted the need to undertake reform of the credit mechanism. The system of credit ceilings and credit deposit ratios at the national level had neither succeeded in ensuring that credit was disbursed to cutting edge business and industry, nor in setting up a viable credit management system. Increasingly, banks were permitted to operate with a freedom that was essentially proscribed only by the new Prudential Regulations (introduced in 1992). The latter was part of the overall reexamination of banking laws in the country. This had become necessary given the rapid growth of financial assets, and the inability of the regulator to evolve with the growing sophistication of the market place. One result was the increasing autonomy granted to the central bank.

As a consequence of these moves, concessionary credit declined from 44.2 percent of total credit in 1990 to 31.4 percent in 2000. This signalled greater profitability for the commercial banks, and the decade also saw some of the highest spreads ever recorded for the banking industry anywhere in the world, with average spreads increased from 4.7 percent in 1980 to 1985 to 6.8 percent in 1990 1995 and 8.2 percent in 1995 to 2000.[26] At the same time there was a shift in bank credit from the government and the public sector enterprises toward the private sector—a trend that continued in 2001 with manufacturing receiving some 60 percent of all private sector credit. The counter argument to the spreads was that they could also be reflective of a deeply fragmented financial sector, and the banks were simply taking advantage of non–market-determined deposit rates, as well as information asymmetries. This suggested that there was still some way to go to achieve levels of efficiency commensurate with international banking. With regard to the direction of credit, gross domestic credit to the government actually increased due to the heavy reliance on SBP credit.

Reforms impacting on the liberalization of interest rates in the financial system had to be accompanied by measures on capital mobility and foreign exchange rate parities. The Pakistani rupee was placed on a free float against a basket of currencies, with the original rate sheet eliminated in early 1998. However, reform of the foreign exchange regime was drastically affected by the country's decision to "go nuclear" in response to the Indian tests of May 1998. A series of sanctions were imposed on Pakistan and India due to their nonsubscription to nonproliferation. With regard to Pakistan these sanctions were in addition to those introduced through the Pressler Amendment and its enforcement by ex-President Bush in 1989. The chief impact was on (a) financial support from the European Community, (b) U.S. financial support for development projects, (c) budgetary support from Japan (of almost $500 million a year), and (d) more stringent conditions from both the multilateral lenders, the IMF, and the World Bank.

Two immediate consequences included a rapid fall of the rupee versus the dollar, as well as equally rapid draining of the limited reserves available to the country. By the year 2001, the rupee was trading at about 30 percent of its value in 1990 against the dollar. The reserves position over the decade actually improved from $0.3 billion to $1.5 billion. However, these reserves also included the foreign currency deposits mobilized by the banking system from resident Pakistanis, and constituted an effective dollar liability owed to the general public. As a result, when the SBP froze all foreign currency accounts, and eliminated depositors' access to these accounts, it effectively generated a default on foreign exchange liabilities internally.[27] This was followed by a default and renegotiation on internal rupee credit granted by the private banking sector, and finally, by the renegotiation of the privately generated debt in the Euromarkets, owed to the Paris Club.

Finally, there was considerable reform in the capital market throughout the decade. This was both the result of and the precursor to the tremendous growth of the main stock exchange in Karachi. The major changes included deregulation of initial public offering pricing and underwriting fees, sanctioning of new financial intermediaries, such as mutual funds, in the private sector, the growth of corporate brokerage houses, availability of discount facilities, automation of exchanges, operational autonomy for the Securities and Exchange Commission of Pakistan, and a revision of the corporate laws. Thus, the period 1991 to 2001 saw a substantial growth of activity in the equity market, despite the recession (1996) and the nuclear tests (1998). The number of listed companies increased from 497 to 762 over the decade, with market capitalization increasing from Rs 90 billion to Rs 392 billion. On the other hand, the Karachi Stock Exchange Index rose from 1855 to an all-time high in 1994 only to fall to about 40 percent of its value in 1998. The Exchange recovered by the year 2000 to 1521, but fell again in 2001 to 1366. Capitalization also declined, to Rs 339 billion, but of greater concern was the decline in funds mobilized from Rs 8 billion (2000) to Rs 3.6 billion in 2001.

By and large, the substantive changes undertaken during the decade of the 1990s largely came to a standstill by the early part of the new century owing to political and economic uncertainty. While the commitment to liberalization during this period had been maintained by successive governments—including two interim governments following the presidential right of dissolving the assemblies under the much maligned Eighth Amendment to the Constitution—, to some extent this liberalization strategy became a cat and mouse game of showmanship with the multilateral lending agencies. The key issue for the country was the uniform absence of sustained foreign investment which would have given industry a boost and provided the playing arena for the relatively sophisticated financial system. In fact, statistics suggest that the total amount of foreign investment entering the country during the decade was in the region of about US$100 to 150 million a year, and this was only because of the receipts generated by the sale of Pakistan Telecommunications Corporation Limited in 1996.

Currently, financial market activity has picked up largely as a result of growth in the cotton sector. Pakistan is not a financial center per se and therefore there is hardly any investment banking activity in the country. Indeed, corporate banking in its conventional meaning was limited to satisfying the needs of the cotton textiles exporting clients through refinancing facilities or providing running finance to large Pakistani or multinational companies, the so-called blue chips or names. Otherwise banks are neither in the forefront of creating new niches or segments such as the potentially rapid growth SME sector, nor are they major corporate innovators.

Consequently, the financial sector is seeing major structural reform through mergers and acquisitions. This is both vertical and horizontal, as smaller commercial banks are swallowed up and as other financial intermediaries merge with commercial banks to create large universal banks. Official policy has encouraged this trend: minimum capital requirements, capital adequacy rules, adjustments in balance sheets to account for credit quality, have all contributed to this change. In all likelihood, Pakistan will see a transition to universal banking in the next five years (including Islamic banking), but the intermediaries will be limited to about four key foreign players, and an equal number of major local players. This will probably also help the government to continue with its policy of stabilization, since it will be easier to coordinate the activities of a few large players through moral suasion, a very common practice in the financial sector in the past.

INSTITUTIONAL REFORM

The Musharraf government continued the reforms that had been started in the previous regimes, under the auspices and watchful eye of the World Bank and the IMF. We have argued that not only were the policies more or less the same, the outcomes were similar as well. The slowdown in the economy, the collapse of investment, the faltering performance of manufacturing, and the relative stagnation in agriculture has been the trend in the last decade. Musharraf policies and reforms have not been able to address and reverse the trend. There have definitely been changes on the financial and monetary side, but these, we have argued, have been the result of international events rather than the outcomes of policy options followed by the Musharraf government.

The Musharraf government had, soon after its inception, clearly stated that institutional reforms would form the backbone of their policy making. The government stated that there would be basic and fundamental changes in the local government, judicial and legal areas, police, bureaucracy, fiscal administration, banking and financial markets, monetary authority, infrastructure provision, regulation, health, education and social welfare, human resource development, and science and technology. But the government was not able to deliver on most of these promises.

The government considered reform in fiscal administration and tax structure to be extremely important. Soon after assuming power the Musharraf government announced a number of initiatives in the fiscal area to increase the tax base, revamp tax administration, reduce rent-seeking by the Central Board of Revenue (CBR) officials, and facilitate compliance by reducing the cost of compliance. These initiatives included a tax survey, carried out with the help of military personnel, of business and residential premises to gather information on potential tax payers, numerous studies to work out the changes that needed to be introduced in the tax administration to facilitate compliance and reduce rent-seeking, induction of private sector people in the CBR, and schemes to "whiten" past assets so that they could be declared and brought into the tax net for the future. But after all of these exercises, very few changes have been implemented successfully in the CBR, and the CBR has successfully resisted government efforts to alter the rules of business in the CBR. Tax collection has not changed significantly in the last three years, none of the taxes have shown the elasticity that was expected, and there has been no qualitative or quantitative change in the perceptions of taxpayers regarding the difficulties of dealing with the tax officials.[28]

The same kinds of results have also taken place in other areas. Reforms in health and education sectors have either failed or have not delivered as yet. Infrastructure provision continues to be considered as a key binding constraint to business expansion and investment. Even the fate of the devolution exercise is still undecided. We will not comment on institutional reforms in noneconomic areas, except to say that in none of the areas have we had results that have been regarded by most commentators as very positive. But these areas should be analyzed by those who have expertise in those areas.

Where the reforms have seemed to work has been in the area of monetary and financial sector institutions. As a result of both donor pressure and the rapid growth of financial intermediation in the country, the government initiated institutional reforms, which led to the restructuring of the SBP. By the end of the decade, the bank had greater operational autonomy, enjoyed more public confidence, and had initiated a series of internal reforms to improve its capability in the arena of banking regulation and monetary management. Another critical area was a restructuring process initiated in a number of state-owned commercial and development banks,[29] with the emphasis on credit risk. The central bank supported these initiatives by establishing a Credit Information Bureau, and, more importantly, through the introduction of Prudential Regulations for banking and nonbanking operations.

A brief compendium of changes in the financial sector in the recent past reflects the strong emphasis on improving governance, especially of the two regulators, the SBP and the Securities and Exchange Commission of Pakistan (SEC). As far as central banking is concerned, the country has seen major revisions to the Prudential Regulations (1992), which have increasingly brought them in line with relevant operational regulations in Europe and the United States. Among the critical changes, there have been structural reforms separating the role of the SBP as regulator of the commercial banks (and also a number of nonbank financial institutions) from its role as a monetary manager and the transfer of this responsibility to the Pakistani SEC. A similar fate is intended for the commercial banks, although such a move has its own risks.[30]

However, as in many countries where institutional development is often not formalized, the degree of autonomy enjoyed by public sector institutions appears to be closely interlinked with the strength and personality of the top management; it is also closely associated with the support that top management can muster from the multilateral lenders. Thus there is a constant concern that the extent of reform is closely associated with the level of support enjoyed by top regulatory management from the multilateral agencies to which they formally belonged. History has shown that civilian governments have frequently reversed such trends toward operational autonomy in the name of democracy.

CONCLUSION

This chapter examined the critical economic and financial issues facing Pakistan as it entered a new century following a decade of political turbulence. The 1990s, which saw successive governments act in a matter detrimental to the democratic process, also saw agreement on certain economic fundamentals. These included a commitment to liberalization, privatization, and a strong emphasis on strategic industry. At the same time, agriculture remained largely at the mercy of the weather, and this was reflected in the largely stagnant position of the country's export sector, which was heavily dependent on agriculture. The financial sector, which to many reflected the country's commitment to reform, had mixed results in terms of achievements.

Many of the problems arose from a liberalization policy, which was the result of a latent desire to fulfill donor expectations and hence qualify for additional financial support, rather than a political commitment to market-based reforms. Consequently, some of the policies were both shortsighted and short lived, including the focus on strategic sectors, as well as the privatization of financial assets. The military coup in 1999, further delayed many announced initiatives. This chapter has largely tried to assess the character of the Musharraf regime in tackling the economic and financial problems carried over from the 1990s and the country's economic performance since then.

Leaving aside the political background of the changes, there is no doubt that a strong commitment toward fiscal and monetary reform was required, much stronger than previous governments had been able to provide. At the same time, this chapter shows how deep structural problems continue to hamper progress, and rather circumstantial events have actually combined to put the Musharraf regime in a position to deal with these problems with the support of the international community. This is a rather ironical situation for the general.

While part of the political isolation of the country was the result of the Kargil fiasco, the events of September 11, 2001, have permitted General Musharraf to carry through a relatively austere economic program, while building up some of the needed institutional capacity, which will attract both local and foreign investment beyond the short run. It could be argued that a complete overhaul of the country's economic and financial institutions alone would justify his takeover of the government. However, areas that need major attention include fiscal reform (which has so far proved elusive), as well as a revival of investment in industry, which is the key to long-term economic stability. These are major challenges for the new civilian government.

NOTES

1. For a recent, relatively nonacademic discussion of Kargil and Kashmir, see Jones.

2. All figures in this chapter, unless otherwise stated, come from the *Economic Survey 2002.*

3. Whether the contention justified the takeover or not is a different matter.

4. The elections to the National Assembly and the provincial legislatures took place on October 10, 2002. The civilian government was in the process of taking over as this chapter was being written.

5. Over the 1990–2001 period wages for unskilled workers have increased by about 140 percent, while the Consumer Price Index (CPI) has risen by 150 percent.

6. See Asian Development Bank (2002).

7. See Table 4.1, p 48, chapter 4 of the *Economic Survey, 2001–2002.*

8. See study by Systems Ltd.

9. Over the last year, the overall increase in the CPI was about 3 percent, but the CPI increase for for the income group earning between Rs 3001 and Rs 5000 per month was about 5.1 percent.

10. This is not out of line with the experience of most developing countries.

11. This has also been a condition of the IMF and the World Bank in lending to Pakistan in the 1990s.

12. See Bari, Cheema, and Haque (2002) and World Bank (2001) for details.

13. Out of the $8.5 billion debt, about $6 billion are held in the State Bank of Pakistan while the remainder is deposited in other banks.

14. It is likely that $1 billion of debt will be written off by the United States in January 2003. Legislation to this effect is in the U.S. Congress currently.

15. The latest guise is the Poverty Reduction Growth Facility (PRGF).

16. It is interesting to note that the growth slowdown in Pakistan has happened at the same time that SAPs have been implemented. The experience of India and Bangladesh stands in sharp contrast to that of Pakistan. In those two countries, growth increased after the introduction of reforms. We do not address the interesting cross-country questions this contrast raises.

17. Agriculture also provides most of the employment for low-income countries.

18. For the high-income countries, most of the workforce is employed in the service sector, followed by industry. Employment in agriculture is a very small proportion of overall employment.

19. See Table 6.3.

20. 67 percent of the Pakistani population lives in rural areas and depends, directly or indirectly, on agriculture for their livelihood.

21. See page 165 of the *Economic Survey 2001–2002* for the exact yearly growth rate figures.

22. There might be some subsidy in the provision of water yet, but others have been removed.

23. For a review of this period see Khan (1998). This section draws heavily on statistics in *Pakistan: Financial Sector Assessment, 1990–2000.*

24. There is some debate that the actual date for the initiation of reforms in Pakistan is 1998, when the government of Pakistan sanctioned the entry of private investment banks through a Presidential Ordinance. Shortly afterward, the government also sold a 10 percent stake in the national airline, Pakistan International Airline. For all practical purposes, the announced reforms in 1991 mark a watershed in the move toward market forces.

25. State Bank of Pakistan, 2002.

26. Ibid.

27. Amounting to $11 billion.

28. This has been established in Bari et al., 2002, and World Bank, 2001.

29. These were called Development Finance Institutions (DFIs), which numbered fourteen institutions at their peak.

30. A more appropriate response would be to create a federally chartered "Pakistan Deposit Insurance Corporation" and transfer responsibility for regulating commercial bank activities to such a body.

BIBLIOGRAPHY

Asian Development Bank, *Poverty in Pakistan: Issues, Causes and Institutional Responses*, Islamabad: Asian Development Bank, 2002.

Bari, F., Cheema A., and Haque E., *Regulatory Impediments, Market Imperfections and Firm Growth: Analyzing the Constraints to SME Growth in Pakistan*, A Study Conducted for the Asian Development Bank (ADB), 2002.

Berry, A., *The Potential Role of the SME Sector in Pakistan in a World of Increasing International Trade,* The Pakistan Development Review, 37:4, Part I (Winter 1998), 25–49.

Cloughly, B., *The Pakistan Army* (Revised Edition), Karachi: Oxford University Press 1999.

Government of Pakistan, *Economic Survey 2001–2002*. Economic Advisor's Wing, Finance Division, Ministry of Finance, 2002.

Jones, O. B., *Pakistan: The Eye of the Storm*, New Haven, Conn.: Yale University Press, 2002.

Khan, B. A., "Financial Markets and Economic Development in Pakistan" in S. R. Khan (ed.), *Fifty Years of Pakistan's Economy*, Karachi: Oxford University Press, 1999.

Majid, N., *Pakistan: Employment, Output and Productivity*, Issues in Development, Discussion Paper 33, International Labor Organization, Geneva, 2000.

State Bank of Pakistan, *Pakistan: Financial Sector Assessment, 1990–2000*, Islamabad, 2002.

State Bank of Pakistan, *Annual Report 2001–2002*. Islamabad, 2002.

Systems Ltd., *Determinants of Primary Level Enrollment in Selected Tehsils of Punjab*, Study for the Multi Donor Support Unit, 2002.

World Bank, *Pakistan: Towards a Private Sector Strategy*, Islamabad: World Bank, 2002.

World Bank, *Pakistan: SME Policy Note*, World Bank, Islamabad, 2001.

7

Implementing Devolution: The New Local Government Scheme

Robert LaPorte Jr.[1]

In response to a request by the government of Pakistan, the World Bank developed "A Framework for Civil Service Reform in Pakistan."[2] The document listed seven problems or shortcomings facing Pakistan, three of which relate directly to the organization and functioning of government and the subject of local government. The three are:

> An *over-centralized organizational structure*, as well as rigid, often irrelevant, and unevenly enforced rules and management [that] are inappropriate for most public sector activities, result in delays in responding to clients and distract senior officers from strategy formulation, policy making, and results-oriented management;
>
> Seriously eroded internal accountability and lack of accountability to the public. As a result of its colonial heritage and long years of military dictatorship, the *civil service's accountability to the public has always been very limited*; and
>
> Politicization of civil service decision-making. Political interference has reduced the effectiveness and professionalism of the civil service, while at the same time *politicians have often failed to exercise their oversight role in the wider public interest.*[3]

Pakistan has been a federal system since Independence in August 1947, but has functioned as a unitary system. Although the provinces have powers separate from the central government, the latter controls finance (95 percent of all public finance is controlled by the center) and the deployment of personnel.[4]

The civil service's limited accountability to the public can be traced back to the early days of independence. Mohammad Ali Jinnah as governor general continued the viceregal system, whereby the governor general (and later the president) dealt directly with civil servants, often bypassing ministers. After Jinnah's death in 1948, successive governors general and later presidents (the 1956 Constitution changed the title of the head of state to president) continued the viceregal system.

There has been a tendency among national leadership—civilian and military alike—to monopolize power and decision making, reducing the oversight role of the average political officeholder. If the amount of leakage and "rent seeking" alleged to take place in Pakistan is accurate, the average officeholder is more concerned with getting his or her "share" than with overseeing the civil service for the greater public good.

In its 1998 report, the World Bank recommended devolution as one means to improve government in Pakistan. However, there is no evidence that the government of Nawaz Sharif (who requested that the World Bank develop the framework for civil service reform) acted on the Bank's recommendations. Instead, reform in government structure and functioning was to await the fourth military takeover in Pakistan's fifty-five year history.

To explore reforms in government focusing on the local level that have taken place since October 1999, we will examine (1) the concept of devolution (Local Government Plan 2000), (2) the implementation of the concept, and (3) reform of police through Police Order 2002. The conclusion will summarize and evaluate briefly, Pakistan's attempts to devolve.

CONCEPTUALIZING DEVOLUTION: LOCAL GOVERNMENT PLAN 2000

Why Devolution?

Upon assuming power after the October 12, 1999 coup, General Pervez Musharraf was confronted with two interrelated political problems of significant dimensions, the polity and the organization and functioning of the government. The third problem was the economy and that is discussed in another chapter in this book. In his address to the nation on October 16, 2000, General Musharraf said that devolution of powers was the sixth point of his seven-point agenda.[5]

For many Pakistanis, the fourth military coup since Pakistan's independence was not a surprise. The takeover met minimal if any opposition. However, to many Western and Pakistani critics, military coups are "out of fashion." Except when foreign policy considerations outweigh rule of law, human rights, civil society, devolution, and other characteristics attributed to democratization, the United States and other Western countries have pushed good governance (defined as democratization accompanied by economic liberalization) as a development agenda item with Third World countries with some vigor since the end of the Cold War.

In 1999, Pakistan's international environment was hostile to the new military-led government. With the withdrawal of Soviet armed forces from Afghanistan in 1989, Pakistan lost its status as a Frontline State. Two years later, President George Bush could no longer maintain that Pakistan was not developing a nuclear bomb and this action triggered an end of U.S. assistance to Pakistan. In the mid-1990s, Pakistan came close to being listed by the U.S. Department of State as a country that harbored terrorists. This did nothing to enhance Pakistan's international reputation. The cultivation of opium poppy, its refinement into heroin, and its transport from Pakistan to Western countries (an issue of contention between the United States and Pakistan since the Soviet invasion of Afghanistan in 1979, when these illicit activities moved across the border into the tribal areas of Pakistan) as well, tarnished the industrialized countries' view of Pakistan and its government. Transparency International's assessment of Pakistan as having one of the world's most corrupt governments[6] was still further condemnation of an almost bankrupt country. Finally, in 1998, Pakistan joined the "nuclear club" by exploding two nuclear bombs. As a result, the United States imposed economic sanctions. The government of Pervez Musharraf had to do something to change world perceptions of Pakistan. To appease both domestic and foreign critics, the government focused first on the devolution of power and resources through the development of a new local government system.

Encouraging developing countries to devolve power and resources internally has been part of international and bilateral development assistance programs for more than a decade. Pakistan's dependence on Official Development Assistance has caused it to be receptive to the development advice of donors.[7] By 1999, Pakistan's new leaders felt compelled to initiate a process that would lead to increased decentralization, if not full-fledged devolution. This is reflected in the World Bank's "Pakistan: A Framework for Civil Service Reform in Pakistan" cited earlier, where the authors of the report attempted to distinguish decentralization from devolution:

> [Pakistani] federal and provincial government officials agree[d in 1998] that "decentralization" can help redress the problems resulting from an unresponsive and unaccountable civil service. [Nevertheless], a distinction needs to be drawn between decentralization (which preserves the line of command from decentralized bodies to the central bureaucracy) and devolution (or the transfer of substantive authority to a lower government tier). For various reasons, there appears to be more willingness to proceed with decentralization than with devolution. [8]

The Process

The Musharraf government initiated the process of what it calls devolution by establishing the National Reconstruction Bureau (NRB) and appointing Lt. Gen. (Rtd.) S. Tanwir H. Naqvi as chairman. The first task of the NRB was to develop a plan. The product was the Local Government Plan 2000 (the Plan will be referred to as LG Plan). The LG Plan 2000 had several authors, including Chairman Naqvi, one District Management Group (DMG) officer and several serving or retired members of the Police Service.[9] The Plan itself is a thirty-three page document with seven sections, including the District, Tehsil, Union, Village Council, City District, Police and Local Government Systems.

The Product: Local Government Plan 2000

The LG Plan begins with a condemnation of the existing (i.e., pre-Musharraf) local government scheme:

> In the existing system of governance at the local level, the province governs the districts and tehsils directly through the bureaucracy at the division, district, and tehsil levels. And the local government for towns and cities exist separately from those of the rural areas. The provincial bureaucratic set-ups are the designated "controlling authorities" of the local governments and tend to undermine and over-ride them, which breeds a colonial relationship of "ruler" and "subject." The separate local government structures engender rural–urban antagonism, while the administration's role as "controlling authorities" accentuates the rural–urban divide.[10]

The LG Plan also criticizes those civil servants (primarily District Management Group [DMG] officers and Provincial Civil Service [PCS] officers) who administered the system, serving as commissioners (of divisions), deputy commissioners (of districts), and assistant commissioners (of sub-districts):

> The two structural and systemic disjoints mentioned above, coupled with the absence of horizontal integration and the consequent inadequacy of functional coordination between the line departments at the division, district, and tehsil levels, lead to inefficiency and corruption and are the root causes of the crisis of governance at the grass root [sic] level. The crisis appears to have been addressed through over concentration of authority, particularly in the office of Deputy Commissioner, which, besides creating the potential for abuse of authority, diffuses operational focus and results in the expedient handling of routine functions through crisis management.[11]

The System's Five Fundamentals

The design of the new Local Government System was

> based on five fundamentals: devolution of political power, decentralization of administrative authority, deconcentration of management functions, diffusion of the power-authority nexus, and distribution of resources to the district level. It is designed to ensure that the genuine interests of the people are served and their rights safeguarded. The new system will create an enabling environment in which the people can start participating in community welfare and be the masters of their own destiny.[12]

The basis of the design included all the keywords and phrases associated with devolution, including devolution, decentralization, deconcentration, diffusion and distribution of power, authority, management functions, power-authority nexus, and resources. On reading this portion of the document, the impression one receives is that the Musharraf government is intent on developing a totally new local government system, eliminating the last vestiges of colonial administration. The district was the keystone of area administration in British India. It continued to be the keystone of independent Pakistan. The LG Plan 2000 promised a serious departure from history and tradition.

Structure

The needs of the districts that do not have large cities within their borders are those addressed by the Local Government System. The principal cities are designated as city districts and for a city district "the Local Government Plan . . . is not an option."[13] Structurally, local governments are:

> formed at three levels: District, Tehsil [sub-district], and Union [a sub-division of a sub-district]. Each will comprise its Nazim ["leader"] and Naib Nazim ["deputy leader"], its elected body, and its administrative structures. To involve people more actively in community development, grassroot organizations like the Village Councils and Citizen Community Boards have been introduced. The scheme provides for monitoring the functioning of government and delivery of services by the citizens and their representatives at all levels.[14]

Each level has a political chief executive (nazim), a council (legislative body), and an administration (headed by a civil servant). With the abolition of divisions (and the commissioners that headed them), the districts deal directly with their provincial governments. With the abolition of the deputy commissioner (held by a civil servant and the most important position in the district prior to the introduction of the new local government system), the District Coordination Officer (DCO) "who will be a Civil Servant [at Grade 20 level]"[15] coordinates the district administration rather than administers the district. The DCO reports to the zila (district) nazim who is "the executive head of the district [with] its administration and the police answerable to him [i.e., the zila nazim]."[16] In terms of power, authority, and resources, the most important level is the district, followed by the teshil, and then the union.

The major change in district administration that the LG Plan called for was in the role of the civil service. The deputy commissioner was replaced with the district coordination officer. The DCO coordinates the district administration and is assisted by executive district officers (who head district offices), district officers (who head suboffices) and deputy district officers "in charge of specific functions located at Tehsils."[17]

Leadership

The most important position at the district level is the zila nazim (district leader). Both the zila nazim and the naib zila nazim (deputy district leader) are elected as joint candidates by the district's electoral college composed of the union councilors of the district. The zila council is composed of union nazims who are elected directly by the people of their union. The zila nazim:

> will provide political leadership for the development of the district and will be in a position to influence policies that could improve both the current quality of life and the future development prospects of a district. In collaboration with the Tehsil Nazims, the Zila Nazim will create a development vision for the district integrating the roles and resources of the administration, private sector, civil society organisations, and local level institutions. This vision will be realised through development plans and budget[s] that the Zila Nazim will submit to the Zila Council for approval."[18]

In addition to serving as the zila nazim's deputy, the niab zila nazim is the speaker of the zila council, playing a liaison role between the zila nazim and the zila council. The zila nazim is not a member of the zila council.

Functions and Responsibilities

The principal function to be performed by the new system is development. Of the eleven suboffices in average district office six of the eleven would include such development activities as:

> *Works and Services:* Housing and Rural Development, Water Supply and Sanitation, Building and Roads, Energy and Industrial Promotion, and Transport.
>
> *Agriculture:* Agriculture (Extension), Livestock, Irrigation and Drainage, Fisheries, and Forests.
>
> *Health:* Public Health, Environment, Basic and Rural Health Units, Child and Woman [sic] Health, and Population Welfare. The Medical Superintendent(s) of hospitals will also function under this office.
>
> *Education:* Boys Schools, Girls Schools, Technical Education, Colleges, and Sports (education).
>
> *Literacy:* Literacy campaigns, Continuing Education, and Vocational Education.
>
> *Community Development:* Local Government Institutional Development, Community Organization, Labor, Social Welfare and Special Education, Sports and Culture, Registration, and Cooperatives.[19]

The other five suboffices were to include Finance and Planning, Information Technology, Revenue, Law, and Magistracy. Missing is the police function, that in earlier local government schemes had the district superintendent of police reporting to the deputy commissioner.

A role played by the district coordination officer is to coordinate the activities of the provincial line agencies (the various provincial departments such as Communications and Works, Irrigation, Agriculture, Education, Health, etc.) in the district but not to command them. These departments report to their respective provincial secretaries and not to either the zila nazim or the DCO.

Implementing the Concept: The New Local Government System

It is one thing to conceptualize, design, and plan a new local government system. It is another to implement or install a new local government system. What will be examined in this section is the extent to which the new local government system introduced by the Musharraf government is, in fact, a significant departure from past practices. In doing so, we will consider the following: the local government elections, the training of elected local officials, local government human resources, and human resources management, the financing of the new system and criticism of the new local government system, and the administrative reforms of the Musharraf government.

Elections

Prior to the promulgation of provincial local government ordinances that installed the new local government system,[20] direct elections were held in five phases in December 2000 for union council members, union nazims, and niab union nazims in all four provinces. Indirect elections for zila nazims, naib zila nazims, tehsil or town nazims, and naib tehsil or town nazims were held in July and August 2001. The elections were held on a non-party basis. Candidates for the offices of zila nazim, naib zila nazim, tehsil or town nazim, naib tehsil or own nazim, union nazim, and naib union nazim "will have academic qualification [sic] of at least matriculation/secondary school certificate, or equivalent."[21] Table 7.1 reveals academic qualifications of the zila nazims indirectly elected in the four provinces.

The table shows that over 84 percent of the zila nazims hold B.A. or higher degrees. It remains to be seen if the quality of district leadership has any relationship to educational credentials. What this table also reveals is the number of districts involved in the new local government system and, consequentially, the size of the task confronting the government in installing the new system.

Table 7.1
Educational Background of Zila Nazims

Province	Matriculate	B.A. Degree or Higher	Total
Balochistan	7	15	22
NWFP	4	20	24
Punjab	2	32	34
Sindhh	2	14	16
Total	15	81	96

Source: NRB, "Local Government Elections," www.nrb.gov.pk, no date.

Voting in Pakistan is often the result of decisions taken by the *biradari* ("brotherhood" or "clan"), one level up from the extended family. There is no evidence than clan voting prevailed in the local government elections, but there is also no evidence that it did not.

What is not known regarding leadership in the new local government system is the extent to which there has been any shift or change in the power of the feudal class. What previously acted as a check on the power exerted in the rural areas by the zamidars in Punjab, the waderas in Sindh, and the sardars and maliks in NWFP and Balochistan was the presence of the commissioners and deputy commissioners as the chief executives of the divisions and the districts. Backed by central and provincial governments, these civil servants could intervene in local disputes to protect or promote the rights of the less powerful in rural Pakistan.[22]

Training

An ambitious plan was developed to train the newly elected local officials. The Think Tank on Capacity Building within the National Reconstruction Bureau:

> assumed the responsibility for developing training modules providing training guidelines, training of master trainers and monitoring training programs in three phases. . .
>
> - Phase 1: Up to 14 August 2001—Training and Orientation of Union Councilors.
> - Phase 2: 15 August to 31 December 2001—Training of other categories of elected representatives, and state functionaries.
> - Phase 3: November 2001 onwards—Follow-on training of all categories of selected representatives.[23]

All local government systems introduced in Pakistan have had some training component either formally (as in the case of the present scheme) or informally attached to them. In the 1960s, President Mohammad Ayub Khan's Basic Democracy Scheme saw the establishment of the Pakistan Academy for Rural Development (PARD) in Peshawar charged with training the Basic Democrats of this local government scheme. Under the Local Bodies Scheme introduced in 1979 by the government of President Mohammad Zia-ul Haq, the National Institutes of Public Administration in Karachi, Lahore, and Peshawar, along with the Pakistan Academy for Rural Development and the National Centre for Rural Development (in Islamabad) provided training to elected local government officials.

Human Resources and Human Resource Management

Although "the provincial government will post [appoint] the District Coordination Officer, District Police Officer and district officers to the district"[24] as head of district administration, the zila nazim "initiate[s] the performance evaluation report of the District Co-ordination Officer (DCO)."[25] The zila nazim also has the authority to transfer the DCO prematurely, but only after giving him a formal warning. In such an eventuality, the zila nazim will state his reasons for the transfer in writing to the chief secretary (the top civil servant in the province), who will be obliged to transfer the DCO within a week.[26]

Under the LG Plan, the DCO is prohibited from bypassing the zila nazim in his—the DCO's—interaction with the provincial government.[27] However, the important function of posting civil servants to the districts remains a federal (through the federal Establishment Division) and provincial power. It appears that the district itself does not appoint civil service officers and has few human resources management responsibilities. In other words, the district is still dependent upon decisions taken in Islamabad and the provincial capitals regarding personnel at the district and sub-district levels and has minimal control over government employees working at the district and subdistrict levels.

Financing the New System

Finance is key to the successful implementation of any government reform effort and the new local government system is no exception. The Finance System section of the LG Plan begins by acknowledging the weaknesses of local government financing in the pre-1999 local government scheme:

> Almost universally, local governments receive some form of fiscal transfer from higher levels of government. In Pakistan, local governments have been receiving 10 to 15 percent fiscal transfers from provincial sources. The level of self-financing of local government in Pakistan has been much higher than in most countries. This is because provincial departments have been responsible

> for carrying out government functions and development at the district level. The transfer and grants system has been weak. There is no formula for distribution of funds to districts and provincial budgets do not specify district expenditures. Districts do not know, with certainty, what they will expect from the provincial departments, which affects planning negatively. This results in political machinations, ad-hocism, and lack of transparency. In order to accomplish a transparent, credible and fair system of transferring funds to the district level, a provincial financial commission will be constituted.[28]

However, the LG Plan also states that: "The principle of the formula for provincial to district transfers is that district and local government should generate their own resources to the extent possible."[29] The tax base in Pakistan is extremely small, "consisting of approximately half a million people out of a population of 140 million."[30] Despite numerous attempts on the part of successive central governments to increase the collection of revenue, "The army's campaign to recover loans and tax revenues registered mixed results and by the end of 2001, the accountability drive seemed to have been shelved."[31] The principal locally derived revenue for districts was from a tax on the movement of goods (*octroi*) into a district. The ability of districts to generate new income sources locally must be viewed as an extremely difficult if not impossible venture.

The LG Plan also promised to reform provincial fiscal transfers to the reformed district governments:

> A formula for provincial fiscal transfers will be devised and implemented. The model provincial formulas will become part of the proposed new provincial finance awards and the resultant formulas developed in conjunction with the provincial governments will be subject to change in a similar fashion as the national finance awards.[32]

However, changes in both national and provincial fiscal transfers to the district await decisions to be taken by the National Assembly and the Provincial Assemblies elected in October 2002.

Finally, here are a few comments on the implementation of the financial powers of the districts under the LG Plan 2000. In an October 29, 2002 article that appears in *The News*,[33] the reporter described the financial morass at the district level:

> To maintain its authority, the bureaucracy has made district governments dependent on the provincial government by centralizing the financial system. Under the financial system, handed down to the districts as part of the devolution plan, [the] District Local Fund was created. All the taxes and revenues were credited to this account. The districts could use this account, but the bureaucratic red-tape created hurdles. As a result, the [District] Local Fund was abolished and replaced with the District Account and all the funds in the District Local Fund were transferred to [the District Account]. Now the districts cannot utilize the revenues collected by them. Although the new system has increased

their revenues, . . . their cash balance has not increased. The banks are under instructions not to show the revenues of the districts as their cash balance unless an [sic] advice is received from the provincial finance department. . . . The spirit of devolution of power demanded that financial powers were devolved to the officers at the district level. However, no change has been made in the Delegation of Financial Powers Rules. . . . The federal government never transferred due amounts to the provinces for onward transfer to the districts. When the funds reached the province, a substantial portion was kept by the [provincial] Finance Department, and the residue was transferred to the [provincial] Local Government and Rural Development Department.

Criticism from Politicians

Neither the LG Plan 2000 nor its implementation has escaped criticism. On April 13, 2000, *Asia Times* reported that Jalal Mehmood Shah, chairman of the Sindhh Thinkers Forum stated: "Local level governance is the subject that should be dealt with by the provincial governments. But the federal government never allowed the provinces the autonomy promised to them in the country's constitution."[34] This article went on to state:

> The Human Rights Commission of Pakistan (HRCP) rejected the plan, saying the military rulers have no mandate to take such steps. "The official local election scheme is incomplete, self-contradictory and divisive and the rulers should announce steps for return of democratic rule," an HRCP resolution said. The Pakistan Muslim League (PML) of Nawaz Sharif and the Benazir Bhutto-led Pakistan People's Party (PPP) have both rejected the military government's overtures and have demanded immediate restoration of democracy. Among critics of Musharraf's plan are hard-line nationalist leaders from the provinces of Sindh and Balochistan, who fear that it interferes with provincial autonomy guaranteed in the country's 1973 Constitution, currently under suspension. The nationalists parties have demanded more autonomy for the provinces along with greater financial and administrative control. . . . The religio-political parties, on the other hand, oppose the devolution plan, saying it is contradictory to the country's cultural values—especially with regard to the mandatory representation for women in district governments.

Behind the criticism was the demand for a return to civilian rule through the electoral process. Opposition to the Musharraf government received its wish when National and Provincial Assembly elections were held in October 2002.

Criticism from the Civil Service

Perhaps the most damaging (to the reforms) criticism so far has come from the civil service. Before discussing this, it is noteworthy to mention that the

Musharraf government has been described as a "government of selected military officers and technocrats."[35] The most recent, publicly released criticism from members of the civil service was revealed in an article that appeared in the November 11, 2002 issue of *The News*.[36] According to this article:

> The entire exercise of National Reconstruction Bureau (NRB) made during [the] last three years to restructure civil services is so flawed that it has been destroyed by just two speeches of senior bureaucrats delivered at the recent meeting of the federal cabinet. . . . General Naqvi's entire exercise has revolved around one focal point that [is] how to demolish the District Management Group (DMG), which is generally perceived to be a representative of colonial legacy, a big hurdle in the way of dispensation of justice and mother of all sins of [the] civil administrative system. . . . The weaknesses and loopholes of the Plan were so well exposed that General Musharraf wasted no time in leaving it to the discretion of the next government.

Lt. General (Retd.) Naqvi has offered his resignation as Chairman of the National Reconstruction Bureau. It cannot be determined if President Musharraf's decision to shelve the reform had anything to do with Naqvi's decision to resign.

Police Order 2002

Before leaving the subject of changes[37] in local government, a few observations should be made regarding a major function of government, police (one of the two pillars of colonial government along with revenue collection). Prior to the implementation of Police Order 2002, the key police officer in the district, the district superintendent of police, reported directly to two civilian officials, the deputy commissioner and the provincial home secretary. In fact, it was the deputy commissioner who often supervised the police and held the police accountable for their actions. With the Police Order 2002, this changed. In Section 37 of the Police Order 2002, the provincial governments "shall establish a District Public Safety Commission in each district consisting of eight, ten, or twelve members depending upon the area and population of the district." Section 38 states that "half of the members of the District Public Safety Commission shall be elected by the Zila Council, from amongst its councilors . . . [while] . . . the other half comprising independent members shall be appointed by the Governor [of the province] from a list of names recommended by the District Selection Board." In effect, the district superintendent of police (SP), now known as the district police officer (DPO), reports to the District Public Safety Commission. The DPO reports to the provincial home secretary only on administrative matters. What this Order does is to provide the DPO with more autonomy in policing the district. The DPO is still part of the Police Service (a Central Superior Service) and neither the District Public Safety Commission nor the district nazim are involved in the appointment police officers (including the DPO) in the district.

CONCLUSION

It is too early to evaluate, comprehensively, the new local government system since the provincial governments promulgated their ordinances to install the new system less than eighteen months ago. However, some observations may be made of the extent to which the new system measures up to the World Bank's definition of devolution.

What Is Devolution?

In its 1998 "Pakistan: A Framework for Civil Service Reform in Pakistan," the authors of the World Bank report stated that:

> Effective devolution would require: (i) constitutional protection to mitigate the risk of arbitrary dismissal of local governments; (ii) appropriate revenue-sharing arrangements to better align agreed expenditure assignments with financial capacity; (iii) strengthening administrative capacity in line with agreed functions at all levels of government. But adding a third (local) layer of bureaucracy without enacting needed managerial, administrative, and personnel expenditure reforms would render such devolution ineffective.[38]

Is Pakistan's New Local Government System Devolution?

Measuring the new local government system against the World Bank's definition of devolution, we find the following:

1. The government of Pakistan has not provided "constitutional protection to mitigate the risk of arbitrary dismissal of local governments."[39] Central and provincial local government ordinances do not substitute for an amendment (or amendments) to the Constitution to give a constitutional base for local government.

2. Appropriate revenue-sharing arrangements to align better-agreed expenditure assignments and financial capacity have not been made and await decisions taken at the national and provincial levels.

3. Administrative capacity in line with agreed functions at all levels of government does not appear to have been strengthened. Some would argue that eliminating the office of deputy commissioner has weakened administrative capacity.

The additional point should be made that is not in the World Bank's definition of devolution and that is control of public personnel at the local level. The appointment of both generalist administrators (district coordination officers, executive district officers, and deputy district officers) and specialists (engineers, teachers, medical doctors, and technical personnel) in the line agencies who work at the district and subdistrict levels still remains in the hands of both central and provincial officials. As a result of the above, the new local government system is, at best, a limited decentralization of political power, administrative authority, management functions, power–authority nexus, and resources to the district level. The new local government system does not attain the "five fundamentals" that were proposed for it in the LG Plan 2000.

The Future of the New Local Government System

C. Mueen Afzal, then secretary general and finance secretary (the highest ranking civil servant in Pakistan), was quoted as saying there would be "no question of reneging on any of the reforms" announced by the government, reforms of the judiciary and police, social services, and government accounting and auditing practices.[40] What he did not include were changes in the local government system. The absence of any reference to local government on the part of the secretary general, combined with President Musharraf's decision to let the newly elected national and provincial assemblies decide the next steps in process, coupled with Lieutenant General (Retired) Naqvi's decision to resign as chairman of the National Reconstruction Bureau does not bode well for the future of the local government system introduced in Pakistan by the Musharraf government.

NOTES

1. The author acknowledges and thanks Ali Ahmed and James D. Mandolfo for their contributions to this work.

2. The World Bank, "Pakistan: A Framework for Civil Service Reform in Pakistan," Report No. 18386-PAK, December 15, 1998.

3. Ibid., i, ii. The italics are mine to emphasize what I consider to be the most important parts of these three problems.

4. The provinces have separate personnel cadres. Each province has a Provincial Civil Service (PCS), which constitutes the general administrator/officer corps. However, major civil service positions at the provincial, division, and district levels are filled by members of the Central Superior Services, especially the District Management Group (DMG) officers.

5. "Devolution of Power to Bring Revolution," *Business Recorder,* December 19, 2000.

6. The government of Pakistan through its Pakistan 2001 Vision Statement said that "Corruption pervades all three branches of government: the executive, the legislative and

the judicial." Cited in "Pakistan: A Framework for Civil Service Reform in Pakistan," op. cit.

7. In response to the question of why Pakistan was trying to privatize many of its state-owned enterprises, former President Ghulam Ishaq Khan said:

> Pakistan is not a "free agent." It has always been greatly affected by what the developed world wants it to do. This is not true for all underdeveloped countries and the developed world has not been consistent in what it wants underdeveloped countries to do. In fact, Pakistan has been forced to do what developed countries want it to do.

(Interview with Robert LaPorte, Jr., Peshawar, April 6, 1995.)

8. The World Bank, "Pakistan: A Framework" iii.

9. The fact that only one DMG officer participated in the development of the new local government system was a sore point with the DMG Association as it was the DMG, among several central superior civil services, that would pay the costs in terms of status and power from the changes that the LG Plan 2000 would make in administration and management at the local level. Interview with DMG officer, October 31, 2002.

10. National Reconstruction Bureau, *Local Government Plan 2002.* The LG Plan may be found on the National Reconstruction Bureau's web site http://www.nrb.gov.pk.

11. Ibid.

12. *Local Government Plan 2000.*

13. Ibid., The integration of the forty-one cantonments (administered by their own cantonment boards) into the local government system "will be reviewed as the district governments start functioning," 19.

14. *Local Government Plan,* 2.

15. Ibid., 4.

16. Ibid.

17. Ibid., 5.

18. Ibid.

19. Ibid., 7.

20. "The provincial governments promulgated the Local Government Ordinance 2000 in their respective provinces to install a new local government system with effect from 14th August 2001 to function within the provincial framework and adhere to Federal and Provincial laws." National Reconstruction Bureau, "The New Local Government System." http://www.nrb.gov.pk/local_government/default.asp. (No access date given.)

21. *Local Government Plan 2000,* pp 3, 9. There were no educational qualifications stated for union councilors.

22. There are exceptions to this statement. When asked why he joined the government service, a DMG officer from a zamindari (land-owning) family from southern Punjab responded by saying that the decision to join the civil service was a family decision. The family wanted a "friend in court" when family interests dictated favorable decisions by local magistrates. Interview with DMG officer in the mid-1980s.

23. National Reconstruction Bureau, "Capacity Building." www.nrb.gov.pk. No date.

24. *Local Government Plan,* 6.

25. Ibid., 5.

26. Ibid., 6.

27. Ibid.

28. Ibid., Sections 138 and 139, 28

29. Ibid., Section 140.

30. Iftikhar H. Malik, "Pakistan in 2000: Starting Anew or Stalemate?" *Asian Survey,* 42:1 (January–February 2001), 110.

31. Iftikhar H. Malik, "Pakistan in 2001: The Afghanistan Crisis and the Rediscovery of the Frontier State," *Asian Survey,* 43:1 (January–February 2002), 208.

32. *Local Government Plan,* 29.

33. Babar Dogar, "Bureaucracy Usurps Districts' Financial Powers," *The News,* October 29, 2002.

34. Muddassir Rizvi, "Opposition Builds Up against Devolution Plans," *Asia Times,* April 13, 2000.

35. Anonymous source. The "technocrats" are high-level civil servants.

36. Amjad Warraich, "Two Speeches Ruined Naqvi's Plan," *The News,* November 11, 2002.

37. I am hesitant to use the term "reform" as *Webster's New Collegiate Dictionary* defines "reform" as "amendment of what is defective, vicious, corrupt, or depraved" and "a removal or correction of an abuse, as wrong, or errors." There seems to be enough debate as to whether or not the reforms contained in the *Local Government Plan 2000* constitute reforms or are simply changes in the local government system.

38. The World Bank, "Pakistan: A Framework," iii.

39. The Constitution of the United States of America does not mention local government, leaving the creation, regulation, and abolition of this level of government to the states. Nearly all U.S. state constitutions have provisions that deal with local government, but none guarantees their existence. In fact, from the 1940s to the 1980s the number of local governments dropped dramatically from over 140,000 to around 85,000 due to decisions taken by states to consolidate local governments.

40. *The Economist,* November 17, 2001.

8

Education in Pakistan: A Survey

Tariq Rahman

Every year the government of Pakistan publishes some report about education. If not specifically about education, at least the annual *Economic Survey of Pakistan,* includes a chapter on education. These reports confess that the literacy rate is low, the rate of participation in education at all levels is low and the country is spending too little in this area. Then there are brave promises about the future such as the achievement of 100 percent literacy and increasing the spending on education which has been hovering around 2 percent of the GNP since 1995 to at least 4 percent and so on. Not much is done, though an increase in the number of schools, universities, and religious seminaries (*madrassas*) is recorded. The private education sector mints millions of rupees and thousands of graduates throng the market not getting the jobs they aspired to. The field of education is a graveyard of these aspirations. The data in Table 8.1 point grimly to where Pakistan stands in South Asia.

Table 8.1: School Attendance in South Asia

	Bangladesh	India	Nepal	Pakistan	Sri Lanka
Children Not Reaching Grade 5 (1995–1999)	30	48	56	50	3
Combined Enrollment as a Percentage of Total	36	54	61	43	66

Source: United Nations Development Program, *Human Development in South Asia: Globalization and Human Development 2001,* (Karachi: Oxford University Press, 2002).

The Historical Legacy

South Asia is heir to a very ancient tradition of both formal and informal learning. These traditions varied from region to region and, more importantly, among different socioeconomic classes. The very poorest people generally got no education at all while those on the upper echelons of the social hierarchy learned languages, literature, theology, and a few other subjects.

According to G. W. Leitner, a well-known functionary of the British empire who said that the British colonial venture had ruined indigenous education in the Punjab, there were 300,000 pupils in indigenous schools before the conquest of that province in 1849 whereas in 1860 to 1861 these numbers had come down to 60,168 pupils (however, Leitner also has a higher figure of 120,000 pupils).[1] Leitner's report does not establish the higher figures, but it is useful in that it tells us what kind of schools existed and names some of the texts taught in them.

To confine ourselves to the education of South Asian Muslims, who are in a majority in Pakistan (96.16 percent), which is the focus of this survey, there were the *maktabs* (Persian schools) and *madrassas* (Arabic schools). As there were more Persian than Arabic schools,[2] it seems that the aim of education was primarily pragmatic—that is, to equip oneself for the business of this world rather than the next. Given that Persian is the language of the highest domains of power—the government, the bureaucracy, the judiciary, education—, it was necessary to learn it in order to function as *munshis* (clerks), *muallims* (teachers), and generally as a functionary of the state.

The British substituted English for Persian[3] and also introduced Urdu, the informal lingua franca of North India but one that had hitherto not been taught formally in schools by Muslim rulers, to the education system.[4] This was a revolution as it created a new basis for socioeconomic stratification. The very poorest people, especially those living in the peripheries, continued to remain illiterate, as there were no schools, or at least not affordable ones, where they lived. Some of them did, however, study in the *madrassas,* which, being charitable organizations, not only charged no tuition fees but even gave free food and lodging. Working-class, lower–middle-class, and middle-class children attended the vernacular medium schools established by the British authorities. The upper classes and children of the higher Indian officers of the British bureaucracy and military attended English-medium institutions. In short, the medium of instruction roughly corresponded to one's position in the hierarchy of wealth and power in the state.

In the areas now comprising Pakistan, Urdu was the most commonly used medium of instruction in government schools. In the province of Sindh, however, Sindhi was also used. There were convent schools and armed forces schools for the rich and the powerful, which used English as the medium of instruction. All higher education, in colleges and universities, was also in English. The *madrassas* used Urdu as well as the indigenous languages as a medium of instruction. Except for the *madrassas* and the private English schools, the government controlled, or at least influenced, all other institutions. They also remained obvious symbols of the educational caste system with the upper classes using English almost as a first language and being completely alienated from both their vernacular-school compatriots and the *madrassa*-educated mullahs (equivalent of clergymen).

EDUCATION IN PAKISTAN

Beginning with the National Education Conference of 1947, there have been at least twenty-two major reports on education issued by the government. Among the most salient ones are: Report of the Commission on National Education (1959); The New Education Policy (1970); The Education Policy, 1972–1980 (1972); National Education Policy (1992); and the National Education Policy: 1998–2010 (1998).[5] The present military government has issued several reports including a controversial and much-criticized Report of the Task Force on Higher Education.[6]

These educational reports touch upon all kinds of educational institutions but they focus more on modern education provided in the government schools, colleges, and universities. For the *madrassas*, however, the government commissioned separate reports, the best known of which are the Report of the National Committee on the Religious Seminaries[7] and the comprehensive report on the *madrassas*.[8] After discounting all the rhetoric about development, several salient features of the states' real educational policy become clear. They follow:

1. To allow the status quo to prevail as far as possible (i.e., a class-based system of education functioning in different languages: the vernaculars for the common people and English for the elite)

2. To use Islam and Pakistani nationalism to prevent ethnic groups from breaking away from the center and to build a modern, cohesive nation out of different linguistic and ethnic groups.

3. To enhance literacy, impart skills, and create an educated workforce capable of running a developing society.

These features were mutually contradictory at times. The first feature, of which the decision makers may not have been conscious, was actually the result of unequal distribution of educational funds and the educational bureaucracy's inertia. Thus, while government schools in the rural areas do not even have chairs for the pupils, the great so-called public schools (public in the sense of the public schools of Britain, such as Eton and Harrow), have not only facilities but even luxuries for their pupils. The second aim, that of nation-building through Islam and Pakistani nationalism, was a conscious objective, but it was not always pursued in the same manner or with equal vigor. During General Zia-ul Haq's rule (1977 to 1988), the Islamization of education and textbooks was more thorough than at any other time. The third aim, that of improving literacy and other educational skills through conscious efforts, suffered as a result of the other two. While elitist children found it much easier to enter elitist domains of power, ordinary government school pupils found it much more difficult, and the students of *madrassas* were, in reality, barred from them. Thus the workforce was almost as class differentiated as a result of the process of education as society otherwise was.

THE PRESENT EDUCATIONAL SCENE

The present educational scene is full of contradictions. On the one hand there are dynamic, fast-moving educational institutions charging exorbitant fees, while, on the other hand, there are almost free or very affordable government schools as well as religious seminaries, which are entirely free. The students of these institutions live in different worlds and operate in different languages. They do not, however, get education in their own mother tongues. These are spoken by the percentages of the population given in Table 8.2 (the total population being 132,352,000).

Table 8.2. Languages Spoken in Pakistan by Percent of Population

Language Spoken	Percent of Population
Punjabi	44.15
Pashto	15.42
Sindhi	14.10
Urdu	7.57
Balochi	3.57
Other	4.66

Source: Census Report of Pakistan. (Islamabad: Population Census Organization, 2001), Table 2.7, p 107.

Such diversity, leading to extreme polarization and divisiveness in society, can be potentially dangerous. Nevertheless, to understand this danger let us look at all major kinds of educational institutions: Schools, religious seminaries (*madrassas*), and institutions of higher education (colleges and universities).

SCHOOLS

The number of schools, students, and teachers is given in Table 8.3 from a recent government source.

Table 8.3: Students and Teachers in Schools

Level	Number	Student Strength	Teachers
Primary	169,089	19,921,232	345,457
Middle	19,180	4,278,392	99,098
Secondary	13,108	1,795,444	66,522

Source: Economic Survey of Pakistan: 2001–2002 (Islamabad: Economic Advisory Wing, 2002), p. 146.

After ten years of schooling, students sit for examinations held by the different Boards of Intermediate and Secondary Education in the country. The teaching and the examinations are both in Urdu except in parts of (mostly rural) Sindh where they are in Sindhi. Some schools do, however, teach in English so that students appear for the matriculation examination in English, too.

Most students from elitist English-medium schools appear for the British Ordinary (O level) and Advanced (A level) school examinations, which demand much higher competence in English than does the Pakistani system. Most of the 511,077 students, who are from Urdu-medium schools, study the textbooks provided by the Textbook Board of the provinces (Punjab, Sindh, NWFP, and Balochistan). These textbooks use Islam and Pakistani nationalism to create a Pakistani nation out of the different linguistic and cultural groups (Punjabis, Sindhis, Pathans, Baloch and Urdu-speaking *Mohajirs*) that constitute Pakistan.[9] There is much glorification of war and the military, and there are many anti-Hindu and anti-India remarks interspersed throughout.[10] Possibly because of such textual propaganda, students of these institutions are more prone to militancy than are their English-school counterparts, as will be discussed later. Table 8.4 indicates the number of schools according to the medium of instruction.

Besides the Urdu- and Sindhi-medium schools, the government also runs some English-medium schools (model schools) in urban centers. The armed forces also run such schools. In addition to these, there were 33,893 English-medium schools spread out all over Pakistani cities and small towns.[11] Almost all such schools I visited claimed to use English, though some did concede that they also used Urdu or Sindhi as an alternative medium of instruction. Such schools much in demand by the public; parents go to incredible lengths, sometimes depriving themselves of basic necessities, to teach their children in schools advertising themselves as "English medium," because they feel that the most powerful and lucrative jobs within the country will be within the reach of their children if only they learn English. Thus, in order to empower themselves—as in other ex-colonies—the people often choose English-medium schools.[12]

For the purposes of the survey I conducted in 1999 to 2000 to record opinions of young people that might be relevant to society and politics, English-medium schools were divided into three categories: ordinary, elitist, and cadet colleges and public schools.[13] In the first category, the ordinary English-medium schools were those charging a monthly tuition fee of Rs 50 to Rs 1,499. They catered to ordinary people—lower-middle class and middle class. Some were English medium in name only, since they actually taught in Urdu, because neither teachers nor students were sufficiently competent in English.

Schools in the second category charged tuition fees from Rs 1,500 to Rs 10,000 or more per month. The teachers and students were much more exposed to English in informal settings—home, peer group, cable television, comic books, foreign travel, and so forth—than were their counterparts in other schools. English was used informally by children in schools that were in upscale residential localities.

Table 8.4: Medium of Instruction

Type of School	Punjab	Islamabad	NWFP (FATA)	Sindh	B'tan	AJK	FANA	Federal Government	Total
Urdu medium	67,490	368	13,556	3,657	9,939	6,009	1,370	167	102,556
Sindhi medium	0	0	0	36,750	0	0	0	0	36,750
Pashto medium	0	0	10,731 (Primary)	0	0	0	0	0	10,731
Mixed medium (Urdu and Sindhi)	No Info	No Info	No Info	1,394	No Info	No Info	No Info	0	1,394
English medium	22,855	309	3,995 326 (FATA)	5,943	465	No Info	No Info	No Info	33,893
Total	90,345	677	28,608	47,744	10,404	6,009	1,370	167	185,324

Source: Sindh Education Profile: 1993–1996. (Karachi: Education Department, Government of Sindh, 1998); Punjab Education Statistics. (Lahore: Punjab Education Management System Government of Punjab, 1998); Census of Private Education Systems. (Islamabad: Federal Bureau of Statistics, 2001).

Schools in the third category, called cadet colleges and public schools, are concerned more with the power elite than with wealth. Most of them are influenced by the armed forces. The tuition fees for the wards of the armed forces are generally lower than that of civilians. While English is the medium of instruction, the students tend to not use it informally with each other. Among such schools are: Cadet College, Pitaro (navy); Military College Sarai Alamgir, Jhelum (army); Burn Hall College, Abbottabad (army); Cadet College, Sargodha (air force), and others. Public schools along the lines of Eton and Harrow, such as the Aitchison College in Lahore, are run by boards of governors (or trustees). In most cases the top brass of the army has a presence on the boards.

STATED POLICY AND REAL POLICY

The stated official policy of the government is that public money will be spent on schools that will use Urdu (and Sindhi only in parts of Sindh) as the medium of instruction. It is often stated that private resources and enterprise run private educational institutions. That being said, even during the British period the English-medium schools, then called European schools, cost more. A report of 1941 puts it this way:

> The cost of European Education is high compared with education in India generally, the cost per pupil in Anglo–Indian and European Institutions being Rs 156 as against Rs. 14 only in all types of institutions from a university to a primary school.

It is explained that the public funds are used to meet only 31 percent of the expenses, whereas the remaining 69 percent comes from fees. However, even this comes to Rs 48.36 per pupil per year, which was Rs 34 more than the average amount (Rs 14) spent on ordinary Indian students. In short, whatever the stated policy might be, the real policy was to subsidize the education of the Anglicized elite. This policy continues to date. In Pakistan the armed forces and the higher bureaucracy use English for official purposes. Thus, they were interested in obtaining young people who were competent in that language. Moreover, the elite, who went for jobs in the modern domains of power, including the officer corps of the armed forces, higher bureaucracy, superior judiciary, commerce, media, and higher education, were very desirous of teaching English to their children. They could either buy it at exorbitant cost at the private elitist schools, or they could establish institutions in which English would be the medium of instruction, but the cost would be lower—at least for their own children. It was for the latter purpose that General Ayub Khan, as commander-in-chief of the Pakistan Army in the 1950s, established "a number of cadet colleges and academies."[15]

In 1966 the students from less-privileged institutions protested against these institutions. A commission on students' welfare and problems agreed that such schools violated the constitutional assurance that "all citizens are equal before law" but defended them as follows:

> Such establishments are intended to produce a better type of students who would be more suitably disciplined and equipped for eventually entering the defense service of the country or filling higher administrative posts and other responsible executive positions in the government and semi-government bodies and private firms and corporations.[16]

As a result, the cadet colleges multiplied. Indeed, the armed forces through the Fauji Foundation (army), Shaheen Foundation (air force), and the Bahria Foundation (navy) created many more institutions from the 1970s onward.

The cadet colleges are subsidized by the state, as the following figures in Table 8.5 indicate.

Table 8.5: Expenses of Cadet Colleges

Institution	Cost in 1998–1999 (Rs)
Cadet College, Palandri	8,181,000
Cadet College, Razmak	11,887,000
Cadet College, Sanghar	5,000,000
Cadet College, Larkana	10,000,000

Source: Details of Demands for Grants and Appropriations, 1999–2000, (Islamabad: Finance Division, 1999). Vol. 1, p 1084; Vol. 2, p 1461–1462.

The cost of an ordinary Urdu-medium school, such as those available to most ordinary children in the country, is Rs 3,580,000 per year. Thus, while cadet colleges have excellent boarding and lodging arrangements, spacious playgrounds, equipped libraries and laboratories, and faculty with master's degrees, the ordinary Urdu-medium (and Sindhi-medium) schools sometimes do not even have benches for pupils to sit on. In short, contrary to its stated policy of spending public funds to provide the same type of schooling to all, the state (and its institutions) actually spend more funds on privileged children for a privileged (English-medium) form of schooling. This perpetuates the socioeconomic inequalities that have always existed in Pakistani society.

SOCIOECONOMIC CLASS AND WORLDVIEW

In Pakistan socioeconomic class affects worldview in general. Relevant to those interested in violent social change, religious militancy, or war with India are questions relating to the distribution of resources, the introduction of Islamic law (Shari'a), and Kashmir. In the survey mentioned previously, the following responses to questions given below in Table 8.6 indicate how socioeconomic class stands in relation to these potentially explosive issues.

Table 8.6. Priorities for Pakistan

		Urdu medium (N=520)	Elitist English medium (N=97)	Cadet Colleges (N=86)	Ordinary English medium (N=119)
Q. What should Pakistan's priorities be?					
a	*Conquer Kashmir*				
	Agree	95.58	62.89	88.37	88.24
	Disagree	2.12	31.96	6.98	6.72
	Don't care	2.31	5.15	4.65	5.04
b	*Develop nuclear weapons*				
	Agree	79.81	64.95	79.09	73.11
	Disagree	13.65	26.80	15.12	18.49
	Don't care	6.54	8.25	5.81	8.40
c	*Implement the Islamic Law*				
	Agree	95.58	52.58	79.07	86.55
	Disagree	1.73	23.71	5.81	1.68
	Don't care	2.69	23.71	15.12	11.76
d	*Give equal rights to religious minorities*				
	Agree	44.04	53.61	33.72	47.90
	Disagree	33.68	22.68	39.54	28.57
	Don't care	23.71	23.71	26.74	23.53
Q. Do you want the language used for higher jobs in the state and the private sector to continue to be English?					
	Yes	27.69	72.16	70.93	45.38
	No	71.15	27.84	29.07	53.78
	No reply	1.15	0	0	0.84

Source: Tariq Rahman, *Language, Ideology and Power*, (Karachi: Oxford University Press, 2002), pp 210–281.

As can be seen, children from lower socioeconomic backgrounds, such as those in the Urdu-medium and the ordinary English-medium schools, support an aggressive foreign policy and more Islamization leading to less tolerance for religious minorities. They are also dissatisfied with policies that make powerful jobs the monopoly of the English-using powerful elites.

Children in the cadet colleges, because they belong to middle-class backgrounds and are subjected to regimentation in their institutions, support aggressive policies but are less supportive of Islamization than their previously mentioned counterparts in Urdu-medium schools. Children of elitist schools, exposed to Western sources of information and role models, are least supportive of militant policies and Islamization. They are also the most tolerant toward religious minorities, but they are alienated from the peoples' culture and aspirations and desire to preserve and perpetuate their privileged position by supporting English as the language of the domains of power in the country.

Such acute divisiveness along socioeconomic class lines, combined with religious intolerance, can lead to further political unrest in Pakistan. Such unrest will probably be expressed though the idiom of religion. However, poverty and alienation from the privileged classes will probably be the major motivating factors for these disgruntled and jobless young men who will come out of the educational institutions for the underprivileged.

MADRASSAS

The *madrassas* are associated with the Taliban rulers of Afghanistan who were students of these institutions.[17] They have also been much in the news for sectarian killings and supporting militancy in Kashmir, They are considered the breeding ground of the *jihadi* culture—a term used for Islamic militancy in the English-language press of Pakistan.

At independence there were 137, or even fewer, *madrassas*. In April 2002, Dr. Mahmood Ahmed Ghazi, the minister of religious affairs, put the figure at 10,000 with 1.7 million students.[18] They belong to the major sects of Islam, the Sunnis and the Shias. Nevertheless, given that Pakistan is a predominantly Sunni country, the Shia *madrassas* are very few. Among the Sunni *madrassas* there are three subsects: Deobandis, Barelvis, and the Ahl-i-Hadith (Salafi). Besides these, the revivalist Jamaat-i-Islami also has its own *madrassas*. Whereas the Deobandis have a strict interpretation of Islam that disallows the veneration of saints, the Barelvis follow popular Islam, which venerates saints and allows folk interpretations of the faith. Ahl-i-Hadith is a puritanical sect close to the Saudi Wahhabi interpretation of Islam. The Saudi Arabia–based organization Haramain Islamic Foundation has been giving funds to the Ahl-i-Hadith, which has made them powerful. Indeed, the Lashkar-i-Toiba, an organization that has been active in fighting in Kashmir, belongs to the Ahl-i-Hadith.[19] In recent years, the Deobandi influence has increased, and many Taliban were trained in their seminaries. According to Khalid Ahmed, one of the most knowledgeable commentators on the religious scene in Pakistan, "The largest numbers of seminaries are Deobandi, at 64 percent, followed by Barelvi, at 25 percent. Only 6 percent are Ahle Hadith. But the increase in the number of Ahle Hadith seminaries or *madrassas* has been phenomenal at 131 percent, going up from 134 in 1988 to 310 2000."[20] Table 8.7 contains information from 1988. It is reproduced here only because there is no reliable information on these lines at present.

If present numbers are to be calculated Khalid Ahmed's data given above may be used in combination with the data of 2002 given here. As mentioned earlier, however, the sect-wise numbers of *madrassas*, enumerated in 2000, are not known me.

The *madrassa* students are the most intolerant of all the other student groups in Pakistan. They are also the most supportive of an aggressive foreign policy. The responses to my questions in Table 8.7 indicate this.

Table 8.7: Priorities of *Madrassa* Students

		Madrassas (N=131)		
Q. What should Pakistan's priorities be?				
		Agree	**Disagree**	**Undecided**
a	*Conquer Kashmir*	99.24	0.00	0.76
b	*Develop nuclear weapons*	96.18	1.53	2.29
c	*Implement Sharia'h*	97.71	0.76	1.53
d	*Give equal rights to religious minorities*	6.87	81.68	11.45
Q. Do you want the language of higher jobs in the state and the private sector to continue to be English?				
		Yes	**No**	**No Reply**
		10.69	89.31	0

Source: Tariq Rahman, *Language, Ideology and Power*, (Karachi: Oxford University Press, 2002), Appendix 14.7, pp. 592–596

The figures are self explanatory. What needs explanation is that the *madrassas*, which were conservative institutions before the Afghan–Soviet War of the 1980s, are both ideologically activist and sometimes militant. According to Peter L. Bergen, author of a book on Osama bin Laden and his Al Qaeda group: "nowhere is bin Laden more popular than in Pakistan's *madrassas*, religious schools from which the Taliban draw many of its recruits."[21] Even with the end of Taliban rule in Afghanistan, the *madrassas* have plenty of zealous young people who can potentially act as crusaders against both Western interests and the moderate regimes, both military and civilian, whom they perceive as the allies of the West.[22]

General Pervez Musharraf's military government, in an attempt to control religious extremism, made a law to control the *madrassas*. This law, the Voluntary Registration and Regulation Ordinance 2002, has, however, been rejected by most of the *madrassas*, which want no state interference in their affairs. The *madrassas* are not "frozen in time," as A. H. Nayyar, an academic and writer on educational matters, wrote of them.[23] The education they impart has two aspects. Most formal courses are, indeed, medieval. They are in Arabic and Persian, the classical languages of Islam in South Asia, which students memorize without much real understanding. This part serves as a symbol of identity and continuity. The other part of the education centers on Urdu textbooks, which are read by the final year graduating students. These are polemical texts that refute the beliefs of the other subsects of Islam as well as of modern ideas. Among the latter are capitalism, socialism, democracy, modernism, and individualism. As *radd* is the Urdu word for refutation, I call them *radd*-texts. These *radd*-texts have a tremendous formative influence on the minds of the young clergymen (mullahs) because they are in Urdu, which they understand very well. Moreover, their arguments are simple and already familiar to them through the sermons of other mullahs. Thus, the clergy is engaged with the modern world but on its own terms and according to its own perceptions of it. Being so actively engaged and having such beliefs about reform, the *madrassas* are not frozen in time; they want to take time into their own hands.

While the refutation of other subsects can lead to sectarian hatred, the refutation of modern ideas leads to opposition to both the modern state and the process of colonization, which introduced modernity to South Asia during the British era.

The *madrassas* became militant when they were used by the Pakistani state to fight in Afghanistan during the Soviet occupation and then in Kashmir so as to force India to leave the state. Pakistan's claim on Kashmir, as discussed by many, including Alastair Lamb,[24] has led to conflict with India, and the Islamic militants (*jihadis*) have entered the fray since 1989. The United States indirectly and sometimes directly helped create militancy among the clergy. For instance, special textbooks in Dari (Afghan Persian) and Pashtu were written at the University of Nebraska, Omaha, with a USAID grant in the 1980s.[25] American arms and money flowed to Afghanistan through Pakistan's Interservices Intelligence (ISI), as several books indicate.[26] At that time all this was done to defeat the Soviet Union. Later, while Pakistan's military kept using the militant Islamists in Kashmir, the United States was much alarmed by them, not without reason as the events of 9/11 demonstrated later.

Apart from the *madrassas* proper, religious parties, such as Lashkar-i-Toiba, Jaish-i-Muhammed, and Harkat-ul-Mujahidin, print militant literature that circulates among the *madrassas* and other institutions. Although these parties have been banned, their members are dispersed all over Pakistani society, especially among the *madrassas*. The *madrassas*, especially the Deobandi *madrassas* of the NWFP, Balochistan, and south Punjab, are potential centers of Islamic militancy in Pakistan.

HIGHER EDUCATIONAL INSTITUTIONS

There are 755 colleges[27] and 80 universities in Pakistan.[28] Out of these, about 35 colleges and 35 universities are in the private sector.

While students join universities after high school in Western countries, they usually go to colleges for their B.A. degrees in Pakistan. Public universities generally begin at the M.A. level, though some universities do have a three-year B.A. (honors) track. The colleges are affiliated with universities. They teach for the B.A. degree for two years, after which students appear for the examination of the university. The lecturers do not evaluate courses; students are evaluated only through the final examinations of the university. Such a system forces stud-

Table 8.8: Breakdown of *Madrassas* by Sect

Province	Deobandi	Barelvi	Ahl-i-Hadith	Shia	Others	Total of Provinces (1988)	Total of Provinces (2002)
Punjab	590	548	118	21	43	1,320	3,100
NWFP	631	32	5	2	8	678	1,200
Sindh	208	61	6	10	6	291	900 (+300 in FATA)
Balochistan	278	34	3	1	31	347	700
Azad Kashmir	51	20	2	—	3	76	Not given
Islamabad	51	20	—	2	3	76	100
Northern Areas	60	2	27	11	3	103	150
Girls' *Madrassas*	Not given	Not given	Not given	Not given	Not given	Not given	448

Source: For 1998 data: Deeni Madaris Ki Jame Report (Islamabad: Islamic Education Research Cell, 1998.)
For 2000 data: The State of Pakistan's Children (Islamabad: SPARC, 2001), p 53.

ents to use cram guides based on past examination papers and to regard all education in light of examinations. The lecturers are promoted on the basis of seniority, not published research. As such, their offerings are generally stagnant, and they have little knowledge of academic development in their fields. Since the tuition fees of public colleges is affordable for even the working classes, they used to be the meeting place of students from elitist English- and Urdu-medium schools. This, however, is changing quickly, because private entrepreneurs are establishing colleges with very high tuition fees. The curricula of these colleges mostly focus on courses pertinent to lucrative fields of employment—information technology, business, commerce, engineering, medicine, and law; but some (out of the thirty-five colleges in the private sector) have emerged recently that cater to the humanities.

Pakistan had only two universities in the public sector in 1947. Today the number is forty-five and still increasing. Moreover, private institutions, calling themselves universities, are mushrooming in all the cities of Pakistan. The University Grants Commission set up by the government of Pakistan does not recognize some of these institutions, but they are flourishing anyway.

The public universities are colonial institutions. Universities were set up by the British colonial government in 1857 to educate the subordinate bureaucracy, because it was very costly to import it from Britain. Moreover, recruiting Indians would strengthen British rule by giving Indians a sense of participation in running state affairs.[29] These universities were dominated by the government, since their chief executive officers (called vice chancellors) were government appointed and the chancellors were governors or viceroys. They lacked funds for quality research or attracting the best minds to academia; they emphasized teaching rather than research; and they were, for the most part, subordinate appendages of the bureaucracy.[30] Because Pakistani universities retained these characteristics after independence, they failed to attract the best minds in the country and, therefore, lacked in quality research.[31]

Recently, the mushrooming of universities has adversely affected the image of the public universities. First, most new public universities have been created in response to the political demand from local pressure groups that their city or region should have a university. The new university hires its faculty from among former college lecturers; certain well-connected people—who are not necessarily academics but former bureaucrats—and military officers become vice chancellors, registrars, and treasurers. This means that the minimal research required in public universities (five research papers for promotion to associate professor and eight for full professorship) is not insisted upon further, reducing the academic credibility of Pakistani academics in general.

The other problem is that funds, already woefully inadequate, have to be distributed more widely. In an article written in 1998, I showed that if the cost per student per year is adjusted with the 1985 prices as base, the real cost per student had decreased for all public universities. In the Quaid-i-Azam University, Islamabad, the foremost institution of higher learning in Pakistan, the cost had decreased in real terms from Rs 37,430 to Rs 13,983 per year per student (see Table 8.9).[32] This trend has occurred in some other major public universities.

Table 8.9. Costs per Student at Selected Public Universities

University	Enrollment	Departments	Unit Cost per Student per Year
University of Peshawar	17,134	35	Rs. 23,497 ($ 338)
University of Punjab	9,972	43	Rs. 59,000 ($975)
University of Karachi	12,255	43	Rs. 27,160 ($ 449)
University of Balochistan	2,000	31	Rs. 77,000 ($ 1,273)

Sources: Database at the University Grants Commission, Islamabad, and the Steering Committee on Higher Education, Islamabad.

While the government spent US$1,080 per student per year in 1987, it spent only $450 in 2001, a reduction of 62 percent. In 2002, with the addition of more public universities, the spending (per student) decreased further. This translates into minimal expensive laboratory equipment, almost no academic journals, very few new books, and no interlibrary loan system for borrowing dissertations and reports. As such, if any academics are doing research in public universities, they are doing so despite the system and not because of it.

The mushrooming of private universities that teach subjects purportedly leading to lucrative employment undermines the concept that, among other things, a university education enlightens a person and gives him or her the knowledge to understand the human significance of policies and advances in knowledge. Moreover, the educational apartheid that starts in schools—with the rich and powerful studying in elitist English-medium private schools and in cadet colleges—continues in the domain of higher education too. Elitist children, after British Ordinary and Advanced school examinations, go on to study in private colleges and universities charging exorbitant tuition fees. The figures in Tables 8.10 and 8.11 show the difference between the fees of the public and the private universities.

Besides the tuition fees, examination, admission, and other types of fees also exist in both kinds of universities; but, of course, they are far higher in the private sector than in the public one.

Table 8.10: Fees at Selected Public Universities

Tuition Fees Structure of Public Universities	
University	**Per Annum Fees at the M.A Level (Pak Rs)**
Punjab University	1320
Quaid-i-Azam University	1350

Source: Universities of Pakistan. (Islamabad: University Grants Commission, 2001.)

Table 8.11: Fees at Selected Private Universities

Tuition Fees Structure of Private Universities			
University	**Fees (Pak Rs)**	**Duration**	**Subject and Level**
Al-Khair	100,000	2 Years	MCS/MIT
Bahai	47,500 227,000	Per Semester Per Year	M.B.A. M.B.B.S.
Greenwich	9,000	Per Course	M.B.A.
Hamdard	8,500 72,000	Per Course Per Year	M.B.A. M.B.B.S.
Iqra	12,000	Per Course	M.B.A.
LUMS (Lahore University of Management Sciences)	174,000	Per Year	M.B.A.
Aga Khan	392,000	Per Year	M.B.B.S.
GIK (Ghulam Ishaq Khan Institute).	150,000	Per Year	B.E.
MCS=Master of Computer Science MIT=Master of Information Technology M.B.B.S.=Bachelor of Medicine, Bachelor of Surgery			

Source: As for Table 8.10.

The fact that private colleges and universities are attended by rich young people who are generally fluent in English and have tremendous self-confidence bordering on arrogance, make them appear to be "good" institutions. The fact is, however, that the faculty is generally part time rather than full time, and this part time faculty is from the public sector universities. Except in some universities, such as Aga Khan, LUMS, and GIK, the faculty members are not published academics. In some they do not even have Ph.D.s or other research degrees. The classes are, generally speaking, air conditioned, and the furniture is better than in the public universities. That being said, taken as a whole, the private universities charge far more than deserved, judging from quality of education they offer.

Nevertheless, the elitist glitter of the private universities has ghettoized the public universities that, like the Urdu-medium schools, are increasingly regarded as substandard, poor, incompetent, "lower-class" institutions. Moreover, the private universities are generally not governed by academics. Thus, the autonomy and power of academics, such as it was, is eroded even further.

Moreover, the idea of the university as a liberal institution where one is exposed to new ideas is also under threat. Most private universities, especially these run by the armed forces, are highly regimented, and academics do not run them. Thus, academics, called "teachers" and not "academics," are treated on par with hired tutors who are supposed to provide a service for payment but have no part in the governance of the institution.

The recently announced policy on higher education contained in the Report of the Task Force on Higher Education has announced more funds for the public universities. However, it has met with considerable criticism from Pakistani academics, because it has neither increased the autonomy of the universities nor given an increased role to faculty members in running universities.[33] The amount of the promised money has not yet been disclosed, and, with so many universities opening up, it is feared that these funds will prove to be inadequate and that the public universities will further suffer from ghettoization. In short, the government's proposed reforms will increase the subordination of the public university, this time to "civil society" (which probably means powerful people from NGOs, the corporate sector, and other powerful institutions) in addition to government bureaucracy, without making it more competent.

CONCLUSION

In summation, the state of education in Pakistan is woefully unsatisfactory. The *madrassas*, the Urdu- and Sindhi-medium schools, and the English-medium schools cater to different socioeconomic classes and further increase the alienation that already exists between these classes. The system is unjust, in that it distributes the most lucrative and powerful jobs most advantageously to the elite, who are educated in English-medium institutions. Meanwhile the *madrassa*-educated people and the failures from the Urdu-medium schools join the increasing army of the unemployed, who use the idiom of religion to express their defused sense of being cheated of their rights. Hence, the unjust system of schooling may increase Islamic militancy in Pakistan, which will be as much an expression of resentment against the present policies of the ruling elite as commitment to Islamizing the society.

The system of higher education is further splitting up the Pakistani educational institutions according to socioeconomic class— the public colleges and universities are increasingly ghettoized; the private institutions are increasingly the coveted, elitist institutions like the English-medium schools are already. With the exception of the upper socioeconomic classes, this trend frustrates everybody, because they feel that they can no longer afford the best higher education for their children.

On the whole, then, Pakistan needs to change its educational policies to end this apartheid, which threatens to disrupt society. This is easier said than done, because a society of over 160 million people needs vast resources for anything as ambitious as providing it adequate and standard education.

APPENDIX A

Educational Levels and Costs in Pakistan

Institutions	Years	Level	Average Monthly Fees	Socioeconomic Class
Madrassas	15–16	Almiya (M.A.)	0 (fee charged in some)	poor and rural children (mostly boys)
Government Schools (Urdu and Sindhi medium)	10	matriculation	0–Rs 25	working classes/ lower–middle classes
English Medium	10	matriculation	Rs 50–1,499	lower–middle classes/middle classes
English Medium (cadet colleges, armed forces schools, etc.)	12	F.A. or F.Sc.	Rs 500–3,000	middle classes (in some cases, wards of officials pay less)
English Medium (private elitist)	11	British Ordinary Level (O Level)	Rs 1,500–10,000+	middle classes and above
English Medium (private elitist)	13	British Advanced Level (A Level)	Rs 6,000–10,000+	upper–middle classes and above
Government Colleges	11–14	F.A. and B.A.	Rs 50–150	lower–middle classes and above
Public Universities	15–16	M.A. or M.Sc. and above	Rs 100–200	lower–middle classes and above
Private Universities/ Colleges	13–16	Bachelor's and Master's degrees	Rs 5,000–15,000	middle classes and above

Source: Field research; NB: US$1=RS 60 in July 2002

APPENDIX B

Essential Facts about Pakistan's Education

Enrollment Ratio	**35.98%**	**41.19% male**	**30.35% female**	**Less in rural =29.11% and more in urban =49.71%**
Educated Persons (school level)	18.30% (below primary)	30.14% (primary, i.e., 5 years)	20.89% (middle, i.e., 8 years)	17.29% (matriculation, i.e., 10 years)
Educated Persons (above school level)	6.56% (12 years)	4.38% (B.A., i.e., 14 years)	1.58% (M.A., i.e., 16 years)	.85% (others, i.e., diplomas, post-graduates, etc.)
Literacy	34.92%	63.08% (urban)	33.64% (rural)	54.81% (male) and 32.02% (female)

Source: Census of Pakistan, 2001

Notes

1. G. W. Leitner, *History of Indigenous Education in the Punjab since Annexation and in 1882.* (1st ed. 1882; Lahore: Republican Books, 1991 reprint).

2. R. Thornton (Comp), *Memoir on the Statistics of Indigenous Education within the North Western Provinces of the Bengal Presidency.* (Calcutta: J. Thomas, Baptist Mission Press, 1850).

3. Tariq Rahman, *Language and Politics in Pakistan.* (Karachi: Oxford University Press, 1996), pp 22–38.

4. Tariq Rahman, *Language, Ideology, and Power: Language Learning among the Muslims of Pakistan and North India.* (Karachi: Oxford University Press, 2002), pp 210–218.

5. The publication details of these reports follow: *Report of the Commission on National Education.* (Karachi: Ministry of Education, Government of Pakistan, 1959); *The New Education Policy.* (Islamabad: Ministry of Education, Government of Pakistan, 1970); *The Education Policy 1972–1980.* (Islamabad: Planning Commission, Government of Pakistan, 1992); *National Education Policy: 1998–2010.* (Islamabad: Ministry of Education, Government of Pakistan, 1998).

6. *Report of the Task Force on Improvement of Higher Education in Pakistan: Challenges and Opportunities.* (Islamabad: Ministry of Education, Government of Pakistan, 2002).

7. *Qaumi Committee Deeni Madaris.* [Urdu: "National Committee About Religious Seminaries"] (Islamabad: Ministry of Education, Government of Pakistan, 1979).

8. *Deeni Madaris Ki Jame Report.* [Urdu: "The Comprehensive Report on the Religious Seminaries"] (Islamabad: Islamic Education Research Cell, Ministry of Education, Government of Pakistan, 1988).

9. For ethnic politics see Tahir Amin, *Ethno-National Movements of Pakistan* (Islamabad: Institute of Policy Studies, 1988); Feroz Ahmed, *Ethnicity and Politics in Pakistan* (Karachi: Oxford University Press, 1998); and Rahman, *Language and Politics.*

10. For detailed analysis see K. K. Aziz, *The Murder of History in Pakistan* (Lahore: Vanguard, 1993); Rubina Saigol, *Knowledge and Identity: Articulation of Gender in Education Discourse in Pakistan* (Lahore: ASR Publications, 1995); Rahman, *Language, Ideology and Politics*, pp 515–524. For a comparison between India and Pakistan see Krishna Kumar, *Prejudice and Pride: School Histories of the Freedom Struggle in India and Pakistan* (New Delhi: Penguin Books India, 2001).

11. Census of Private Educational Institutions, Table 1: 12.

12. Alistair Pennycook, "Language, Ideology, and Hindsight: Census from Colonial Language Policies," in Thomas Ricento, ed., *Ideology, Politics and Language Policies: Focus on English* (Philadelphia: John Benjamins Company, 2000).

13. Rahman, *Language, Ideology and Politics,* Appendix 14.

14. *Education in India in 1938–39*. (Delhi: Manager of Publications, 1941), p 113.

15. Muhammad Ayub Khan, *Friends Not Masters*. (Karachi: Oxford University Press, 1967), p 43.

16. *Report of the Commission on Student's Problems and Welfare*. (Islamabad: Ministry of Education, Government of Pakistan, 1966), p 18.

17. Ahmed Rashid, *Taliban: Islam, Oil and the New Great Game in Central Asia.* (London: I.B. Tauris, 2000).

18. *Pakistan: Madrassas, Extremism and the Military*. (Brussels: International Crises Group, Asia Report No. 36, 2002), p 2.

19. Khalid Ahmed, "The Power of the Ahle Hadith," *The Friday Times* (Lahore). 12–18 July 2002, p 10.

20. Ibid.

21. Peter L. Bergen, *Holy War Inc.: Inside the Secret World of Osama bin Laden.* (New York: Simon and Schuster, 2001), p 150.

22. For Central Asia parallels see Ahmed Rashid, *Jihad: The Rise of Militant Islam in Central Asia*. (Lahore: Vanguard, 2002).

23. A. H. Nayyar, "*Madrassas* Education: Frozen in Time," Pervez Hoodbhoy, ed., *Education and the State: Fifty Years of Pakistan*. (Karachi: Oxford University Press, 1998), pp 215–250.

24. Alistair Lamb, *Incomplete Partition: The Genesis of the Kashmir Dispute 1947–1948*. (Karachi: Oxford University Press, 1997).

25. Joe Stephens and David B. Ottway, "The ABC's of Jihad in Afghanistan," *The Washington Post*, 23 March 2002, Sec. A, p 1.

26. John K. Cooley, *Unholy Wars: Afghanistan, America and International Terrorism*. (London: Pluto Press, 1999).

27. Colleges of Pakistan. (Islamabad: University Grants Commission, 1999).

28. *The News* (Rawalpindi), 17 July 2002.

29. A. N. Basu, ed., *Indian Education in Parliamentary Papers: Part I* (Bombay: Asia Publishing House, 1952).

30. Edward Shils, "The Academic Profession in India," Edward Leach and S. N. Mukherjee, eds., *Elites in South Asia*. (Cambridge: Cambridge University Press, 1970), pp 172–200.

31. Tariq Rahman, *Language, Education and Culture*. (Karachi: Oxford University Press, 1999), pp 120–142.

32. Ibid..

33. Rahman, *Language, Ideology and Power.*

9

Fifty-Five Years of Archaeological Research in Pakistan: The Prehistoric Periods

Jonathan Mark Kenoyer and Richard H. Meadow

Archaeological research in Pakistan is an international endeavor involving scholars from many nations and institutions. While the breadth of academic involvement has been stimulated by the diversity of the archaeological record, fieldwork in Pakistan would not have been—and would not be—possible without the policy of active cooperation and assistance followed by the government of Pakistan and, for archaeology, by the Department of Archaeology and Museums of the Federal Ministry of Culture and Heritage in particular. The recognition of the importance of international collaboration has resulted in much joint research between Pakistani and non-Pakistani scholars, and this in turn has promoted a better understanding of the archaeology and early history of the region. Even so, the archaeology and early history of the geographical area encompassed by Pakistan is still rather poorly known. Although great strides have been made since the founding of Pakistan, there remains much to do, particularly given the pace of industrial and agrarian development.

The purpose of this chapter is not to present a summary of all of the major discoveries made in the last fifty–five years, but rather to highlight those that have resulted in major shifts in research paradigms and interpretive frameworks. The main focus is on studies of the prehistoric period, beginning even before the earliest evidence for toolmaking hominids and continuing through the rise and decline of the Indus Valley Civilization. Special emphasis is placed on contributions by American scholars and Pakistani archaeologists trained in America and on collaborative projects that are helping to build a foundation for the next fifty years of research.

Although American contributions to archaeological research in northwestern South Asia began before Pakistan's independence, there was a marked increase beginning in the 1950s and continuing until the present. Many American scholars have been based in Departments of Anthropology, with the result that projects have tended to be multi-disciplinary including personnel specializing in Physical Anthropology (study of hominoid and hominid remains), Ethnology (study of material culture in its present context), Zooarchaeology (study of animal remains from archaeological sites), Palaeoethnobotany (study of plant remains resulting from human activity), Palynology (study of pollens), Geoarchaeology (study of past human influence on the landscape), Experimental Archaeology (attempting to replicate past technological processes), and

Ethnoarchaeology (study of modern practices to formulate models useful for investigating past behaviors). For the earliest periods, specialists in Geology (study of rock deposits), Paleontology (study of premodern faunas including Taphonomy, Paleoecology, and Biostratigraphy), and Chronostratigraphy (use of various dating techniques) have also played a major role. In addition to site survey, collection, mapping, and excavation, various field projects have included site and object conservation, training courses, and site and museum development.

PRIMATE EVOLUTION AND EARLY TOOLMAKERS IN PAKISTAN

Pakistan has a largely untapped geological resource of fossils that covers the evolution of most organisms, beginning as early as the Archaean Epoch, some 3.8 billion years ago, and continuing to the present. In 1933, the Yale–Cambridge expedition to what is now northern Pakistan and Kashmir, led by Helmut de Terra and T. T. Paterson, began studying Stone Age sequences in Kashmir and on the Potwar Plateau of the Punjab (de Terra & Teilhard de Chardin 1936; de Terra & Paterson 1939). Although many of their original interpretations have since been modified and updated, their studies provided an important basis for future research on early environments and cultures in South Asia.

The Potwar Plateau of northern Pakistan contains some of the world's richest fossil beds from the Miocene Epoch. Beginning in the early 1970s a number of American teams initiated long-term research projects in collaboration with the Geological Survey of Pakistan to investigate the biostratigraphy and chronostratigraphy of the Siwalik deposits of this region. Eventually coming to work closely together, investigators from Dartmouth College (Noye Johnson and Gary Johnson), the University of Arizona (Everett Lindsay), LaMonte Geophysical Laboratory (Neil Opdyke later at the University of Florida, Gainesville), and Yale University (David Pilbeam, continuing the project now from Harvard University, Elwyn Simons, Grant Meyer, and S. Mahmood Raza) focused on the Potwar Plateau with forays into the Suleiman and Bukhti ranges. At about the same time a team from Howard University (Taseer Hussein) worked in the Trans–Indus region. The result of this research has been the establishment of a remarkable chronological sequence into which almost any geological outcrop can be situated to within about 100,000 years (see Table 10.1). The Siwalik sequence in the Potwar is now the best collected, best dated, and best documented long land sequence in the world for the Miocene, comparable in quality to that established for the subsequent five million years in East Africa (Pilbeam et al. 1977; Badgley & Behrensmeyer, eds. 1995; Barry et al. 2002). In the course of these investigations many new species of mammals—large and small—have been identified. Of particular importance has been the recovery of rodent remains through a comprehensive program of screen washing of sediments. This biostratigraphic work together with the results of isotope studies has permitted identification of significant climatic and related temperature and environmental shifts in the late Miocene (10.7 to 5.7 Ma). At that time when the Himalaya were being formed, the climate became increasingly seasonal, with the carbon dioxide content of the atmosphere being affected and C-4 (more arid-adapted) grasses replacing C-3 (more temperate/tropical) grasses in the area of study. In addition, numerous fragments of Miocene primate fossils (especially *Sivapithecus*) were recovered, providing important data for reconstructing the complex evolutionary processes that preceded the emergence of hominids (Pilbeam 1978, 1979).

Table 10.1. Geological and Archaeological Terms and Dates

Epoch	Approximate Dates
Holocene	Present to 10,000/12,000 BP
Pleistocene:	
Upper/Late Pleistocene	10,000 to 100,000 (or 127,000) BP
Middle Pleistocene	100,000 BP to about 1 (or 0.7) Ma
Lower/Early Pleistocene	1 my to about 2 (or 1.9 or 1.7) Ma
Pliocene	2 my to about 5 (or 5.26) Ma
Miocene	5 my to about 25 (or 23) Ma
Oligocene	25 my to about 36 Ma
Archaeological Periods	**Approximate Dates**
Neolithic (Food Production)	9000 to 8000 BP and later
Epipaleolithic (Transitional period)	10,000 to 9000 BP
Upper Paleolithic (Hunting–Gathering)	30,000 to about 10,000 BP
Middle Paleolithic (Hunting–Gathering)	100/70,000 to about 30,000 BP
Lower Paleolithic (Hunting–Gathering)	+ 2 Ma to 100/70,000 BP

Key: Ma = million years ago, BP = before present

Fragmentary deposits dating to the Pliocene (circa 5 to 2 Ma) have been located in the Potwar, but so far no hominid fossils have been discovered. At present, the earliest hominid fossils, such as Australopithecus, Paranthropus, and Homo have been found only in Africa, dating to the Pliocene and Pleistocene Epochs. On the basis of fossils in Africa, most scholars assume that the earliest toolmaking species, *Homo habilis* (2.3 to 1.7 Ma) and later *Homo erectus* (1.8 or 1.5 Ma) originated in Africa and migrated to Europe and Asia. Nevertheless, the presence of early hominids in Pakistan is suggested by finds in dated contexts of what are thought by some researchers to be stone tools. Since 1979 the British Archaeological Mission to Pakistan, working in collaboration with the Geological Survey of Pakistan, has been studying the geology and documenting

Paleolithic sites in the Potwar Region (Dennell 1991). In 1983 and 1988 members of the project discovered near the town of Riwat what appeared to be stone tools dating to before 2 million years ago (Dennell 1984; Dennell et al. 1988; Hurcombe & Dennel 1992; Rendell et al. 1989). Although there has been controversy regarding the identification of these flaked stone pieces as tools and with the dating of the geological strata, discoveries of Lower Palaeolithic tools in the Jammu area from Upper Siwalik beds dating to before 2.8 Ma (Sharma 1995:105 in Korisettar 2002:13) also suggests the presence of early hominids in this part of the world. Only further work in the region will resolve the debate. Once such work is begun we expect that it will be only a matter of time before more widespread evidence is turned up.

By 500,000 years ago there is considerable evidence for the descendants of the earlier toolmakers throughout most of the subcontinent. Most recently, surveys by an Italian team in collaboration with Shah Abdul Latif University, Khairpur, have discovered evidence for Paleolithic tools at sites in the Rohri Hills of northern Sindh (Biagi & Pessina 1994; Negrino & Kazi 1996), which provide good evidence for the antiquity of human populations in the heart of the Indus Valley itself. Presumably these individuals were some form of *Homo erectus*, or an archaic Asian form of *Homo* that has not been preserved in the fossil record (Allchin & Dennell 1990; Dennell et al. 1990; Allchin 1994).

These discoveries have two major implications. First, South Asia, and specifically northern Pakistan, was an important region of development for hominoids. Second, tool-using hominids may have been present in South Asia as early as they existed in Africa. If the latter is true, as some have argued, then we will have to rethink the models currently proposed for human origins (Lukacs 1984; Dennell et al. 1990; Kennedy 1994).

EARLY FOOD-PRODUCING COMMUNITIES

Following the Paleolithic, the next important phase in the archaeology of Pakistan is the period of initial settling down and the beginnings of plant and animal domestication. Until recent discoveries at the site of Mehrgarh, it was assumed that the staple domestic grains and animals were brought to South Asia from Western Asia. Now it is possible to suggest more complex models that include aspects of an indigenous transition from hunting and gathering to food production. While regions of Balochistan and the Indus valley were not isolated from what was going on farther west, there was considerable indigenous potential that seems to have contributed to the local domestication of some plants and animals.

The foundation for current research by Pakistani and international projects was established through the pioneering efforts of several scholars who surveyed and excavated in the rugged terrain of Balochistan, Makran, and Sindh, following up on earlier surveys conducted during the period of British rule. This work in Pakistan has been complemented by surveys in Afghanistan to the west and in the deserts of India to the east.

Although the work of Louis Dupree (e.g., 1992) focused primarily on Afghanistan, it is appropriate to recognize his important contributions involving the investigation of Upper Paleolithic and early Neolithic sites that had connections with what was going on in Balochistan and the Indus Valley. Dupree's evidence suggests that in Northern Afghanistan, during the Middle Paleolithic and especially during the Upper Paleolithic (30,000 to 15,000 BP), potential domesticates such as wild sheep and goat, and possibly cattle, were being heavily exploited (Perkins 1972; Shaffer 1978a; Meadow 1989).

Some of these same sites have nonceramic Neolithic occupations with the remains of domesticated sheep/goat and possibly domesticated cattle being reported. Sickle blades, stone hoes, ground stone querns, and mullers have also been recovered along with the faunal materials, but no architectural structures were discovered. Dupree suggested that these Neolithic sites, dating to perhaps as early as 8500 BC, represent the temporary camps of specialized pastoral populations. (All BC dates cited in this paper are in calibrated years, which approximate calendar years.) Although he was never able to follow up on his discoveries, research by other scholars in Balochistan, and specifically the excavations at Mehrgarh support the possibility that there were mobile communities in the highlands and that these communities were interacting with settled agriculturists and artisans and moving in seasonal migration patterns of vertical transhumance (highlands to lowlands and back).

Although Dupree's projects included a more anthropological approach to archaeological research in the region, the major credit for introducing American archaeological methods to Pakistan belongs to Walter Fairservis, a class fellow of Dupree, who began his graduate studies at Harvard University in 1948. Starting with his initial Ph.D. research in 1949, and continuing throughout his association with the American Museum of Natural History in New York, Fairservis conducted numerous surveys in Balochistan and Afghan Seistan (Fairservis 1952, 1956, 1959, 1961). During the course of these surveys he and his team members located many sites belonging to prehistoric and historic periods. Small-scale excavations at the site of Kili Gul Mohammad and Damb Sadaat near Quetta revealed the presence of preceramic Neolithic and early Chalcolithic occupations that anticipated the more extensive discoveries at the site of Mehrgarh some twenty years later. He also conducted surveys in the Las Bela valley and excavated at the Harappan site of Allahdino near Karachi (Fairservis 1982). His exhaustive studies of prehistoric figurines, ceramics, and other artifacts have remained a point of reference for all subsequent research.

In addition to his new discoveries, Fairservis was introducing new ways to analyze and interpret the data that he recovered. This resulted in a major clash with the leading British scholar of the day, Sir Mortimer Wheeler (Fairservis 1985). Wheeler did not believe that there was much evidence for the development in Balochistan of cultural practices that would lead to the Indus Civilization, and even though he began to modify his views in his later years, he preferred to invoke the mechanisms of diffusion to explain culture change (Wheeler 1968; Fairservis 1985).

Fairservis drew part of the inspiration for his work from Jim Ford (an archaeologist who worked in Peru) and Robert Redfield (an anthropologist who worked in Mexico and wrote about the Near East). In contrast to Wheeler's "orthogenetic interpretation of history whereby period followed period much as do Egyptian dynasties, or the succession of monarchs in England," Fairservis viewed the stratigraphic units in his excavations "as arbitrary units in a time flow within which cultural stability and change could be discerned" (Fairservis 1985: 344–345). He used ethnographic observations from Balochistan and other regions of the world to argue for a cultural evolution that linked the early settled communities in Balochistan to the emergence of the Harappan or Indus Civilization.

The importance of Balochistan in the overall development of the Indus Valley region that was anticipated by the work of Fairservis has to some extent been confirmed through the research in Afghanistan and Balochistan by Shaffer (Shaffer 1974, 1978b), Dales and Flam (Dales & Flam 1969; Dales 1971, 1973, 1977a, 1977b), and numerous other scholars (e.g., Mughal 1974, 1977; Tosi 1979; Besenval 1992, 1994). The most important confirmation has come from excavations at the site of Mehrgarh, located at the foot of the Bolan Pass, which connects the Indus Valley with the highland plateau of Quetta.

The site of Mehrgarh was excavated by the French Archaeological Mission to Pakistan under the direction of Jean-François Jarrige from 1974 to 1986 (Jarrige & Lechevallier 1979; Jarrige & Meadow 1980; C. Jarrige et al. 1995) and again from 1996 to 2000 (Jarrige 2000). A major contribution of these excavations is the picture they present of the process of settling down and establishing domestic plants and animals as the major source of subsistence. In contrast to the purely diffusionary models proposed by earlier scholars (e.g., Wheeler 1968), the transition to food production in northwestern South Asia can now be seen as a process with major indigenous components that is likely to have involved communities throughout the highland region and all along the piedmont zone of Balochistan (Costantini 1984; Meadow 1995, 1999; Meadow & Patel 2002). In Balochistan itself the earliest highland villages have not yet been located or excavated, possibly because they are hidden under large mounds or modern villages. Kili Gul Mohammed in the Quetta Valley is the only site yet excavated in the highlands where there is possible evidence for the early exploitation of cereals (Fairservis 1956, 1975). Yet from remains found at Kili Gul Mohammed and Mehrgarh, we can determine that the early food-producing communities probably had trade networks extending from the highlands to the west, out into the Indus Plains to the east, and south to the Makran coast (Kenoyer 1995b; Possehl 1999).

The population of Mehrgarh Periods I-IIA is well represented by numerous burials found between the mud-brick structures. After carefully studying the shape of the teeth in these early burials, John Lukacs (University of Oregon) feels that they do not reflect peoples who moved into the region from the West because they do not have strong links in dental morphology to known Neolithic populations of West Asia (Lukacs 1989). On the contrary, characteristics of their teeth associate them with a distinctively Asian gene pool. This early pattern is the more significant because there is a distinct change in tooth shapes during the later Chalcolithic period (Mehrgarh Period III) when the dental remains begin to show greater similarities to West Asian populations (Lukacs 1989). This change could be explained by an increase in trade, communication, and other forms of interaction and corresponding gene flow between the Indus region and West Asian cultures during the fifth and fourth millennia BC.

In conjunction with the biological evidence, the material culture of the Neolithic occupation at Mehrgarh, from ca. 6500 to 5500 BC shows how the basic subsistence economy of the Indus Valley became established and how trade and craft specialization developed. The subsistence of the earliest inhabitants of Mehrgarh was focused primarily on hunting and gathering, supplemented by cultivation of barley and some wheat (Costantini 1984) and the herding of domestic goats (Meadow 1981, 1984, 1993b, 1995, 1999; Meadow & Patel 2002). By the end of the aceramic Neolithic, domestic plants and animals became the dominant subsistence resources and with barley being the dominant cereal and cattle the dominant animal.

In the earliest Neolithic period, there is evidence for local production of stone and bone tools (Russell 1995), but most of the ornaments appear to have been traded to the site as finished objects (Jarrige & Meadow 1980; Kenoyer 2000). During the later Chalcolithic periods at Mehrgarh there was a dramatic change in production strategies whereby raw materials from distant areas were brought to the site and processed locally. The general trends in the production, display, and eventual deposition of tools and ornaments during the Neolithic and Early Chalcolithic period at Mehrgarh provide important background for understanding later developments at sites in the Indus valley itself. No centralized structures for political, economic, or ideological control have been found at the site, and yet there is a change from the trade of finished goods to the localized production and redistribution. Along with this change in economic strategies, craft production itself was gradually transformed from relatively simple forms of processing to highly specialized manufacture involving both local and exotic materials and complex pyrotechnologies.

Additional evidence for these important transitions comes from surveys and excavations in Balochistan (Franke-Vogt et al. 2000; Franke-Vogt 2001; Besenval 1994, 1997), Punjab (Mughal 1970, 1981, 1982, 1990, 1997; Mughal et al. 1996), Sindh (Flam 1986, 1993b), and the Northwest Frontier Province (Dani 1970–1971, 1975; Durrani 1986, 1988; Khan et al. 1990; Durrani et al. 1991; Khan 1992). In addition, the continued efforts by scholars from Shah Abdul Latif University, Sindh, have opened up a new perspective on the Neolithic and early Chalcolithic cultures in the regions around Rohri and in the Thar desert of Sindh (Shaikh 1997, Mallah 1998, 2000).

During the next 2,500 years the communities living in the Indus Valley and adjacent regions developed new technologies to produce pottery and figurines of terracotta, elaborate ornaments of stone and metal, tools and utensils, and architectural styles that together reflect regional cultures named after the sites where they were first identified. Of these the most important are the Amri and Kot Diji cultural phases that are found in the southern and northern regions of the Indus Valley, respectively. By approximately 3000 BC there is evidence for the expansion of Kot Dijian interaction networks, linking them to the southern Amrian regions, and by 2800 BC we see the first development of large settlements surrounded by smaller villages and hamlets.

Dr. M. Rafique Mughal, then a field officer in the Department of Archaeology and Museums, government of Pakistan, was the first to show systematically that these cultures represent the formative stage of the later Indus Valley urban civilization (Mughal 1970). Although his interpretations and the name he applied to the phenomenon—"Early Harappan"—were criticized by many scholars in both Pakistan and India, some of whom had been trained by Wheeler, his propositions have subsequently been confirmed through surface surveys and excavations at numerous sites.

Mughal's interpretation goes one step beyond that proposed by Fairservis. Whereas Fairservis focused on the role played by the highland villages of Balochistan, Mughal argued that the foundation for the emergence of cities on the Indus plain came from people inhabiting the plain itself. It was they who developed the basic technologies, trade networks, subsistence practices, and sociopolitical organization that underlay the establishment of cities. While there were certainly some population movements within the Indus Valley and between the Indus Valley and surrounding areas, there is currently little evidence to support the model proposed by Fairservis of a population shift from the highlands to the plains during the first half of the third millennium BC (Kenoyer 1998, 2000).

One of the most important sites of the Kot Diji Phase is Rehman Dheri excavated by Dr. F. A. Durrani of Peshawar University (Durrani 1986, 1988). Rehman Dheri provides concrete evidence for the establishment of planned settlements with massive mud-brick walls and the early use of graffiti and seals during the period just prior to the rise of the Indus cities. Other sites in Pakistan that have demonstrated the important changes and continuities leading to the urbanism of the Harappa Phase are the site of Harappa itself (Kenoyer 1991a, 1991b; Meadow & Kenoyer 1994, 1997, 2000), Ghazi Shah in Sindh (Flam 1993a, 1993b), and Nausharo in Balochistan (Jarrige 1986, 1988, 1989, 1990; Jarrige & Meadow 1992; Quivron 1994; C. Jarrige et al. 1995). Of particular importance are Louis Flam's survey and subsequent excavation work in Sindh Kohistan. Following Sir M. Aurel Stein (1931) and Robert Raikes (1965), Flam has underlined the importance of the massive installations of diversion and check dams in the hills and foothills to the west of the Indus Valley. In addition he has defined for this region a pattern of "acro-sanctums"—high mounds overlooking lower settlements—that was previously thought to exist only for the urban Harappan settlements. Finally, working in part with geomorphologists Stanley Schumm, Michael Harvey, and David Jorgensen, he has provided us with a good understanding of the dynamics of the Indus River with particular reference to changes in its course through time and their significance for understanding settlement patterns in Sindh (Flam 1976, 1981, 1993c, 1999; Jorgensen et al. 1993).

Discoveries from these various excavations and new interpretations, such as those presented by Mughal, required a major reassessment of the models used to understand developments leading to the first urban civilization of South Asia. In light of major changes in American archaeological theory and methodology that took place in the 1960s and 1970s, it is not surprising that critical summaries and new interpretive models were presented (Possehl 1977; Jacobson 1979; Dyson 1982). In 1984 Jim Shaffer proposed a comprehensive framework for discussing the increasingly complex sets of archaeological data that had been accumulated though surveys and excavations. The central concept of his scheme was the Tradition—"persistent configurations of basic technologies and cultural systems within the context of temporal and geographical continuity" (Shaffer 1992b). He identified three major cultural traditions that existed in the geographical regions extending from Eastern Iran to the Greater Indus Valley: the Indus Valley Tradition, the Balochistan Tradition, and the Helmand Tradition. He further divided each of these Traditions into Eras and Phases. The Early Food Producing Era refers to a cultural context in which the economy is based on food production and there is an absence of ceramics (e.g., Mehrgarh, Period IA). The Regionalization Era refers to cultures that are becoming regionally differentiated in artifact styles (e.g., ceramics). These artifact styles cluster in time and space (without fixed boundaries), and are connected by regional interaction networks (e.g., the Kot Dijian and Amrian phases). The Integration Era refers to a period of pronounced homogeneity in material culture over a large geographical area, reflecting an intense level of interaction between social groups (e.g., the urban Harappan Phase). Finally, the Localization Era sees the breakdown of integration and the emergence of local cultures with interaction networks that are different from those present during previous eras.

Shaffer's framework is flexible enough to allow for the definition of new analytical units, such as the Ravi Aspect of the Hakra Phase at Jalilpur and Harappa (Kenoyer & Meadow 2000), and it can be expanded to incorporate later cultural developments of the early Historic period (Kenoyer 1995a, 1997a).

There is still much to learn about the formative stages of the Indus Civilization, and several research projects are examining the earlier periods in conjunction with more extensive excavations of the urban Indus or Harappan Phase.

INDUS CIVILIZATION

One of the leading American scholars to study settlements of the urban Harappan Phase of the Indus Civilization was George F. Dales. Dales undertook a survey along the Makran coast in 1961 with his wife Barbara, T. Cuyler Young, Jr., and

M. Rafique Mughal. They sank some test trenches into the important Harappan outpost of Sutkagen Dor and discovered another at Sotka Koh (Dales 1962a, 1962b; Dales & Lipo 1992). In 1964 to 1965 Dales excavated at Mohenjo-daro for one season using modern excavation and collection techniques. On the basis of a new approach to one of the most important sites in Pakistan, he was able to reveal information that challenged many of the earlier theories about the character of the urban settlement as well as reasons for its decline (Dales 1964, 1965, 1966, 1984; Dales & Kenoyer 1986). Returning to the coastal zone he excavated at the Harappan coastal town of Balakot (Dales 1979a & b; also Franke-Vogt 1997) bringing a team of students and specialists who are continuing to analyze the data from that project relating to chronology, site planning, fishing, crafts, trade, and subsistence. Then in 1986 he began a long-term research project at Harappa (Dales 1989) where he and his team were able to establish the first detailed chronology of an Indus urban center, excavate in the important Harappan cemetery, and collect new information on the origin of the most ancient city of the subcontinent. In all of his excavations Dales made a special effort to train students and collaborate with Pakistani scholars, a program that is still being implemented at Harappa. Detailed analysis of specific categories of artifacts, the careful redocumentation of the excavated ruins, and the study of surface distributions of craft indicators and other artifacts (Jansen 1991, 1993) are all part of that program.

Harappa, however, was accessible for excavation. Beginning in 1986, the Harappa Project, directed by George F. Dales and J. Mark Kenoyer in collaboration with the Department of Archaeology and Museums, government of Pakistan, established a permanent research facility with an on-site conservation laboratory (Dales 1989; Dales & Kenoyer 1993). Three major goals of the project were to understand the growth and development of the ancient city, to conserve the objects and excavation areas, and to train American and Pakistani students in modern archaeological research methods.

THE HARAPPA ARCHAEOLOGICAL RESEARCH PROJECT

Until the recent excavations at Harappa, urban aspects of the Indus Civilization were known primarily from discoveries made in the 1920s and 1930s at the sites of Mohenjo-daro and, to a lesser extent, at Harappa. The architecture, artifacts, and internal organization particularly of Mohenjo-daro in Sindh came to be the standard against which all discoveries at other sites were compared. Today, careful stratigraphic and spatial recording and quantitative studies are revealing new information about development, structure, and change at Indus sites and in ancient Indus society. Thus, although no excavations have been allowed at Mohenjo-daro since 1965, a new understanding of the site was obtained in the 1980s through the detailed analysis of specific categories of artifacts, the careful redocumentation of the excavated ruins, and the study of surface distributions of craft indicators and other artifacts (Jansen 1991, 1993).

The authors of this paper served respectively as Field Director and Zooarchaeologist, until 1992 when the ill health of Dr. Dales led to Dr. Meadow assuming the role of Project Director while Dr. Kenoyer has continued to serve as Co–Project Director and Field Director (Meadow & Kenoyer 1993). At this time Dr. Rita P. Wright became Assistant Project Director, and since 1995 she has been involved in a regional survey of the region around Harappa in collaboration with Dr. M. R. Mughal and Dr. Joseph Schuldenrein. Numerous scholars and students from the United States of America, Pakistan, Europe, and Japan have collaborated in this project and continue to conduct research on the many categories of artifacts and data recovered from the excavations.

Since its inception, the Harappa Project has been the principal focus of American involvement in the pre- and protohistoric archaeology of Pakistan. Between 1986 and 2002, a total of 163 team members (not including local labor or assistants) were associated with the project of whom 83 were Pakistani, 64 American, 16 of other nationalities. While training of both Pakistani and American students has taken place during all field seasons (1986 to 1990; 1992–2002), for four seasons (1994–1997) a formal training program was cosponsored by PIATR (Pakistan Institute for Archaeological Training and Research, Lahore) and partly funded by Fulbright Foundation (USEFP) grants to J. M. Kenoyer and Steven Weber.

In addition to those enrolled in the training program, more than a score of educated young men from Harappa City and surrounding communities have been integrated into the project and have received training in many different aspects of field archaeology. A local potter and local carpenter have also been closely affiliated with the project and have also been closely affiliated with the project and have been guided in their attempts to replicate ancient techniques and styles of craftsmanship. In sum, the HARP has been intensively and continuously involved in the training of both Pakistani and American students and young professionals.

Current excavations and conservation research are implementing new techniques, which are proving quite successful. Of particular importance has been the on-site objects conservation laboratory staffed by conservators from the Conservation Analytical Laboratory of the Smithsonian Institution. As the result of more than a decade and a half of commitment to field conservation, the materials recovered from Harappa are among the most stable of any excavated in South Asia. Integrating conservation with excavation has been extremely successful in advancing general knowledge about the ancient city, stabilizing and conserving specific areas of the site, providing archaeological remains for visitors to see, and educating the local inhabitants about the cultural heritage that they need to protect and develop.

THE INDUS CIVILIZATION AND HARAPPA

The earliest levels of the site, currently thought to date to before 3300 BC, have revealed the remains of a village culture making primarily stone and bone tools but with the use of copper tools beginning as well (Kenoyer & Meadow 2000) (see Table 10.2). Pottery was almost solely hand-built with minimal if any use of the potter's wheel and then only for final finishing of the upper part of the vessel. Vessels included both heavy coarse ware cooking pots and delicate pieces with polychrome decorations. These early settlers developed extensive trade contacts with surrounding resource areas to obtain copper, lapis lazuli, and carnelian (Kenoyer in press). Their technological accomplishments included glazing steatite (soapstone) beads, growing wheat and barley, and husbanding animals—especially humped (zebu) cattle and sheep.

Table 10.2. Provisional Prehistoric Chronology of Harappa

Periods 1A and 1B: Ravi Aspect of the Hakra Phase	> 3300 BC–ca. 2800 BC
Period 2: Kot Diji (Early Harappa) Phase	ca. 2800 BC–ca. 2600 BC
Period 3A: Harappa Phase A	ca. 2600 BC–ca. 2450 BC
Period 3B: Harappa Phase B	ca. 2450 BC–ca. 2200 BC
Period 3C: Harappa Phase C	ca. 2200 BC–ca. 1900 BC
Period 4: Harappa/Late Harappa Transitional	ca. 1900 BC–ca. 1800 BC(?)
Period 5: Late Harappa Phase	ca. 1800 BC(?)–< 1300 BC

By 2800 BC, during the Early Harappa or Kot Diji Phase, the site had expanded to a large town. It was at this time that the basic structure of Indus cities emerged. Streets and houses were oriented to the cardinal directions, wheel-made pottery became common, and the initial stages of a formalized writing system manifested itself in the form of incised graffiti on pottery vessels. At this time the first glazed steatite seals were produced, anticipating the later development of the distinctive Indus seals (Kenoyer 1998).

The full urban phase of the city is associated with the Harappa Phase occupations, from 2600 to 1900 BC. By this time the settlement had developed into a complex city organized into distinct walled sectors with craft areas, bazaars, and domestic structures as well as some impressive monumental public buildings (e.g., Meadow & Kenoyer 1993, 1994, 1997, 2000, in press a & b).

Studies of the artifacts recovered during the recent excavations are providing new information on the organization of craft production (Kenoyer 1992a; Wright 1991, also 1993), social hierarchy as reflected in ornament styles and material wealth (Kenoyer 1992b, 1998, 2000), and the distribution of crafts within the city (Kenoyer 1993; Miller 1997a & b, 1999; Kenoyer & Miller 1999). One of the most important new developments in the study of Indus crafts is the on-going analysis of raw materials being undertaken by Randall Law (in press a, b, & c). After conducting extensive surveys of potential raw material source areas throughout Pakistan and parts of western India, he has begun to compare these samples with materials from the site of Harappa using a variety of high-resolution techniques. Preliminary results indicate that it will be possible to differentiate specific sources for steatite, chert, different types of sandstone, granite, gypsum, lead, and many other varieties of minerals and lithic materials. Other areas of study that are still in progress are the analysis of ceramic assemblages from the Cemetery and the habitation areas of the site by Chris Jenkins (1994, 2000) and the stylistic and chronological analysis of terracotta figurines by Sharri Clark (in press a & b).

Analyses of the mammalian fauna (Meadow 1991, 1993a; L. Miller, in progress) as well as of fish remains (Belcher 1991, 1993, 1994a, 1994b, 1997, 1998), together with study of carbonized plant remains (Weber 1998, 1999), are providing insights into the acquisition of subsistence resources and their distribution within the city.

Excavations in the Harappan cemetery and studies of the human remains have led to a new understanding of mortuary practices (Dales & Kenoyer 1989, 1990, 1991) as well as of the physical characteristics and health of the people of this early urban community (Hemphill et al. 1991). The individuals buried in the Harappan cemetery were generally quite healthy when they died with little evidence of trauma, disease, or malnutrition (Kennedy 1984, 1990, 1992; Lovell 1994, 1997; Lovell & Kennedy 1989). The major problem area appears to have been in the realm of dental health, as many of the older individuals exhibited high incidences of caries, antemortem tooth loss, and abscesses (Lukacs & Pastor 1990; Lukacs & Minderman 1992).

During the urban period, the city was part of extensive trade networks spanning the greater Indus Valley, western India, Afghanistan, and Central Asia. Important new discoveries relate to massive gateways and city walls used to limit and control access into and out of the city and the control of craft production as an important factor in state economy (Meadow & Kenoyer 1994; Kenoyer 1997a). Large numbers of new seals and other inscribed objects have been recovered that provide a new window on the use of writing (Meadow & Kenoyer 1994, 2000; Kenoyer & Meadow 1996) and eventually may help in the decipherment of the still enigmatic Indus script (Possehl 1996).

In the Late Harappan or Cemetery H levels, from approximately 1800 BC to perhaps as late as 1500 BC, the city continued to be a major center for regional trade and technological developments. The earliest glass beads in South Asia were formed along with exquisite glazed faience ornaments made to imitate turquoise and lapis lazuli (Kenoyer 1997b). During this period, the disappearance of the Indus script and standardized weights, along with changes in burial customs have traditionally been associated with the rise of a new culture associated with the introduction of Vedic Aryan religion and culture. It is clear however that the changes were not the result of an invasion, but reflect local transformations of social organization and ideology (Shaffer & Lichtenstein 1989; Kenoyer 1995a).

In conjunction with the excavations at Harappa, Dr. Rita P. Wright and Dr. Joseph Schuldenrein conducted a regional survey project in collaboration with Dr. M. R. Mughal and the Punjab Survey of the Department of Archaeology and Museums. They reexamined sites originally discovered by the Punjab Survey to the south and west of Harappa along the bed of the Old Beas River. In addition to documenting more details about cultural aspects of the settlements, they have tried to reconstruct the landscapes that surrounded the sites before, during, and after their occupation (Schuldenrein 2002). Combining information from various sampling procedures they have been able to define three complete cycles of alluviation and soil formation. Two of these cycles span the end of the Pleistocene and the present and represent 11,000 years of warm and moist environments. Initial examination of the sites and surrounding landscapes indicates that a comprehensive chronostratigraphic and paleoenvironmental context can be developed for the Beas settlement area that will have important ramifications for the reconstruction of landscapes associated with the establishment of Harappan culture.

Many questions about the origins and character of Harappa still remain to be answered, but our recent work at the site clearly demonstrates that this city and the civilization of which it was a part can no longer be described as monotonous and unchanging. These studies reveal a society that was continuously reinventing itself in response to a wide range of pressures, and there is now absolutely no basis for the earlier notion that the Indus Civilization burst onto the scene fully formed and then, after a period of fluorescence, suddenly disappeared. Through careful excavation and artifact analysis it is possible to make inferences about continuity and change in social, economic, and ideological aspects of this society even without the aid of written texts. Furthermore, many of the patterns revealed in the archaeological record are similar to those that result from cultural processes that still occur in the modern cities of South Asia. Continued excavations into the ancient city of Harappa and ethnoarchaeological studies in the living city of Harappa will serve to promote an ever better understanding of the birth, life, and transformation of one of the oldest cities of the ancient world.

OTHER CONTRIBUTIONS

Although the major focus of this article has been on archaeological research in Pakistan, it is not possible to understand any of the prehistoric periods of the northwestern subcontinent without consideration of discoveries taking place in northwestern India. Whereas most of the advances in these regions have been made by Indian scholars, some American scholars have been involved in major excavation and survey projects. Jim Shaffer's research in Haryana and the Eastern Punjab has provided important new information on the Harappan settlements and their cultural transformations (Bhan & Shaffer 1978; Shaffer 1987). His more recent work in South India is opening up a whole new area of research on the peninsular cultures that were contemporaneous with the Early

Harappan and Harappan Phases of the Indus Valley (Shaffer 1991, 1992a). Another scholar who has greatly impacted Pakistan archaeology from his work in India is Gregory Possehl (University of Pennsylvania). While he has also made significant contributions to the archaeology of Pakistan (Possehl 1967, 1975, 1986) his major focus has been on the region of Gujarat, India. Here he implemented a series of long-term research projects that included the sites of Rojdi, Oriyo Timbo, and Babar Kot in Saurashtra. The results of his research and that of Indian colleagues from M.S. University of Baroda, Deccan College (Pune), the Gujarat State Department of Archaeology, and the Archaeological Survey of India (summarized yearly in *Indian Archaeology, a Review*) have shown that this region, which had previously been considered peripheral, played an important role in shaping the character of the Indus Civilization (Possehl & Raval 1989; Possehl 1990, 1992, 1999, 2002; Possehl & Mehta 1994).

CONCLUSION

In the preceding summary we have focused on studies, and especially those by American and Pakistani scholars, that have had a major impact on our understanding of the ancient foundations of modern cultures in northwestern South Asia. We have seen that there have been important strides made for the very early periods (e.g., the Late Miocene) and for the Middle Holocene (c. 7000–2000 BC), while there are tantalizing clues for the Late Pliocene and Early Pleistocene. Otherwise, there remain major gaps. Those of particular significance are (1) during the Late Pleistocene and Early Holocene just before the development of agricultural and pastoralism, and (2) during the period immediately following the fluorescence of the Indus Civilization when the foundations were being formed for the Gangetic Civilization of the first millennium BC. And even the period during which farming and herding began is known in detail only from one site—Mehrgarh. Indeed for an area so rich in ancient remains, we have only just begun to scratch the surface. In this regard it is important to note that the continued promise of such research in Pakistan depends to a great extent on the growing number of Pakistani scholars and their continued collaboration with their foreign colleagues.

ACKNOWLEDGMENTS

The first draft of this paper was prepared for the "Pakistan at 50" Conference of the American Institute of Pakistan Studies held at Wake Forest University 28 to 31 August 1997. We wish to thank the organizers of that conference for stimulating this contribution and Craig Baxter, who was president of the institute at the time of the Wake Forest conference, for seeing the updated version into press.

The Harappa Archaeological Research Project is particularly grateful for the assistance and support of the government of Pakistan through its officials in the Ministry of Culture and Heritage and the Ministry of Education. Both of these ministries have played key roles in facilitating archaeological and anthropological research in Pakistan.

Support for our ongoing research at Harappa and on the Indus Civilization in general has been provided by numerous organizations. We would like to thank the National Science Foundation, the National Endowment for the Humanities, the National Geographic Society, the Smithsonian Institution, American School of Prehistoric Research (Peabody Museum, Harvard University), the Fulbright Foundation, University of Wisconsin and Harvard University, the Kress Foundation, and private donors. We particularly wish to acknowledge the collegial support of all our colleagues working in Pakistan. Only through the open sharing of information and frank exchanges of ideas can we make further advances in this complex field of study. Finally, we apologize for not being able to provide references to all of the many studies done by other scholars and graduate students, both Pakistani and non-Pakistani.

BIBLIOGRAPHY

Allchin, B.

1994 Palaeolithic sites in the plains of Sind and their geographical implication. *Ancient Sindh* 1: pp 131–151.

Allchin, B. & R. W. Dennell

1990 Palaeolithic survey in Potwar region 1980–88: history and results. *Pakistan Archaeology* 24: pp 1–20.

Badgley, C. & A. K. Behrensmeyer, eds.

1995 Long records of continental ecosystems. *Palaeogeography, Palaeoclimatology, Palaeoecology* 115 (1–4): whole issue.

Barry, J. C., M. E. Morgan, L. J. Flynn, D. Pilbeam, A. K. Behrensmeyer, S. M. Raza, I. A. Khan, C. Badgley, J. Hicks & J. Kelly

2002 Faunal and environmental change in the Late Miocene Siwaliks of northern Pakistan. *Paleobiology Memoirs* 3, supplement to *Paleobiology* 28(2).

Belcher, W. R.

1991 Fish resources in an early urban context at Harappa. In *Harappa Excavations 1986–1990*, edited by R. H. Meadow, pp 107–120. Prehistory Press, Madison.

1993 Fishing of the third millennium B.C.: ongoing research in the Greater Indus Valley. *Marine Reference Collection Centre Newsletter* 1(3): pp 2–3.

1994a Butchery practices and the ethnoarchaeology of South Asian fisherfolk. In *Proceedings of the 7th meeting of the ICAZ Fish Remains Working Group*, edited by W. VanNeer, pp 170–176. Annales du Musée Royal de l'Afrique Centrale, Science Zoologiques, Tervuren.

1994b Riverine fisheries and habitat exploitation of the Indus Valley Tradition: an example from Harappa. In *South Asian Archaeology 1993*, edited by A. Parpola & P. Koskikallio, pp 71–80. Suomalainen Tiedeakatemia, Helsinki.

1997 Marine and riverine resource use during the Indus Valley Tradition: a preliminary comparison of fish remains from Balakot and Harappa. In *South Asian Archaeology 1995*, edited by B. & R. Allchin, pp 173–185. Oxford & IBH, New Delhi.

1998 *Fish Exploitation of the Baluchistan and Indus Valley Traditions: an Ethnoarchaeological Approach to the Study of Fish Remains*. Ph.D. Dissertation. University of Wisconsin, Madison.

Besenval, R.

1992 Recent archaeological surveys in Pakistani Makran. In *South Asian Archaeology 1989*, edited by C. Jarrige, pp 25–36. Prehistory Press, Madison.

1994 The 1992–1993 field-seasons at Miri Qalat: new contributions to the chronology of protohistoric settlement in Pakistani Makran. In *South Asian Archaeology 1993*, edited by A. Parpola & P. Koskikallio, pp 81–92. Suomalainen Tiedeakatemia, Helsinki.

1997 Entre le Sud–Est iranien et la plaine de l"Indus" le Kech-Makran: Recherches archéologiques sur le peuplement ancien d'une marche des confins indo-iraniens. *Arts Asiatiques* 52: pp 5–36.

Bhan, S. & J. G. Shaffer

1978 New discoveries in northern Haryana. *Man and Environment* 2: pp 57–68.

Biagi, P. & A. Pessina

1994 Surveys and Excavations in the Rohri Hills (Sindh, Pakistan): a Preliminary Report on the 1993 campaign. *Ancient Sindh* 1: pp 13–76.

Clark, S. R.

(in press a) Representing the Indus Body: Sex and Gender and the Anthropomorphic Terracotta Figurines from Harappa. *Asian Perspectives* 42(2).

(in press b) In search of the "Mother Goddess": The Terracotta Figurines from Harappa and Cultic Interpretations. In *South Asian Archaeology 2001*, edited by C. Jarrige & V. Lefèvre. Paris.

Costantini, L.

1984 The beginning of agriculture in the Kachi Plain: the evidence of Mehrgarh. In *South Asian Archaeology 1981*, edited by B. Allchin, pp 29–33. Cambridge University Press, Cambridge.

Dales, G. F.

1962a Harappan outposts on the Makran Coast. *Antiquity* 36: pp 86–92.

1962b A search for ancient seaports. *Expedition* 4(2): pp 2–10, 44.

1964 The mythical massacre at Mohenjo-daro. *Expedition* 6(3): pp 36–43. [also pp 293–296 in *Ancient Cities of the Indus*, edited by G. L. Possehl. Vikas Publishing House, New Delhi, 1979.]

1965 New investigations at Mohenjo-daro. *Archaeology* 18(2): pp 145–150. [also pp 192–195 in *Ancient Cities of the Indus*, edited by G. L. Possehl. Vikas Publishing House, New Delhi, 1979.]

1966 The decline of the Harappans. *Scientific American* 214(5): pp 92–100. [also pp 307–312 in *Ancient Cities of the Indus*, edited by G. . Possehl. Vikas Publishing House, New Delhi, 1979.]

1971 Early human contacts from the Persian Gulf through Baluchistan and southern Afghanistan. In *Food, Fiber and the Arid Lands*, edited by W. G. McGinnies, B. J. Goldman & P. Paylore, pp 145–170. University of Arizona Press, Tucson.

1973 Archaeological and radiocarbon chronologies for protohistoric South Asia. In *South Asian Archaeology*, edited by N. Hammond, pp 157–169. Duckworth, London.

1977a Shifting trade patterns between the Iranian Plateau and the Indus Valley in the third millennium B. C. In *Le plateau iranien et l'Asie Centrale des origines à la conquête islamique*, edited by J. Deshayes, pp 67–78. C. N. R. S., Paris.

1977b Hissar IIIC stone objects in Afghan Sistan. In *Mountains and Lowlands: Essays in the Archaeology of Greater Mesopotamia*, edited by L. D. Levine & T. C. Young, Jr., pp 17–27. Bibliotheca Mesopotamica 7. Undena Publications, Malibu.

1979a The Balakot Project: summary of four years of excavations in Pakistan. *Man and Environment* 3: pp 45–53.

1979b The Balakot Project: summary of four years excavations in Pakistan. In *South Asian Archaeology 1977*, edited by M. Taddei, pp 241–274. Istituto Universitario Orientale, Seminario di Studi Asiatici, Naples.

1984 Sex and stone at Mohenjo-daro. In *Frontiers of the Indus Civilization*, edited by B. B. Lal & S. P. Gupta, pp 109–115. Books & Books, New Delhi.

1989 Harappa: a new look at the type site of the Indus Civilization. In *Old Problems and New Perspectives in the Archaeology of South Asia*, edited by J. M. Kenoyer, pp 127–131. Wisconsin Archaeological Reports 2. Department of Anthropology, University of Wisconsin, Madison.

Dales, G. F. & L. Flam

1969 On tracking woolly Kullis and the like. *Expedition* 12(1): pp 15–23.

Dales, G. F. & J. M. Kenoyer

1986 *Excavations at Mohenjo Daro, Pakistan: The Pottery*. University Museum Press, Philadelphia.

1989 Excavation at Harappa—1988. *Pakistan Archaeology* 24: pp 68–176.

1990 Excavation at Harappa—1989. *Pakistan Archaeology* 25: pp 241–280.

1991 Summaries of five seasons of research at Harappa (District Sahiwal, Punjab, Pakistan) 1986–1990. In *Harappa Excavations 1986–1990*, edited by R. H. Meadow, pp 185–262. Prehistory Press, Madison.

1993 The Harappa Project 1986–1989: new investigations at an ancient Indus city. In *Harappan Civilization*, second revised edition, edited by G. L. Possehl, pp 469–520. Oxford & IBH, New Delhi.

Dales, G. F. & C. P. Lipo

1992 *The Makran Coast of Pakistan: A Search for Ancient Seaports*. Archaeological Research Facility, University of California, Berkeley.

Dani, A. H.

1970–1971 Excavations in the Gomal Valley. *Ancient Pakistan* 5: pp 1–177.

1975 Origins of Bronze Age cultures in the Indus basin—a geographic perspective. *Expedition* 17(2): pp 12–18.

Dennell, R. W.

1984 The Importance of the Potwar Plateau, Pakistan, to the studies of early man. In *South Asian Archaeology 1981*, edited by B. Allchin, pp 10–20. Cambridge University Press, Cambridge.

1991 *Pakistan's Prehistory: A Glimpse at the First Two Million Years*. Ancient India and Iran Trust, Cambridge.

Dennell, R. W., L. Hurcombe, R. Jenkinson & H. Rendell

1990 Preliminary results of the Palaeolithic Programme of the British Archaeological Mission to Pakistan, 1983–1987. In *South Asian Archaeology 1987*, edited by M. Taddei, pp 17–30. IsMEO, Rome.

Dennell, R. W., H. M. Rendell & E. Hailwood

1988 Late Pleistocene Artefacts from Northern Pakistan. *Current Anthropology* 29(3): pp 495–498.

Dupree, L.

1972 Prehistoric research in Afghanistan (1959–1966). *Transactions of the American Philosophical Society* 62(4): pp 1–84. Philadelphia.

Durrani, F. A.

1986 *Rehman Dheri and the Origins of Indus Civilization*. Ph.D. Dissertation. Department of Anthropology, Temple University.

1988 Excavations in the Gomal Valley: Rehman Dheri Excavation Report No. 1. *Ancient Pakistan* 6: pp 1–232.

Durrani, F. A., I. Ali & G. Erdosy

1991 Further excavation at Rehman Dheri. *Ancient Pakistan* 7: pp 61–151.

Dyson, R. H.

1982 Paradigm changes in the study of the Indus Civilization. In *Harappan Civilization*, edited by G. L. Possehl, pp 417–427. Oxford & IBH, New Delhi

Fairservis, W. A.

1952 Preliminary report on the prehistoric archaeology of the Afghan–Baluchi areas. *Novitates*, American Museum of Natural History No. 1587.

1956 Excavations in the Quetta Valley, West Pakistan. *Anthropological Papers of the American Museum of Natural History* 45(2): pp 165–402.

1959 Archaeological Surveys in the Zhob and Loralai Districts, West Pakistan. *Anthropological Papers of the American Museum of Natural History* 47(2): pp 273–448.

1961 Archaeological studies in the Seistan Basin of southwestern Afghanistan and eastern Iran. *Anthropological Papers of the American Museum of Natural History* 48(1): pp 1–128.

1975 *The Roots of Ancient India*. University of Chicago Press, Chicago.

1982 Allahdino: an excavation of a small Harappan site. In *Harappan Civilization*, edited by G. L. Possehl, pp 107–112. Oxford & IBH, New Delhi.

1985 Sir Mortimer Wheeler and I: archaeological methodologies in the Indo–Iranian Borderlands. In *Orientalia Iosephi Tucci Memoriae Dicata*, edited by G. Gnoli & L. Lanciotti, pp 343–354. IsMEO, Rome.

Flam, L.

1976 Settlement, subsistence and population: a dynamic approach to the development of the Indus valley civilization. In *Ecological Backgrounds of South Asian Prehistory*, edited by K. A. R. Kennedy and G. L. Possehl, pp 76–93. Cornell University Press, Ithaca, NY.

1981 *The Paleogeography and Prehistoric Settlement Patterns in Sind, Pakistan (c. 4000–2000 BC).* Ph.D. Dissertation. University of Pennsylvania, Philadelphia.

1986 Recent explorations in Sind: paleography, regional ecology and prehistoric settlement patterns. In *Studies in the Archaeology of India and Pakistan*, edited by J. Jacobson, pp 65–89. Oxford & IBH, New Delhi.

1993a Excavation at Ghazi Shah, Sindh, Pakistan. In *Harappan Civilization*, second revised edition, edited by G. L. Possehl, pp 457–467. Oxford & IBH, New Delhi.

1993b Excavations at Ghazi Shah 1985–1987: an interim report. *Pakistan Archaeology* 28: pp 131–158.

1993c Fluvial geomorphology of the lower Indus basin (Sindh, Pakistan) and the Indus Civilization. In *Himalaya to the Sea*, edited by J. F. Shroder, Jr., pp 265–287. Routledge, London and New York.

1999 Ecology and population mobility in the prehistoric settlement of the lower Indus Valley, Sindh, Pakistan. In *The Indus River: Biodiversity, Resources, Humankind*, edited by A. Meadow & P. S. Meadows, pp 313–323. Oxford University Press, Oxford.

Franke–Vogt, U.

1997 Reopening research on Balakot: a summary of perspectives and first results. In *South Asian Archaeology 1995*, edited by R. and B. Allchin, pp 215–235. Oxford & IBH, New Delhi.

2001 The Southern Indus Valley during the later 2nd and 1st millennia BC: The Dark Age. In *Migration und Kulturtransfer*, edited by R. Eichmann and H. Parzinger, pp 247–290. Rudolph Habelt, Bonn.

Franke-Vogt, U., S. S. ul-Haq & M. H. K. Khattak

2000 Archaeological exploration in the Kanrach Valley (Las Bela, Balochistan). In *South Asian Archaeology 1997*, edited by M. Taddei and G. De Marco, pp 189–213. Istituto Italiano per l'Africa e l'Oriente, Rome.

Hemphill, B. E., J. R. Lukacs & K. A. R. Kennedy

1991 Biological adaptations and affinities of Bronze Age Harappans. In *Harappa Excavations 1986–1990*, edited by R. H. Meadow, pp 137–182. Prehistory Press, Madison.

Hurcombe, L. and R. W. Dennell

1992 A Pre-Acheulean, Lower Palaeolithic industry in the Pabbi Hills, Northern Pakistan. In *South Asian Archaeology 1989*, edited by C. Jarrige, pp 133–136. Prehistory Press, Madison.

Jacobson, J.

1979 Recent developments in South Asian prehistory and protohistory. *Annual Review of Anthropology* 8: pp 467–502.

Jansen, M.

1991 Mohenjo-Daro—a city on the Indus. In *Forgotten Cities on the Indus*, edited by M. Jansen, M. Mulloy & G. Urban, pp 145–165. Phillip von Zabern, Mainz am Rhein.

1993 Mohenjo-daro: type site of the earliest urbanization process in South Asia. In *Urban Form and Meaning in South Asia: The Shaping of Cities from Prehistoric to Precolonial Times*, edited by H. Spodek & D. M. Srinivasan, pp 35–52. National Gallery of Art, Washington.

Jarrige, C., J.-F. Jarrige, R. H. Meadow & G. Quivon, editors

1995 *Mehrgarh Field Reports 1975 to 1985—From the Neolithic to the Indus Civilization*. Department of Culture and Tourism, Government of Sindh and the French Foreign Ministry, Karachi.

Jarrige, J.-F.

1986 Excavations at Mehrgarh-Nausharo. *Pakistan Archaeology* 10–22: pp 63–131.

1988 Excavations at Nausharo. *Pakistan Archaeology* 23: pp 149–203.

1989 Excavation at Nausharo 1987–88. *Pakistan Archaeology* 24: pp 21–67.

1990 Excavation at Nausharo 1988–89. *Pakistan Archaeology* 25: pp 193–240.

2000 Mehrgarh Neolithic: new excavations. In *South Asian Archaeology 1997*, edited by Maurizio Taddei and Giuseppe de Marco, pp 259–283. Istituto Italiano per l'Africa e l'Oriente, Rome.

Jarrige, J.-F. & R. H. Meadow

1980 The antecedents of civilization in the Indus Valley. *Scientific American* 243(2): pp 122–133.

1992 Mélanges Fairservis: a discourse on relations between Kachi and Sindh in prehistory. In *South Asian Archaeology Studies*, edited by G. L. Possehl, pp 163–178. Oxford & IBH, New Delhi.

Jarrige, J.-F. & M. Lechevallier

1979 Excavations at Mehrgarh, Baluchistan: their significance in the prehistoric context of the Indo-Pakistan borderlands. In *South Asian Archaeology 1977*, edited by M. Taddei, pp 463–536. Istituto Universitario Orientale, Seminario di Studi Asiatici, Naples.

Jenkins, P. C.

1994 Cemetery R37: new perspectives on style and chronology. In *From Sumer to Meluhha: Contributions to the Archaeology of South and West Asia in Memory of George F. Dales, Jr.*, edited by J. M. Kenoyer, pp 105–112. Madison, Department of Anthropology.

2000 The pottery from Cemetery R37: chronology and the changing social structure of Harappan society. In *South Asian Archaeology 1997*, edited by M. Taddei & and G. DeMarco, pp 35–53. Istituto Italiano per l'Africa e l'Oriente, Rome.

Jorgensen, D. W., M. D. Harvey, S. A. Schumm, and L. Flam

1993 Morphology and dynamics of the Indus river: implications for the Mohen jo Daro site. In *Himalaya to the Sea*, edited by J. F. Shroder, Jr., pp 288–326. Routledge, London and New York.

Kennedy, K. A. R.

1984 Trauma and disease in the ancient Harappans. In *Frontiers of the Indus Civilization*, edited by B. B. Lal & S. P. Gupta, pp 417–424. Books & Books, New Delhi.

1990 Reconstruction of trauma, disease and lifeways of prehistoric peoples of South Asia from the skeletal record. In *South Asian Archaeology 1987*, edited by M. Taddei, pp 61–78. IsMEO, Rome.

1992 Biological anthropology of human skeletons from Harappa: 1928–1988. *Eastern Anthropologist* 45(1–2): pp 55–86.

1994 Evolution of South Asian Pleistocene hominids: demic displacement or regional continuity? In *South Asian Archaeology 1993*, edited by A. Parpola & P. Koskikallio, pp 337–344. Suomalainen Tiedeakatemia, Helsinki.

Kenoyer, J. M.

1991a The Indus Valley Tradition of Pakistan and Western India. *Journal of World Prehistory* 5(4): pp 331–385.

1991b Urban process in the Indus Tradition: a preliminary model from Harappa. In *Harappa Excavations 1986–1990*, edited by R. H. Meadow, pp 29–60. Prehistory Press, Madison.

1992a Harappan craft specialization and the question of urban segregation and stratification. *Eastern Anthropologist* 45(1–2): pp 39–54.

1992b Ornament styles of the Indus tradition: evidence from recent excavations at Harappa, Pakistan. *Paléorient* 17(2—1991): pp 79–98.

1993 Excavations on Mound E, Harappa: A systematic approach to the study of Indus urbanism. In *South Asian Archaeology 1991*, edited by A. J. Gail & G. J. R. Mevissen, pp 165–194. F. S. Verlag, Stuttgart.

1995a Interaction systems, specialized crafts and culture change: The Indus Valley Tradition and the Indo–Gangetic Tradition in South Asia. In *The Indo–Aryans of Ancient South Asia: Language, Material Culture and Ethnicity*, edited by G. Erdosy, pp 213–257. W. DeGruyter, Berlin.

1995b Shell trade and shell working during the Neolithic and Early Chalcolithic at Mehrgarh. In *Mehrgarh Field Reports 1975 to 1985—From the Neolithic to the Indus Civilization*, edited by C. Jarrige, J.-F. Jarrige, R. H. Meadow & G. Quivron, pp 566–581. Department of Culture and Tourism, Government of Sindh and the French Foreign Ministry, Karachi.

1997a Early city–states in South Asia: comparing the Harappan Phase and the Early Historic period. In The *Archaeology of City–States: Cross Cultural Approaches,* edited by D. L. Nichols & T. H. Charlton, pp 51–70. Smithsonian Institution Press, Washington, D. C.

1997b Trade and technology of the Indus Valley: new insights from Harappa, Pakistan. *World Archaeology* 29(2): pp 262–280.

1998 *Ancient Cities of the Indus Valley Civilization*. Oxford University Press, Karachi.

2000 Wealth and socio-economic hierarchies of the Indus Valley Civilization. In *Order, Legitimacy and Wealth in Early States*, edited by J. Richards & M. Van Buren, pp 88–109. Cambridge University Press, Cambridge.

(in press) Bead technologies at Harappa, 3300–1900 BC: a comparative summary. In *South Asian Archaeology 2001*, edited by C. Jarrige & V. Lefèvre. Paris.

Kenoyer, J. M. & R. H. Meadow

1996 New inscribed objects From Harappa. *Lahore Museum Bulletin* 9(1): pp 1–29.

2000 The Ravi Phase: a new cultural manifestation at Harappa (Pakistan). In *South Asian Archaeology 1997*, edited by M. Taddei and G. DeMarco, pp 55–76. Istituto Italiano per l'Africa e l'Oriente, Rome.

Kenoyer, J. M. & H. M. -L. Miller

1999 Metal technologies of the Indus Valley Tradition in Pakistan and western India. In *The Archaeometallurgy of the Asian Old World*, edited by V. C. Pigott, pp 107–151. University Museum Monograph 89 & MASCA Research Papers in Science and Archaeology 16. University of Pennsylvania Museum, Philadelphia.

Khan, F.

1992 Recent discoveries from the North–West Frontier, Pakistan. *South Asian Studies* 8: pp 67–80.

Khan, F., J. R. Knox & K. D. Thomas

1990 Sheri Khan Tarakai: A Neolithic village in Bannu District, NWFP. In *South Asian Archaeology 1987*, edited by M. Taddei & P. Callieri, pp 111–127. IsMEO, Rome.

Korisettar, R.

2002 The archaeology of the South Asian Lower Palaeolithic: history and current status. In *Indian Archaeology in Retrospect, Volume 1 (Prehistory: Archaeology of South Asia)*, edited by S. Settar and R. Korisetttar, pp 1–66. Indian Council of Historical Research, New Delhi.

Law, R.

(in press a) Potential steatite source areas of the Indus Valley Civilization. *Proceedings of the International Colloquium on Indus Civilization, April 6–8, 2001*, Islamabad.

(in press b) Regional interaction in the prehistoric Indus Valley: initial results of rock and mineral sourcing studies at Harappa. In *South Asian Archaeology 2001*, edited by C. Jarrige & V. Lefèvre. Paris.

(in press c) Moving mountains: the trade and transport of rocks and minerals within the greater Indus Valey region. In *An Odyssey of Space: 2001: 34th Chacmool Conference Proceedings*. University of Calgary Press, Calgary.

Lovell, N. C.

1994 Spinal arthritis and physical stress at Bronze Age Harappa. *American Journal of Physical Anthropology* 93: pp 149–164.

1997 Anemia in the ancient Indus Valley. *International Journal of Osteoarchaeology* 7(2): pp 115–123.

Lovell, N. C. & K. A. R. Kennedy

1989 Society and disease in prehistoric South Asia. In *Old Problems and New Perspectives in the Archaeology of South Asia*, edited by J. M. Kenoyer, pp 89–92. Wisconsin Archaeological Reports 2. Department of Anthropology, University of Wisconsin, Madison.

Lukacs, J. R.

1984 Hominoid adaptations and hominid origins: evidence from South Asia. In *Studies in the Archaeology and Palaeoanthropology of South Asia*, edited by K. A. R. Kennedy & G. L. Possehl, pp 1–16. Oxford & IBH, New Delhi.

1989 Biological affinities from dental morphology: the evidence from Neolithic Mehrgarh. In *Old Problems and New Perspectives in the Archaeology of South Asia*, edited by J. M. Kenoyer, pp 75–88. Wisconsin Archaeological Reports 2. Department of Anthropology, University of Wisconsin, Madison.

Lukacs, J. R. & L. L. Minderman

1992 Dental pathology and agricultural intensification from Neolithic to Chalcolithic periods at Mehrgarh (Baluchistan, Pakistan). In *South Asian Archaeology 1989*, edited by C. Jarrige, pp 167–180. Prehistory Press, Madison.

Lukacs, J. R. & R. F. Pastor

1990 Activity induced patterns of dental abrasion in prehistoric Pakistan. In *South Asian Archaeology 1987*, edited by M. Taddei, pp 79–110. IsMEO, Rome.

Mallah, Q. H.

1998 Archaeological survey in southeastern Pakistan: the Thar Desert of Sindh. *Scientific Sindh* 5: pp 165–178.

2000 *Archaeology and Ethnoarchaeology of the Thar Desert*. Ph.D. dissertation, University of Wisconsin, Madison.

Meadow, R. H.

1981 Early animal domestication in South Asia: a first report of the faunal remains from Mehrgarh, Pakistan. In *South Asian Archaeology 1979*, edited by H. Härtel, pp 143–180. Dietrich Reimer Verlag, Berlin.

1984 Animal domestication in the Middle East: a view from the eastern margin. In *Animals and Archaeology: 3. Early Herders and their Flocks*, edited by J Clutton-Brock and C. Grigson, pp 309–337. BAR S202. British Archaeological Reports, Oxford.

1989 Prehistoric wild sheep and sheep domestication on the eastern margin of the Middle East. In *Early Animal Domestication and its Cultural Context*, edited by P. J. Crabtree, D. Campana & K. Ryan, pp 24–36. MASCA Research Papers in Science and Archaeology, Special Supplement to Volume 6. The University Museum of Archaeology and Anthropology, Philadelphia.

1991 Faunal remains and urbanism at Harappa. In *Harappa Excavations 1986–1990*, edited by R. H. Meadow, pp 89–106. Prehistory Press, Madison.

1993a The past, present, and future of bioarchaeological studies in Pakistan with specific reference to Mohenjo-daro and the Indus Civilization. *Pakistan Archaeology* 28: pp 183–215.

1993b Animal domestication in the Middle East: a revised view from the eastern margin. In *Harappan Civilization*, second revised edition, edited by G. L. Possehl, pp 295–320. Oxford & IBH, New Delhi.

1995 The origins and spread of agriculture and pastoralism in South Asia. In *The origins and spread of agriculture and pastoralism in Eurasia*, edited by D. R. Harris, pp 390–412. Institute of Archaeology, University College London, London.

1999 Pre- and proto-historic agricultural and pastoral transformations in northwestern South Asia. *The Review of Archaeology* 19(2): pp 12–21.

Meadow, R. H., editor

1991 *Harappa Excavations 1986–1990*. Prehistory Press, Madison.

Meadow, R. H. & J. M. Kenoyer

1993 Excavation at Harappa 1992 &1993. *Pakistan Archaeology* pp 28: 55–107.

1994 Excavations at Harappa 1993: the city walls and inscribed materials. In *South Asian Archaeology 1993*, edited by A. Parpola & P. Koskikallio, pp 451–470. Suomalainen Tiedeakatemia, Helsinki.

1997 Excavations at Harappa 1994–1995: new perspectives on the Indus script, craft activities, and city organization. In *South Asian Archaeology 1995*, edited by R. & B. Allchin, pp 139–172. Oxford & IBH, New Delhi.

2000 The "tiny steatite seals" (incised steatite tablets) of Harappa: some observations on their context and dating. In *South Asian Archaeology 1997*, edited by M. Taddei and G. DeMarco, pp 321–340. Istituto Italiano per l'Africa e l'Oriente, Rome.

(in press a) Harappa excavations 1998–1999: new evidence for the development and manifestation of the Harappan phenomenon. In *South Asian Archaeology 1999*, edited by K. R. van Kooij & E. M. Raven. Leiden.

(in press b) Excavations at Harappa 2000–2001: new insights on chronology and city organization. In *South Asian Archaeology 2001*, edited by C. Jarrige & V. Lefèvre. Paris.

Meadow, R. H. & A. K. Patel

2002 From Mehrgarh to Harappa and Dholavira: prehistoric pastoralism in northwestern South Asia through the Harappan Period. In *Indian Archaeology in Retrospect, Volume 2 (Protohistory: Archaeology of the Harappan Civilization)*, edited by S. Settar and R. Korisettar, pp 391–408. Indian Council of Historical Research, New Delhi.

Miller, H. M. -L.

1997a Locating ancient manufacturing areas: high-temperature manufacturing debris from surface surveys at Harappa, Pakistan. In *South Asian Archaeology 1995*, edited by R. & B. Allchin, pp 939–946. Oxford & IBH, New Delhi.

1997b Pottery firing structures (kilns) of the Indus Civilization during the third millennium B.C. In *The Prehistory and History of Ceramic Kilns*, edited by P. Rice & D. Kingery, pp 41–71. Ceramics and Civilization 7. American Ceramic Society, Columbus, Ohio.

1999 *Pyrotechnology and Society in the Cities of the Indus Valley*. Ph.D. Dissertation. University of Wisconsin, Madison.

Mughal, M. R.

1970 *The Early Harappan Period in the Greater Indus Valley and Northern Baluchistan (c. 3000–2400 B.C.)*. Ph.D. Dissertation. Department of Anthropology, University of Pennsylvania, Philadelphia.

1974 Explorations in northern Baluchistan, 1972: new evidence and fresh interpretation. In *Proceedings of the 2nd Annual Symposium on Archaeological Research in Iran*, edited by F. Bagherzadeh, pp 276–286. Iranian Centre for Archaeological Research, Tehran.

1977 Cultural links between Pakistan and Iran during the pre-historic period. In *Iran–Pakistan: A Common Culture; Articles written by twenty six Pakistani scholars*, pp 33–82. Iran Pakistan Institute of Persian Studies, Islamabad.

1981 New research on the origins of the Indus Civilization. *Sind Quarterly* 9(3): pp 45–51, 60.

1982 Recent archaeological research in the Cholistan desert. In *Harappan Civilization*, edited by G. L. Possehl, pp 86–95. Oxford & IBH, New Delhi.

1990 Archaeological field research in Pakistan since Independence: an overview. *Bulletin of the Deccan College Post-Graduate & Research Institute* 49: pp 261–277.

1997 Ancient Cholistan: Archaeology and Architecture. Ferozsons, Rawalpindi.

Mughal, M. R., F. Iqbal, M. A. Khan & M. Hassan

1996 Archaeological sites and monuments in Punjab: preliminary results of explorations: 1992–1996. *Pakistan Archaeology* 29: pp 1–474.

Negrino, F. & M. M. Kazi

1996 The Paleolithic industries of the Rohri Hills (Sindh, Pakistan). *Ancient Sindh* 3: –38.

Perkins, D.

1972 The fauna of Aq Kupruk caves: a brief note. *Transactions of the American Philosophical Society* 62(4): p 73.

Pilbeam, D.

1978 Rethinking human origins. *Discovery* 13(1): pp 2–9.

1979 Recent finds and interpretations of Miocene hominoids. *Annual Review of Anthropology* 8: pp 333–352.

Pilbeam, D., G. E. Meyer, C. Badgley, M. D. Rose, M. H. L. Pickford, A. K. Behrensmeyer, S. M. Ibrahim Shah

1977 New hominoid primates from the Siwaliks of Pakistan and their bearing on hominoid evolution. *Nature* 270(5639): pp 689–695.

Possehl, G. L.

1967 The Mohenjo Daro floods: a reply. *American Anthropologist* 69(1): pp 32–40.

1975 The chronology of gabarbands and palas of western South Asia. *Expedition* (Winter): pp 33–39.

1977 The end of a state and continuity of a tradition. In *Realm and Region in Traditional India*, edited by R. G. Fox, pp 234–254. Duke University Program in South Asian Studies, Durham, N.C.

1986 *Kulli: An Exploration of an Ancient Civilization in South Asia*. Carolina Academic Press, Durham, N.C.

1990 The Sorath Harappan: a new regional manifestation of the Indus urban phase. In *South Asian Archaeology 1987*, edited by M. Taddei, pp 295–320. IsMEO, Rome.

1992 The Harappan Civilization in Gujarat: The Sorath and Sindhi Harappans. *Eastern Anthropologist* 45(1–2): pp 117–154.

1996 *Indus Age: The Writing System*. University of Pennsylvania Press, Philadelphia.

1998 Sociocultural complexity without the state: the Indus Civilization. In *Archaic States*, edited by G. M. Feinman and J. Marcus, pp 261–291. School of American Research Press, Santa Fe.

1999 *Indus Age: The Beginnings*. University of Pennsylvania Press, Philadelphia.

2002 *The Indus Civilization: a contemporary perspective*. AltaMira Press,

Possehl, G. L. & D. P. Mehta

1994 Excavations at Rojdi, 1992–1993. In *South Asian Archaeology 1993*, edited by A. Parpola & P. Koskikallio, pp 599–602. Suomalainen Tiedeakatemia, Helsinki.

Possehl, G. L. & M. H. Raval

1989 *Harappan Civilization and Rojdi*. Oxford & IBH and AIIS, New Delhi.

Quivron, G.

1994 The pottery sequence from 2700 to 2400 BC at Nausharo, Baluchistan. In *South Asian Archaeology 1993*, edited by A. Parpola & P. Koskikallio, pp 629–644. Suomalainen Tiedeakatemia, Helsinki.

Raikes, R.

1965 The ancient gabarbands of Baluchistan. *East and West*, n.s. 15: pp 3–12.

Rendell, H. M., R. W. Dennell & M. A. Halim

1989 *Pleistocene and Palaeolithic Investigations in the Soan Valley, Northern Pakistan*. BAR S544. British Archaeological Reports, Oxford.

Russell, N.

1995 The bone tool industry at Mehrgarh and Sibri. In *Mehrgarh Field Reports 1975 to 1985—From the Neolithic to the Indus Civilization*, edited by C. Jarrige, J.-F. Jarrige, R. H. Meadow & G. Quivon, pp 583–613. Department of Culture and Tourism, Government of Sindh and the French Foreign Ministry, Karachi.

Schuldenrein, J.

2002 Geoarchaeological perspectives on the Harappan sites of South Asia. In *Indian Archaeology in Retrospect, Volume 2 (Protohistory: Archaeology of the Harappan Civilization)*, edited by S. Settar and R. Korisetttar, pp 47–80. New Delhi, Indian Council of Historical Research.

Shaffer, J. G.

1974 The prehistory of Baluchistan: some interpretative problems. In *Arctic Anthropology*, Supplement 11: pp 224–235.

1978a The later prehistoric periods. In *The Archaeology of Afghanistan: From Earliest Times to the Timurid Period*, edited by F. R. Allchin & N. Hammond, pp 71–186. Academic Press, London.

1978b *Prehistoric Baluchistan*. B & R Publishing, Delhi.

1987 Cultural development in the eastern Punjab. In *Studies in the Archaeology of India and Pakistan*, edited by J. Jacobson, pp 195–236. Oxford & IBH, New Delhi.

1991 Archaeological Research at Watgal, Raichur District, Karnataka: A Report on the 1990–1991 Activities. Department of Anthropology, Case Western Reserve University, Cleveland, Ohio.

1992a Archaeological Research at Watgal, Raichur District, Karnataka: a Report on the 1991–1992 Activities. Case Western Reserve University, Cleveland, Ohio.

1992b The Indus Valley, Baluchistan and Helmand Traditions: Neolithic through Bronze Age. In *Chronologies in Old World Archaeology* (3rd Edition), edited by R. Ehrich, Vol I: pp 441–464; Vol. II: pp 425–446. University of Chicago Press, Chicago.

Shaffer, J. G. & D. A. Lichtenstein

1989 Ethnicity and change in the Indus Valley cultural tradition. In *Old Problems and New Perspectives in the Archaeology of South Asia*, edited by J. M. Kenoyer, pp 117–126. Wisconsin Archaeological Reports 2. Department of Anthropology, University of Wisconsin, Madison.

Shaikh, N.

1997 Recent Exploration of Archaeological Sites and Monuments of Khairpur District. In *South Asian Archaeology 1995*, edited by F. R. Allchin and B. Allchin, pp 309–322. Oxford & IBH, New Delhi.

Sharma, K. K.

1995 Quaternary Stratigraphy and Prehistory of the Upper Indus Valley, Ladakh. In *Quaternary Environments and Geoarchaeology of India*, edited by S. Wadia, R. Korisettar & V. S. Kale, pp 98–108. Geological Society of India, Bangalore.

Stein, Sir M. A.

1931 *An Archaeological Tour in Gedrosia*. Memoirs of the Archaeological Survey of India 43. Calcutta.

de Terra, H. & P. Teilhard de Chardin

1936 Observations on the Upper Siwalik formation and later Pleistocene deposits in India. *Proceedings of the American Philosophical Society* 76: pp 791–822.

de Terra, H. & T. T. Paterson

1939 *Studies on the Ice Age in India*. Publication 493. Carnegie Institute, Washington, D.C.

Tosi, M.

1979 The Proto-urban cultures of Eastern Iran and the Indus Civilization. Notes and suggestions for a spatio-temporal frame to study the early relations between India and Iran. In *South Asian Archaeology 1977*, edited by M. Taddei, pp 149–171. Istituto Universitario Orientale, Seminario di Studi Asiatici, Naples.

Weber, S. A.

1998 Out of Africa: The initial impact of millets in South Asia. *Current Anthropology* 39(2): pp 267–274.

1999 Seeds of urbanism: palaeoethnobotany and the Indus Civilization. *Antiquity* 73: pp 813–826.

Wheeler, R. E. M.

1968 *The Indus Civilization* (Third Edition). Cambridge University Press, Cambridge.

Wright, R. P.

1991 Patterns of technology and the organization of production at Harappa. In *Harappa Excavations 1986–1990*, edited by R. H. Meadow, pp 71–88. Prehistory Press, Madison.

1993 The Harappa Museum pottery collections: some typological and technical evidence. *Pakistan Archaeology* 28: pp 231–241.

Chronology of Important Events in Pakistan: October 1999 to October 2002

Scott Kofmehl

1999

October 12. A bloodless military coup brings Army Chief General Pervez Musharraf to power. Deposed Prime Minister (PM) Sharif is arrested and placed under house arrest.
October 15. The State Bank of Pakistan directs commercial banks to freeze all local and foreign currency accounts of hundreds of politicians suspected of corruption.
October 17. In a television address, Musharraf pledges that "the armed forces have no intention to stay in charge any longer than is absolutely necessary to pave the way for true democracy to flourish in Pakistan."
October 17. Military government begins with an anticorruption program against politicians.
October 18. An emergency meeting of eight Commonwealth foreign ministers in London condemns the coup and effectively suspends Pakistan from the Commonwealth.
October 25–27. On his first foreign trip, Musharraf visits Saudi Arabia and the United Arab Emirates.
October 26. Musharraf announces the new appointments to the National Security Council and a civilian Cabinet.
November 3. Pakistan's Kashmir region holds election for local Northern Areas Legislative council. The elections had been ordered by ex-PM Sharif and confirmed by Musharraf.
November 4. Violence flared up in Kashmir between Pakistani militant Lashkar-i-Toiba and the Indian army.
November 5. Musharraf announces the trial of ex-PM Sharif for tax evasion and defaulting on loans.
November 8. Musharraf intends to return to democracy as soon as better conditions are installed.
November 9. Pakistani and Indian troops clash in Kashmir in the first escalation of conflict since the military coup. At least twenty-one soldiers are killed.
November 11. Pakistan's authorities additionally accuse ex-PM Sharif of hijacking, kidnapping, and attempted murder. Charges are made in connection with the attempted diversion of a plane carrying Musharraf on the day of the coup. Charges could result in the death penalty.

November 15. The Pakistan Muslim League (PML) files a petition in the Supreme Court claiming that the October 12 military coup was "immoral, illegal, and unconstitutional."
November 30. Musharraf intends to establish up to 100 special courts for corruption and loan default trials.
December 3. Mohammed Yaqub, former governor of the State Bank of Pakistan, resigned from the National Security Council.
December 4. Musharraf announces that he will restore democracy at the district level by the end of 2000, while to return to national parliamentary democracy will take longer.
December 7. Musharraf complains about India's cool reaction to his peace offer. He stresses the importance of the Kashmir conflict in Indo-Pakistani relations.
December 8. The Pakistan People's Party (PPP) demands the restoration of the constitution and early general elections, warning that the present situation could give rise to fundamentalism.
December 8. In the Sharif case, the prosecution filed charges of hijacking, kidnapping, attempted murder, and plotting to wage war against the state.
December 9. Musharraf meets Iran's president Khatami and supreme leader Khamenei in order to hold talks over the countries' different views on the Taliban issue and the sectarian violence against Iranians in Pakistan.
December 13. Pakistan's Central Bank orders a freeze on all funds of the Taliban movement, in accordance with UN sanctions.
December 15. Musharraf announces $363 million aid program to the poorest regions of Pakistan.
December 21. Musharraf reinforces his statement that Pakistan's parliament will not be restored soon.
December 23. Pakistan's Supreme Court upholds a ruling of the lower Federal Sharia Court declaring interest (*riba*) is un-Islamic and directs the government to introduce an interest-free economy by 2001. The ruling raises grave concern regarding the effects on the economy.
December 24. Pakistan permits an Indian Airlines plane, hijacked by Kashmiri separatists who are believed to be members of the Lashkar-i-Toiba, to land and refuel in Lahore. The aircraft then proceeded to Kandahar, Afghanistan, where after negotiations the surviving crew and passengers (one passenger was killed) were released in exchange for three terrorist prisoners held in Indian jails. India agreed to this method of terminating the hijacking episode on December 31.
December 26. Foreign Minister Sattar accuses India that it used the hijacking to isolate Pakistan. Sattar makes it clear that Pakistan is opposed to all forms of terrorism.
December 27. Pakistan launches second major crackdown on corruption and loan defaulting. Authorities arrest thirty-three people, including former provincial chief ministers.

2000

January 1. Pakistan and India exchange lists of nuclear sites in order to comply with a 1988 agreement not to attack nuclear facilities.
January 3. Foreign Minister Sattar rejects India's allegation that Pakistan was involved in the recent hijacking.
January 11. Pakistan's foreign ministry says that Pakistan does not allow terrorism on its soil, which is a crime under the 1997 Anti-Terrorism Act.
January 13. One U.K. and two U.S. delegations separately visit Pakistan and Musharraf to remind him of his pledge to restore democracy soon. U.S. delegations also meet officials from the PML and the PPP.
January 17. Musharraf visits China in order to reaffirm Pakistan's ties with China.
January 17. Musharraf offers peace dialogue on the Kashmir issue. He denies that the hijackers of the Indian plane are in Pakistan.
January 19. Ex-PM Sharif and six codefendants are formally charged with kidnapping, hijacking, attempted murder, and terrorism. The original charges of treason were not included. Sharif and the co-defendants pleaded not guilty to all charges.
January 23. Heavy fighting continues between Pakistani and Indian troops in Kashmir.
January 24. U.S. officials say they have evidence that the Harkat-ul-Mujahideen group hijacked the Indian plane, operating with the support of Pakistani military and intelligence service.
January 25. U.S. President Clinton contradicts the State Department statement that Pakistan supported the hijacking of the Indian plane.
January 27. Freed Harkat-ul-Mujahideen cleric Mohammad Masood Azhar who calls on Islamabad to be prepared for a holy war against India.
February 4. Masood Azhar launches a new party, Jaish-i-Muhammad (the army of the Prophet Muhammad), in Karachi. The party's aim is to wage a holy war in Kashmir against India.
February 7. Musharraf says that there is no danger of war with India, but India unnecessarily increases tensions.
February 9. U.S. President Clinton says that he is "profoundly concerned" about the discord between nuclear rivals India and Pakistan and he hopes to do something before leaving office.
February 14. Iraq and Pakistan announce broader relations in all fields between the two countries. They particularly agree to restrict U.S. influence in the region.
February 15. Interior Minister Haider announces a nationwide ban beginning in March that prohibits people from carrying arms and ammunitions in public.
February 16. The U.S. distributes photos of Osama bin Laden and offers US$5 million reward for his arrest.
February 16. U.S. President Clinton offers to mediate between Pakistan and India in their dispute over Kashmir.

February 25. U.S. State Department criticizes the Pakistani military government for not setting election after the October 1999 coup.
February 25. In the Sharif case, the defense team resigned, bringing the case to a halt.
February 29. Pakistan rejects the U.S. human rights report that criticizes Pakistan's human rights record.
March 10. Iqbal Raad, a leading defense lawyer for Sharif, and two assistants, are murdered.
March 15. Pakistan's independent human rights commission criticizes the country's human rights record, particularly its treatment of women, child abuse, and restriction of freedom of speech.
March 16. Pakistan's military government bans open-air political rallies.
March 16. A judge convicted Javed Iqbal of killing 100 children. Iqbal was sentenced public strangulation, after which his body was to be cut into 100 pieces and dissolved in acid.
March 20. Pakistan's chief justice Irshad Hasan Khan summons the attorney general to appear before a court the next week to justify the ban on open-air political rallies and strikes.
March 21. U.S. President Clinton and Indian PM Vajpayee meet to discuss the Kashmir conflict. Vajpayee denies the threat of war. Clinton asks that India respect the Line of Control (LOC) and renew the dialogue process with Pakistan.
March 23. Musharraf announces a plan for "a devolution of power and establishing the foundation of democracy." He outlines a timetable for restoring democracy at a local level.
March 25. U.S. President Clinton arrives in Islamabad for a five-hour visit in Pakistan. Clinton presses Musharraf on the return to democracy and to use influence to bring bin Laden to justice. In a nationwide broadcast, Clinton tells the Pakistani people that there is no military solution to the fifty-two–year dispute over Kashmir.
March 30. Musharraf reiterates his priorities in Pakistan's internal affairs. Outlines plans for elections, pushes privatization efforts, and justifies that 19 percent of the budget is used for defense.
March 30. Musharraf states that he is prepared to discuss the Kashmir issue with India whether it is through bilateral relations or through mediation or through facilitation.
April 3. A team of IMF officials arrives in Pakistan to discuss debt rescheduling, a poverty-alleviation program, and a possible US$2 billion loan facility.
April 6. Ex-PM Sharif is sentenced to life in prison for terrorism and hijacking. The court clears Sharif of the kidnapping and attempted murder charges. Sharif announces appeal.
April 9. Musharraf leaves for a G77 summit in Havana, Cuba, with a short stop in France. The summit will be followed by visits to Egypt and Libya.

April 11. Gunmen killed at least fourteen minority Shia Muslims and wounded thirty-four others in a congregation in a mosque in Malowali.
April 12. Musharraf meets UN Secretary General Annan at the G77 summit in Havana. They discuss the Kashmir conflict, Indo-Pakistani relations, and the democratization plan.
April 19. Pakistan's government agrees to a gas pipeline project from Iran via Pakistan to India.
April 21. Musharraf announces major steps to improve human rights. He highlights women's rights improvements, prison rights, and the restriction of a controversial blasphemy law.
April 27. A Lashkar-i-Toiba convention in Muridke calls *jihad* a religious duty for all Muslims. The convention asks the Pakistani government to resist any restriction against *jihad*.
April 30. The annual U.S. terrorism report accuses Pakistan of harboring and aiding known terrorists, but does not place Pakistan on the list of terrorist states.
May 1. Pakistan rejects U.S. terrorism report as unfounded.
May 4. Pakistan's Chief Justice Khan urges provincial judges to speed up cases on the recovery of $2 billion in defaulted loans, a key demand by the IMF.
May 7. Science and Technology Minister Rehman announces that the information and technology (IT) budget will be raised from $21 million to $300 million in fiscal year 2000/2001.
May 11. Pakistan's major traders announce a three-day strike from May 19 to protest against a general sales tax plan.
May 12. Pakistan's Supreme Court rules that the October 12, 1999 coup was legal ("justified on grounds of state necessity") but set a three-year deadline to hold elections.
May 17. Musharraf withdraws a key change to a controversial blasphemy law to appease fundamentalist religious parties.
May 18. An IMF mission arrives in Islamabad to discuss a new loan package that would fund a three-year economic program. It would replace the stalled $1.56 billion program.
May 19. Retailers in major Pakistani cities shut their businesses at the start of a three-day strike in protest against the government's plans to broaden the tax net.
May 25. Musharraf says he will adhere to the Supreme Court ruling and restore democracy within three years.
May 25. India's PM Vajpayee says he is prepared to resume talks with Pakistan, but Pakistan must end the cross-border terrorism, honor bilateral agreements, and maintain the LOC.
May 30. Protesting merchants vow to shut their shops for another two days to try to force the government to back away from carrying out a plan to widen the country's tax net.
June 2. Ex-PM Sharif is charged with tax evasion in connection with a purchase of a helicopter.

June 5. Pakistan faces intense pressure to devalue the rupee to bring a bulging trade deficit under control and fend off speculation in financial markets.
June 7. India's PM Vajpayee says that it is India's earnest desire to be friends with Pakistan.
June 9. Interior Minister Haider announced plans to bring the estimated 40,000 madrassas (Islamic schools) under government control and curb the network of Islamic militants.
June 9. Pakistan government accepts two key demands of striking retailers: not to reopen income tax returns filed for 1998–1999 and not to make an on-the-spot assessment of the stocks of traders.
June 10. Pakistan's wheat output in 1999–2000 will be more than 21 million tons, upgrading GDP growth forecasts to 5 percent (from earlier forecast of 4.5 percent). Inflation rate is 3.4 percent.
June 15. Foreign Minister (FM) Abdus Sattar and U.S. Deputy Secretary of State Strobe Talbott held talks in Washington, D.C. to discuss issues of nuclear security.
June 17. Pakistan presents 2000–2001 budget. Government expects to collect 24 percent more taxes, the defense budget will total $2.56 billion, and budget deficit is 4.6 percent of GDP.
June 21. International Court of Justice says that it does not have jurisdiction to rule in a dispute between Pakistan and India over the shooting down of a naval plane last year.
June 23. Musharraf says that Pakistan feels threatened by India, but war should be avoided through deterrence and diplomacy.
June 26. Pakistan burns more than 48 tons of narcotics worth hundreds of millions of dollars. Interior Minister Haider says Pakistan is close to becoming opium poppy–free by year's end.
July 1. Pakistan's Central Bank abolishes a requirement for importers under which they have to pay a cash margin in rupees for opening a letter of credit for imports.
July 1. A policeman opens fire on protesting traders in Multan, wounding four people.
July 3. Musharraf meets opposition politicians of PML and some smaller parties to discuss reform policies and listened to their views. PPP representatives were excluded from the talks.
July 16. Musharraf issued a decree reviving the Islamic provisions of the country's suspended constitution, to be incorporated in the Provisional Constitution Order.
July 16. Ten people were killed and thirty injured when a bomb exploded on a commuter train in Hyderabad. At least nineteen people have died and sixty injured in four separate bombings in July 2000.
July 18. Iran's police intercept a band of drug traffickers at the Pakistani border and seize 2.5 tons opium.

July 22. A Pakistani Accountability Court sentences ex-PM Sharif to fourteen years' hard labor and bans him from politics for twenty-one years after convicting him on corruption charges.
July 25. India vetoes Pakistan's application for membership in ASEAN.
August 2. India's PM Vajpayee blames Pakistan for backing militant groups that committed a series of massacres in Kashmir in which ninety people were killed.
August 2. Finance Minister Aziz announces a new tax amnesty scheme, asking individuals to declare their hidden assets, after a similar program brought in $194 million.
August 2. Musharraf says former prime ministers Benazir Bhutto and Nawaz Sharif have no place in the country's politics and that he is trying to create a "new leadership" growing from the grassroots level through nonparty local council elections announced for mid-2001.
August 6. A Lahore court sentences a man to death for blasphemy after he claimed to be a prophet of God.
August 6. The All-Parties Conference, uniting forty parties and other groups (including the PML and PPP), meets in Lahore to challenge the military rule. The common aim is to restore democracy.
August 9. Musharraf issues a decree amending the Political Parties Act, effectively barring Bhutto and Sharif from holding party offices because of court convictions.
August 9. Pakistan's economy grew by 4.9 percent in the last fiscal year.
August 14. Musharraf outlines the election plans and changes, including plans to hold local elections from December 2000 to August 2001, to give one-third of seats to women and 5 percent to minorities, and to reduce the minimum voting age from twenty-one to eighteen.
August 15. Musharraf reshuffles his top policy-making National Security Council (NSC). He removes five civilian members, brings in four key ministers, and creates a new seven-person NSC.
August 24. Bangladesh launches an initiative to try to reduce tension between India and Pakistan.
September 3. Bangladeshi PM Hasina Wajid will hold bilateral talks with India and Pakistan at the upcoming UN Millennium Summit in New York. She will also address the UN Security Council.
September 6. Musharraf, in his first appearance at the UN, offers talks with India "at any level, at any time, and anywhere." He wants a no-war pact and seeks to rid South Asia of nuclear weapons.
September 10. The PPP issues a declaration after a national convention in Lahore declaring Bhutto its chairperson for life and the next candidate for prime minister.
September 19. Sixteen people are killed and eighty others are injured when a bomb explodes in an Islamabad market. Government blames Indian-sponsored terrorists for this bombing and more than forty other bombings.

September 29. Karachi-based *Dawn* newspaper group complains that a raid on its offices by soldiers and electricity inspectors this week was aimed at intimidating the media.
October 2. Musharraf says he will hold national elections in 2002, but gives no specific date.
October 10. Musharraf says that his government has halted economic decline in the year since ousting the civilian rulers. Economic revival and good governance will remain top priorities.
October 11. Human Rights Watch says conditions have deteriorated since last year's coup and calls for international pressure to force an end to military rule.
October 12. Pakistan marks its first anniversary of last year's military coup without any significant protests, largely due to preventive police measures, including detention of political leaders.
October 18. Pakistani government warns politicians that seek more autonomy for their provinces that they would deal with them severely.
October 26. The National Accountability Bureau investigators filed five corruption charges against former PM Benazir Bhutto and her husband Asif Ali Zardari.
October 30. The High Court in Karachi upheld the April conviction of Sharif for hijacking and confirmed his sentence of life in prison. The court sustained his appeal against the conviction for terrorism and turned down an appeal by the prosecution to impose the death penalty.
November 6. Pakistan's Central Bank says the economy will grow at 4.5 percent in the fiscal year that began in July, down from the original forecast of 4.8 percent.
November 7. Chief executive of Pakistan-ruled part of Kashmir, Sultan Mahmood Chaudhry, calls for a joint anti-India "freedom struggle" by Kashmiris and Sikhs.
November 21. The United States waves sanctions against China for past missile technology transfers to Iran and Pakistan but imposes them on the two receiving nations for buying the equipment.
November 30. IMF approves a $596 million standby loan, restoring aid cut off in May 1999 because of Pakistan's failure to stick to the last agreement.
December 3. Alliance for the Restoration of Democracy, headed by Nawabzada Nasrullah Khan, emerges as union among PPP, PML, and sixteen other parties opposed to the military government.
December 10. Former PM Sharif was released from prison and flown into exile in Saudi Arabia together with eighteen family members. Musharraf justified his decision to exile Sharif, saying that the best way to cleanse Pakistan of the corruption of a "feudal political culture" was to remove him from the country.
December 31. Local elections, the first phase of the government's program for a staggered return to full democracy, were held in 18 of 106 districts.

2001

January 9. Minister of Religious Affairs Zakat announced that all bank transactions and financial dealings would be conducted in strict accordance with sharia, beginning July 1.

January 18. Pakistan admits failure to meet all IMF conditions, particularly the budget deficit and tax revenue targets.

January 23. Paris Club agrees to debt rescheduling program for Pakistan.

February 2. Musharraf calls Indian PM Vajpayee about the earthquake and relief efforts in Gujarat. This is the first conversation between the leaders since the October 1999 coup.

February 4. Pakistan newspaper *Jang* reports that Pakistan's Shaheen II ballistic missile had an increased range of 3,500 km and had entered production for the army.

February 14. Musharraf said that introduction of sharia into Pakistan's banking system would not affect Pakistan's international financial transactions and debt commitments.

February 21. Rear Admiral Tahir said that the navy was ready to equip its submarines with nuclear missiles to deter a threat from Indian submarine-borne missiles.

February 21. U.S. President Bush presses for peace talks between Pakistan and India.

February 26. The Supreme Court ordered the government to answer allegations that the April 1999 conviction of Benazir Bhutto had been politically manipulated.

March 1. The government arrested up to 1600 activists of the opposition Alliance for the Restoration of Democracy (ARD) before a rally planned for March 23 in Lahore.

March 1. Since September 2000, 170,000 refugees have entered Pakistan.

March 10. UN Secretary General Annan is prevented from visiting Jalozai refugee camp in the North–West Frontier Province (NWFP) where some 80,000 Afghans are taking refuge.

March 21. The second phase of local elections was held in twenty districts.

March 21. Pakistan says it feels threatened by India's 14 percent increase in defense expenditures.

March 30. The IMF approved a loan of $133 million to Pakistan, part of the standby agreement.

March 31. At least 36 people die and 125 were injured in stampede at a Muslim shrine.

April 6. The Supreme Court orders a retrial for former prime minister Benazir Bhutto, overturning her 1999 conviction of corruption.

May 1. A planned pro-democracy rally was suppressed by a weeklong crackdown by the authorities in which 4,000 ARD supporters were arrested.

May 6. Musharraf states that ban on public activities by political parties would be maintained until after the general elections, scheduled to be held before October 2002.
May 11–15. China's PM Zhu visits Pakistan to mark fifty years of diplomatic relations.
May 31. The third phase of the local elections was held in twenty districts.
June 13–14. During a visit to the U.K., FM Sattar said that Pakistan was unable to continue to provide shelter for "economic refugees" from Afghanistan. Pakistan has absorbed 2.5 million political and economic refugees since 1979.
June 20. Musharraf dismisses President Rafiq Tarrar and appoints himself as his replacement. Musharraf also dissolves the National Assembly and the four provisional assemblies. Musharraf will continue to hold positions of army chief of staff and chief executive.
June 20. The federal Cabinet approves a new antiterrorism law to curb all forms of sectarian and ethnic violence and terrorism.
July 2–4. The fourth and final phase of local elections was held in twenty-nine districts. The second stage of the return to democracy would be the election of provincial assemblies.
July 25. The death toll in flash floods caused by monsoon rains reached 200.
August 14. Musharraf announces that the elections for the provincial legislatures and the bicameral federal legislature would be held between October 1 and October 11, 2002. He also announced a ban on two militant Islamic organizations, the Sunni Lashkar-e-Jhangvi and the Shiite Sipah-i-Mohammed, making a plea for religious tolerance.
August 23. It is reported that Bhutto's PPP enjoyed widespread success in the Sindh province in recent local elections.
August 25. Musharraf reportedly held a meeting with senior PPP leader Mahkdoom Amin Fahim.
September 19. Musharraf addresses the nation to justify his agreement to cooperate with the U.S. military action against Osama bin Laden and his Al Qaeda network. Pakistan was one of three states to recognize the Taliban as the legitimate government of Afghanistan.
September 20. Gallup opinion poll shows that 62 percent of Pakistani respondents were opposed to the government siding with the United States.
September 21. Three protestors were shot dead by police in Karachi during a day of nationwide protests and strikes organized by the Pakistan and Afghan Defense Council.
September 23. U.S. President Bush waives sanctions on development aid and military sales that had been imposed in May 1998 after Pakistan had conducted a series of nuclear tests.
September 24. U.S. and Pakistan officials sign an agreement to reschedule US$379 million of Pakistan's debts to the United States.
September 26. The IMF announces the release of a further US$135 million to complete Pakistan's one-year standby agreement.

September 29. The government orders Harkat-ul-Mujahadeen (Movement of the Holy Warriors), a militant group declared a terrorist organization by the United States, to shut its seven offices in the country.

October 5. U.K. Prime Minister Tony Blair visits Pakistan.

October 7. Musharraf consolidated his hold on power by extending indefinitely his expiring three-year term as army chief of staff.

October 7. The Afghan Defense Council calls for a *jihad.*

October 8. Musharraf announces a reshuffling of top military commanders that is designed to distance the government from Islamic militancy and Afghanistan's Taliban regime.

October 9. In the worst street violence since the start of the U.S.-led bombing, four people were shot dead by police.

October 14. About 5,000 demonstrators attempt to storm Jacobabad air base in Sindh province, one of two bases Musharraf is allowing the U.S. military to use. Demonstration in Karachi of 20,000 people.

October 15–16. U.S. Secretary of State Colin Powell visits Pakistan.

October 24. Police arrested two top Pakistani nuclear scientists. They are later released.

October 27. Thousands of armed men leave Pakistan for Afghanistan to join Taliban forces.

October 28. Sixteen Christian worshippers are killed when six gunmen open fire on a church in Bahawalpur.

October 28. Pakistan agrees to reopen its border to allow up to 300,000 of the most vulnerable Afghan refugees to enter Pakistan.

November 7. Musharraf starts a six-day foreign tour that includes Iran, France, the U.K., and the United States.

November 19. FM Sattar states that Pakistan no longer has any relations with the Taliban regime.

November 22. Pakistan orders the closure of the Taliban's embassy in Islamabad, its last anywhere.

December 7. The IMF approve a three-year arrangement for Pakistan under the poverty reduction and growth facility worth a total of US$3.322 billion, of which US$109.6 million is now available.

December 10. The European Union (EU) admits Pakistan to its Generalized System of Preferences from January 1, 2002.

December 13. Finance Minister Aziz secures a debt restructuring agreement with the Paris Club. Analysts said that it was one of the most generous arrangements ever agreed to by the Paris Club.

December 20–24. Musharraf visits China to meet with President Jiang and reassert strong ties.

December 24. Pakistan will increase its forces along the 1,500 km northern border with Afghanistan to 60,000 regular troops in addition to 65,000 police and paramilitary troops.

December 25. Authorities arrest the leaders of two Islamic militant groups alleged by India to have perpetrated the December 13 attack on the Indian federal parliament.

2002

January 12. In a nationwide television address, Musharraf presents his reform policies that will allow Pakistan to be a "progressive and dynamic Islamic welfare state."
January 23. Daniel Pearl, a U.S. journalist for the *Wall Street Journal*, disappears in Karachi while being taken by intermediaries to interview a radical cleric, Mubarak Ali Shah Gilani.
January 24. Musharraf confirms that general elections would be in October 2002.
January 28. The National Movement for the Restoration of Pakistan's Sovereignty claimed to be holding Pearl, according to e-mails under the account name "kidnapperguy."
February 12–14. Musharraf made an official visit to the United States to hold talks with President Bush.
February 12. Ahmed Omar Sheikh, the main suspect in Daniel Pearl's kidnapping, is arrested in Lahore by government authorities.
February 13. Moody's announces an upgrading of Pakistan's external debt rating from Caa1 to B3.
February 14. Sheikh appeared in court and admitted responsibility for kidnapping and that—"as far as I understand"—Pearl was dead.
February 22. The search for U.S. journalist Daniel Pearl became a murder hunt after the U.S. consulate general in Karachi had been given a videotape that included a scene of Pearl's "execution."
February 26. Twelve people are killed and fifteen others wounded when gunmen open fire on worshippers in a Shiite Muslim mosque in Rawalpindi. Musharraf blames extremist Islamic groups.
February 27. The U.S. State Department offered a US$5 million reward for information leading to Pearl's killers.
March 7. Pakistan Information Minister Memon attended a South Asian Association for Regional Cooperation in Islamabad and met India's Information and Broadcasting Minister Swaraj, the first Indian cabinet minister to visit Pakistan for more than two years.
March 9. About 600 of the estimated 2,000 Islamic militants detained for membership in banned extremist groups are to be released as a part of a government amnesty.
March 14. It is reported that leading Islamic militant groups banned in January 2002, such as Lashkar-i-Toiba and Harkat-ul-Mujahideen, had relocated to Pakistan-controlled Kashmir.

March 17. Five people, including two Americans are killed, and forty-five others wounded in a grenade attack on a Protestant church near the U.S. embassy in Islamabad.
March 22. U.K.-born militant Ahmad Omar Sayeed Shaikh and three other men were charged in Karachi with the kidnap and murder of Daniel Pearl.
April 22. The trial of Ahmad Omar Sayeed Shaikh and the three other men began.
April 26. Twelve people, all women and children, are killed and at least twenty-three others wounded when a bomb explodes in a women's section of a mosque in Bukker.
May 1. Official results from yesterday's nationwide referendum show that 97.7 percent of voters, 42.8 million of the 43.9 million total, approved the extension of President Musharraf's tenure for another five years. The government says voter turnout was 50 percent. The referendum contained three questions: (i) do you support the policies of economic reform? (ii) do you support the policy of fighting extremism? (iii) do you want General Musharraf to be president for another five years?
May 8. A suicide bomber detonated a car bomb next to a bus outside the Karachi Sheraton hotel, killing sixteen people as well as himself and injuring seventeen people.
May 12. Musharraf announces the creation of a new federal anti-terrorism task force.
May 14. Police shot dead Riaz Basra, the leader of Lashkar-i-Toiba, who was being sought in connection with some 100 sectarian killings.
May 17. Police believe they found the dismembered remains of Daniel Pearl in a compound on the edge of Karachi.
May 22. Britain urges its citizens to leave Pakistan, orders the departure of 160 personnel from the Islamabad High Commission (embassy), and closes its consulates after warnings of bomb attacks on Westerners.
May 29. *The Times* (London) reports that Pakistan has moved thousands of troops away from the NWFP to its confrontation with India on the LOC.
May 31. Pakistan's security forces working with the U.S. FBI arrested fourteen Al Qaeda members in NWFP.
June 7. FM Sattar resigned due to health reasons.
June 14. Thirteen people are killed and forty are injured when a suicide car bomber detonates a bomb outside the U.S. consulate general in Karachi. The Karachi mission was shut down until June 18 and the U.S. embassy in Islamabad and consulates in Lahore and Peshawar were closed temporarily.
July 15. An antiterrorism court sentences Sheik Omar Saeed to death for his role in organizing the kidnapping and murder of American journalist Daniel Pearl. Three other religious militants are sentenced to twenty-five years in prison for their roles in the conspiracy to kidnap Pearl.
June 19. Foreign Secretary Inamul Haq was announced as the new foreign minister.

June 19. The federal Cabinet approved an ordinance for the registration of madrassas (Islamic schools).
June 24. Musharraf issued a Chief Executive's Order requiring all candidates for future elections to the federal and provincial legislatures to hold a university degree.
June 26–27. Musharraf unveiled an array of radical constitutional reforms that would strengthen his own grip on power and give the military a permanent role in government.
July 6. Musharraf issues a decree barring anyone from seeking a third term as prime minister or provincial chief minister, disqualifying Bhutto and Sharif.
July 9. Pakistan paramilitary forces hold a press conference where captured members of Harkut-ul-Mujahideen al-Alami admitted that they had organized the suicide bombing outside of the U.S. consulate in Karachi in June.
July 10. Musharraf announced that the National Assembly and provincial assembly elections would be held on October 10.
July 10. An accountability court convicted in absentia former PM Benazir Bhutto in relation to a charge that in 1994 she received a US$10 million kickback for granting a gold import license.
July 15. Ahmad Omar Sayeed Shaikh was sentenced to death and three codefendants, Salman Saqib, Fahad Nasim, and Shaikh Mohammed Adil, were sentenced to life in prison.
July 17. It is reported that the police are holding three more suspects in relation to Pearl's murder.
August 4. At least six people are killed and three others injured when as many as five gunmen attack a Christian boarding school near Murree.
August 9. Three nurses and twenty-three other people are killed in a grenade attack on a Christian missionary hospital in Taxila.
August 21. Musharraf unilaterally redraws the constitution, imposing twenty-nine amendments that expand his powers, including the ability to make further amendments at will, dissolve parliament, and appoint the country's military leaders and Supreme Court justices. The changes also institutionalize the political role of the military by allotting it seats on a newly created National Security Council, a civilian-military body that will monitor future governments.
August 24. The trial began for the three men charged with the attack on the Karachi U.S. consulate general.
August 30. Officials in Larkana rejected the nomination of former PM and leader of the PPP Benazir Bhutto as a candidate for a seat in the upcoming National Assembly election.
September 1. An antiterrorism court found six men guilty in a gang rape case and sentenced the men to death by hanging.
September 13. An election tribunal in Karachi dismissed appeals by Bhutto that bar her from entering the National Assembly election. Sharif, in a gesture of solidarity, withdrew from the election.

September 25. Unidentified gunmen killed seven men and wounded two others in an attack on the offices of a Christian charity, the Institute of Peace and Justice, in central Karachi.

October 13. Results from parliamentary election, the first since Musharraf came to power, show that the PML (Quaid-i-Azam), a new party loyal to Musharraf, won 78 of 272 constituency seats in the 342 seat parliament. The PPP, led by Benazir Bhutto, received 62 seats. Mutahidda Majilis-e-Amal, a coalition of conservative Islamic groups, earned 45 seats. The EU said the elections were "seriously flawed."

October 17. The government says it will pull back hundreds of thousands of troops who have been stationed along its border with India since December 2001, matching a similar statement made by New Delhi the previous day.

Sources: The chronology was compiled from *Keesing's Record of World Events* and FAST's Chronology of Pakistan. They are available on the Internet at http://www.isn.ethz.ch/onlinepubli/publihouse/fast/suppdata/pakistan/pak.01.chron.pdf. Additional information was obtained from the *Middle East Journal* and newspapers.

Index

About the Contributors

Faisal Bari is Associate Professor of Economics at the Lahore University of Management Sciences. He received a Ph.D. from McGill University and was a Visiting Rice Fellow at Yale University from 2000 to 2001. His research interests include corporate governance and industrial organization in developing countries as well as growth and investment in those countries.

Craig Baxter is Professor Emeritus of Politics and History at Juniata College. He was a Foreign Service officer with assignments in India, Pakistan, and Bangladesh and was Visiting Professor of Social Sciences at West Point. He holds a Ph.D. from the University of Pennsylvania. He has written extensively on South Asia. He was president of the American Institute of Pakistan Studies from 1993 to 1999.

Devin T. Hagerty is Assistant Professor of Political Science at the University of Maryland, Baltimore County. He has a Ph.D. from the University of Pennsylvania and has taught at the University of Sydney, Australia, and the University of Illinois, Urbana–Champaign. While at the Kennedy School at Harvard University, he wrote *The Consequences of Nuclear Proliferation: Lessons from South Asia* (1998).

Robert LaPorte Jr. is Professor Emeritus of Public Administration and Political Science at the Pennsylvania State University. He has long been involved in research, writing, lecturing, and consulting on Pakistan, especially concerning its public policy and public administration. He has written three books on the country as well as a number of articles and chapters in books. He holds a Ph.D. from Syracuse University.

Jonathan Mark Kenoyer is Professor of Anthropology at the University of Wisconsin, Madison. His work focuses on the Indus Valley Civilization where he is Field Director of the Harappa Archaeological Research Project. He holds a Ph.D. from the University of California, Berkeley, and is author of *Ancient Cities of the Indus Valley Civilization* (1998, with support from the American Institute of Pakistan Studies.)

Bashir Ahmad Khan is Associate Professor of Banking and Finance at the Lahore University of Management Sciences. He holds a Ph.D. from the University of Oxford and studied in the United Kingdom as a Commonwealth Scholar from 1991 to 1993 and as a Fellow of the Charles Wallace Trust in 2003. His current studies pertain to structure, performance, and risk in banks in developing countries.

Scott Kofmehl graduated from Juniata College in 2003. He has been chosen as a Thomas Pickering Foreign Affairs Fellow in a program sponsored by the U.S.

Department of State and administered by the Woodrow Wilson National Fellowship Foundation. He has been a Boren National Security Education Program Scholar and was the president of the Juniata College student body. He is now studying at the Kennedy Center at Harvard University.

Zulfikar Khalid Maluka is an attorney with a law degree from Punjab University and a master's degree in international relations from Quaid-i-Azam University. He taught international law and politics at Quaid-i-Azam University in the 1980s. He wrote *The Myth of Constitutionalism in Pakistan* (1995) and has published many papers in Pakistani and international journals.

Richard H. Meadow is Director of the Zooarchaeology Library at the Peabody Museum, Harvard University, and is Senior Lecturer in Anthropology at the university. He is also Director of the Harappa Archaeological Research Project. His specialty is the study of animal remains in Indus Valley sites. He holds a Ph.D. from Harvard University. He has also worked in Iran, Oman, Thailand, and Turkey.

Tariq Rahman is Professor of Linguistics and South Asian Studies at Quaid-i-Azam University. His did his graduate work in Great Britain where he obtained a Ph.D. He has lectured in Denmark and at several institutions in the United States. He has written extensively on language and education in Pakistan.

Rasul Bakhsh Rais is Professor of Political Science at the Lahore University of Management Sciences. He was the Quaid-i-Azam Visiting Professor of Pakistan Studies at Columbia University from 1991 to 1994. He taught for about twenty-two years at the Quaid-i-Azam University in Islamabad and has visited several universities in the United States. His Ph.D. is from the University of California at Santa Barbara.

Thomas P. Thornton teaches at the Johns Hopkins University from which he received his Ph.D. He had a long career in the United States government as, among other things, a senior member of the Policy Planning Staff of the Department of State and a member of the staff of the National Security Council. He has written extensively on matters pertaining to South Asia and on American foreign policy.

Andrew R. Wilder is author of *The Pakistani Voter: Electoral Politics and Voting Behaviour in Pakistan* (1999). He was born in Pakistan and has spent many years there. He holds a Ph.D. from the Fletcher School of Law and Diplomacy, Tufts University. Currently he is based in Kabul as Director of the Afghanistan Research and Evaluation Unit.